Irving Fisher (1867–1947)
Arthur Hadley (1856–1930)
Ragnar Frisch (1895–1973)
Friedrich von Hayek (1899–1992)
Allyn Young (1876–1929)
Ugo Mazzola (1863–1899)

Pioneers in Economics

Series Editor: Mark Blaug

Professor Emeritus, University of London
Consultant Professor, University of Buckingham
Visiting Professor, University of Exeter

This important series presents critical appraisals of influential economists from the 17th century to the present day. It focuses in particular on those economists who were influential in their own time and whose work has had an impact – often inadequately recognized – on the evolution and development of economic thought. The series will be indispensable for a clear understanding of the origin and development of economic ideas and the role played by the leading protagonists of the past.

A full list of published titles in this series is printed at the end of this volume.

Irving Fisher (1867–1947)
Arthur Hadley (1856–1930)
Ragnar Frisch (1895–1973)
Friedrich von Hayek (1899–1992)
Allyn Young (1876–1929)
Ugo Mazzola (1863–1899)

Edited by

Mark Blaug

Professor Emeritus,
University of London

An Elgar Reference Collection

Published by
Edward Elgar Publishing Limited
Gower House
Croft Road
Aldershot
Hants GU11 3HR
England

Edward Elgar Publishing Company
Old Post Road
Brookfield
Vermont 05036
USA

A CIP catalogue record for this book is available from the British Library

A CIP catalogue record for this book is available from the US Library of Congress

ISBN 1 85278 505 5

Contents

Acknowledgements vii
Introduction ix

1. William R. Allen (1977), 'Irving Fisher, F.D.R., and the Great Depression', *History of Political Economy*, **9** (4), Winter, 560–87 1
2. John H. Crockett, Jr. (1980), 'Irving Fisher on the Financial Economics of Uncertainty', *History of Political Economy*, **12** (1), Spring, 65–82 29
3. Melvin Cross and Robert B. Ekelund, Jr. (1980), 'A.T. Hadley on Monopoly Theory and Railway Regulation: An American Contribution to Economic Analysis and Policy', *History of Political Economy*, **12** (2), Summer, 214–33 47
4. Jens Christopher Andvig (1981), 'Ragnar Frisch and Business Cycle Research During the Interwar Years', *History of Political Economy*, **13** (4), Winter, 695–725 67
5. Paul B. Trescott (1982), 'Discovery of the Money-Income Relationship in the United States, 1921–1944', *History of Political Economy*, **14** (1), Spring, 65–88 98
6. Charles P. Blitch (1983), 'Allyn A. Young: A Curious Case of Professional Neglect', *History of Political Economy*, **15** (1), Spring, 1–24 122
7. Michael Hudson (1985), 'German Economists and the Depression of 1929–1933', *History of Political Economy*, **17** (1), Spring, 35–50 146
8. Laurence S. Moss and Karen I. Vaughn (1986), 'Hayek's Ricardo Effect: A Second Look', *History of Political Economy*, **18** (4), Winter, 545–65 162
9. Orhan Kayaalp (1988), 'Ugo Mazzola and the Italian Theory of Public Goods', *History of Political Economy*, **20** (1), Spring, 15–25 183

Name Index 195

Acknowledgements

The editor and publishers wish to thank the following who have kindly given permission for the use of copyright material.

Duke University Press for articles: William R. Allen (1977), 'Irving Fisher, F.D.R., and the Great Depression', *History of Political Economy* **9** (4), 560–87; John H. Crockett, Jr. (1980), 'Irving Fisher on the Financial Economics of Uncertainty', *History of Political Economy*, **12** (1), 65–82; Melvin Cross and Robert B. Ekelund, Jr. (1980), 'A.T. Hadley on Monopoly Theory and Railway Regulation: An American Contribution to Economic Analysis and Policy', *History of Political Economy*, **12** (2), 214–33; Jens Christopher Andvig (1981), 'Ragnar Frisch and Business Cycle Research During the Interwar Years', *History of Political Economy*, **13** (4), 695–725; Paul B. Trescott (1982), 'Discovery of the Money-Income Relationship in the United States, 1921–1944', *History of Political Economy*, **14** (1), 65–88; Charles P. Blitch (1983), 'Allyn A. Young: A Curious Case of Professional Neglect', *History of Political Economy*, **15** (1), 1–24; Michael Hudson (1985), 'German Economists and the Depression of 1929–1933', *History of Political Economy*, **17** (1), 35–50; Laurence S. Moss and Karen I. Vaughn (1986), 'Hayek's Ricardo Effect: A Second Look', *History of Political Economy*, **18** (4), 545–65; Orhan Kayaalp (1988), 'Ugo Mazzola and the Italian Theory of Public Goods', *History of Political Economy*, **20** (1), 15–25.

Every effort has been made to trace all the copyright holders but if any have been inadvertently overlooked, the publishers will be pleased to make the necessary arrangement at the first opportunity.

In addition the publishers wish to thank the library of the London School of Economics and Political Science and The Alfred Marshall Library, Cambridge University, for their assistance in obtaining these articles.

Introduction

Irving Fisher was one of the greatest and certainly one of the most colourful American economists who ever lived. A writer and teacher of prodigious scope and power, his works are distinguished by their unusual clarity of exposition, the ideas being typically set out verbally, algebraically and geometrically with all complications carefully deferred until the essential principles are established. In addition, they run the entire gamut from mathematical economics to mathematical statistics, from the theory of value and prices to the theory of capital and interest. The now familiar distinction between stocks and flows is almost entirely due to his masterpiece, *The Nature of Capital and Income* (1906). The modern theory of the real rate of interest stems from his *Theory of Interest* (1930), a revised version of an earlier book entitled *The Rate of Interest* (1907). His famous 'ideal index' of prices – a geometric mean of two indices in which prices are weighted by their base year and end-year quantities – was defended in *The Making of Index Numbers* (1922). Finally, *The Purchasing Power of Money* (1911) restated the old quantity theory of money in modern dress. In reading these books today one needs continually to remind oneself of the dates at which they were published because they sound so modern and require almost no revision of any kind to accommodate intervening theoretical developments.

Irving Fisher was born in up-state New York in 1867 and took his B.A. in mathematics at Yale University in 1898, followed by a Ph.D. in economics in 1901. For three years he taught mathematics at Yale, switching to the economics department in 1895 after establishing an international reputation with his startingly original Ph.D. thesis, *Mathematical Investigations in the Theory of Value and Prices* (1892), which contained, among other things, the design of a machine to illustrate general equilibrium in a multi-market economy. He remained at Yale until his retirement in 1935. He was director of Remington Rand (now the Rand Corporation), a founder and president of the Eugenics Research Association, the Stable Money League, the Econometric Society, the American Statistical Association and simply dozens of other companies and agencies.

The purpose of *The Nature of Capital and Income* was to provide a theoretical foundation for the science of accounting, both at the level of the individual enterprise and of the economy as a whole. Fisher defined 'capital' as any stock of wealth that yields a flow of services over time – land, machines, buildings, raw materials, natural resources, human skills – and 'income' as the surplus of that flow of services above those necessary to maintain and replace the stock of wealth. The link between capital and income is the rate of interest because the value of capital is nothing but the present value of the future flow of income from it, discounted, that is, at the going rate of interest. It is not capital that confers value on income but rather income that confers value on capital because economic activity is essentially forward-looking. It follows that, strictly speaking, capital is the only factor of production; that all distributive income consists of interest, wages being merely interest payments on the stock of human capital; and that national income consists entirely of consumption expenditure. It is evident that the Fisherian notion of ignoring investment in the measurement of national income was eventually rejected. Nevertheless, virtually every other element of this most brilliant of Fisher's many brilliant books has entered without qualification into modern economics.

The Purchasing Power of Money (1911), dedicated to Simon Newcomb, was organized around the 'equation of exchange': $MV + M^1V^1 = PT$, with M and M^1 standing for the stock of notes, currency and bank deposits in circulation, V and V^1 for their respective velocities of circulation, P for the level of prices (the reciprocal of 'the purchasing power of money') and T for the total volume of transactions, all variables being defined for an identical time period, say one year. Fisher was fully aware that the quantity *theory* of money had frequently been defended as a truism rather than a theory. As a theoretical proposition, PT is only brought into equality with $MV + M^1V^1$ by a transmission mechanism linking an increase in the stock of M or M^1 to the flow of expenditure. Thus, in what Fisher called 'transition periods' between two comparative static equilibria, the right-hand side of the equation of exchange is not equal to the left-hand side; indeed, it is this possibility of an inequality between them that allows us to speak of a quantity *theory* of money. He was always aware that much of the theory in question was hidden behind the quantity equation of exchange – for example, the role of the rate of interest in the so-called 'indirect mechanism' linking money to prices as distinct from the 'direct mechanism' which operates through the real value of the cash balances normally held by economic agents. Despite the fact that the book contains virtually no errors either of omission or commission, and despite Fisher's pioneering efforts to quantify the parameters of the equation of exchange, the balance of argument in the book was such as to suggest an intransigent defence of the quantity theory of money, minimizing the weight of transition periods to the point where they practically disappear from view. The book never enjoyed the unqualified success of most of his other works and it failed altogether in resolving the great controversy over what was meant by the quantity theory of money. Even modern monetarists have found it necessary to start all over again in defining the problem of just how an increase in the supply of money affects prices.

Fisher's *Theory of Interest* made no claims to say anything new, its greatness as a book lying wholly in its outstanding pedagogic qualities. It was dedicated to 'the memory of John Rae and of Eugen von Böhm-Bawerk, who laid the foundations upon which I have endeavored to build', and amounted to a demonstration that the real rate of interest is determined by both demand and supply – by the demand for production and consumption loans on the one hand and the supply of savings on the other. Most of the book is devoted to theory relating to the determination of the real rate of interest, although a distinction between the real and the money rate of interest is made at the outset of the volume and is taken up again in the closing chapters.

Three of Fisher's works were devoted to projects for monetary reform: *Stabilizing the Dollar* (1920), *Stamp Scrip* (1933) and *100% Money* (1935); and two others, *Booms and Depressions* (1932) and *Inflation* (1933), were designed to strengthen his proposals for monetary reform. *Stabilizing the Dollar* contained an ingenious scheme for stabilizing the purchasing power of money under a convertible gold standard by varying the official price of gold inversely with an index of prices, a system which could be adopted by one country combined with a flexible exchange rate for its currency or by all countries operating with fixed exchange rates. *Booms and Depressions* and *Stamp Scrip* took up the old proposal of Silvio Gesell (1862-1930) of stamping notes each month at a post office without which stamp the notes would cease to be legal tender. The object of the scheme was to discourage the hoarding of notes, which it would certainly succeed in doing if it were also extended to cover bank deposits, a point which Fisher quickly observes. *100% Money* was intended to show that business cycles are largely due to bank credit and the power of banks in a fractional reserve system to 'create money' at will. The solution was to insist on 100 per cent reserve backing for deposits held; depositors would pay charges to cover the cost of managing their deposit accounts and banks would then have to make loans with funds borrowed in the capital market. Fisher candidly admitted that this idea was as old as banking itself; in particular, he gave credit to a group of economists from the University of Chicago (including Henry Simons, Frank Knight and Paul Douglas) who had advocated a similar scheme only two years earlier; it is still supported by many economists today, principally Milton Friedman.

Having made a private fortune early in life from the invention of a visible card-index file system, Fisher spent most of it in later years campaigning for a great number of causes to which he was passionately devoted, including prohibition, preventive medicine, eugenics, world peace and 100 per cent deposit reserves. His enormous influence on the American economic profession (not to mention his private wealth) effectively came to an end in 1929: not only did he fail to predict the Wall Street crash but afterwards he went on insisting month after month that the upturn to a new boom was just around the corner. Nevertheless, he went on publishing until the age of 75, dying five years later in 1947.

Fisher never founded a school. He had many pupils but few disciples. Many of his later works were unfavourably received, perhaps because the aura of a crank increasingly began to surround Fisher's name. It was no doubt difficult for fellow economists not to suspect the ideas of a man whose book on *How to Live: Rules for Healthful Living Based on Modern Science* (1915) had become a national bestseller, translated into ten languages. Possibly if Fisher had been more cautious about the Great Depression, his reputation would not have suffered its extraordinary eclipse in the last two decades of his life.

Arthur Hadley was America's leading railway economist in the last quarter of the nineteenth century. His *Railway Transportation* (1885) synthesized the theory of price discrimination under monopoly and applied Cournot's marginal rule for profit maximization to railways. His textbook *Economics: An Account of the Relations Between Private Property and Public Welfare* (1896) anticipated Marshall's period analysis and enjoyed considerable success in American universities and colleges, being only effectively replaced by Ely's *Outline of Economics* (1908) and Taussig's *Principles of Economics* (1911).

Hadley was educated at Yale University and the University of Berlin. He became a professor of Yale in 1891 and president of Yale in 1899, a post he held until 1921. He chaired a number of influential commissions on the problems of railways and came close to being nominated for high political office in the Republican Party.

Ragnar Frisch was a pioneer of 'econometrics', a name which he himself coined – that union of mathematical and statistical methods applied to the testing of economic hypotheses which, he firmly believed, would at long last establish economics as a science. He founded the Econometric Society in 1930, edited *Econometrica* from 1933–5, and in 1969 was awarded the first Nobel Prize in Economics (jointly with Jan Tinbergen) for his services to econometric modelling and measurement. But he was also the nearest equivalent in our times to the economist as Plato's 'philosopher-king': for over 30 years, he exerted an overwhelming influence on economic thought and economic policy in his native country of Norway.

Curiously enough, most of his writings remain unpublished, but what he did publish had the uncanny quality of becoming instant classics. These included essays such as 'Propagation Problems and Impulse Problems in Dynamic Economics' (1933), reprinted in R.A. Gordon and L.R. Klein (eds.), *Readings in Business Cycles* (Richard D. Irwin, 1965), 'On the Notion of Equilibrium and Disequilibrium', *Review of Economic Studies*, February 1936, and 'Alfred Marshall's Theory of Value', *Quarterly Journal of Economics*, November 1950, as well as books such as *Theory of Production* (Reidel, 1965; Rand McNally, 1965). In the closing years of World War II, he took an increasing interest in problems of economic planning, of which *Planning for India* (Asia Publishing House, 1960) and *Economic Planning Studies: A Collection of Essays* (Reidel, 1976) provide only an imperfect impression. His macroeconomic 'decision models', as he liked to call them, were large-scale optimization models, embodying input-output and behavioural equations which he never managed to put to serious practical use. Nevertheless, he made an impact on the planning literature, not just in Western but also in Eastern Europe, through personal contacts, memoranda to governments, letters to colleagues and unpublished drafts of manuscripts.

Frisch was born in Oslo (Norway) in 1895. As a young man he worked in his father's gold and silver workshops, earning a certificate as a goldsmith, while at the same time studying economics at the University of Oslo. Upon graduation in 1919, he went to France to prepare his doctoral dissertation in mathematical statistics. After the award of his Ph.D. in 1926, he left, like so many other inter-war European economists, to travel to America on a Rockefeller Foundation Fellowship. Returning to Norway in 1928, he became a lecturer at the University of Oslo but two years later went back to America as Visiting Professor at Yale University. A new professorship was especially created to bring him back to Norway: in 1931 he was appointed to the Chair of Economics at the University of Oslo which he held until his retirement in 1965. Throughout the 1930s and again in the early post-war years, he advised the Labour Party of Norway along lines which resembled the ideas of Keynesian policy-makers in Britain and America, except for a greater emphasis on central planning in respect of the key industries of the economy.

Hayek's reputation has gone through a remarkable cycle. An eminent exponent of the Austrian theory of business cycles in the 1930s, he was worsted in the battle over Keynes' *Treatise on Money* (1930) and retreated into capital theory, an esoteric branch of the subject in which few economists then took an active interest. Even the immensely popular *Road to Serfdom* (Routledge & Kegan Paul, 1944; University of Chicago Press, 1956) – an indictment of government intervention in modern economies as representing 'creeping socialism' – failed to reinstate him to the front ranks. He gave up economics altogether after the war and took up psychology, political philosophy, the philosophy of law and the history of ideas. And then, gradually, his fame as a 'libertarian' began to spread. After receiving the Nobel Prize in Economics in 1974, shared jointly with Gunnar Myrdal, he came back to mainstream economics as a leading critic of Keynesianism and an advocate of free banking as the answer to the scourge of inflation. Even when elderly, articulate, austere and infinitely urbane, he reigned supreme as the kind of moral philosopher and political economist that the discipline had not seen since Adam Smith.

Hayek was born in 1899 in Vienna, the capital of the Austro-Hungarian Empire, in an academic family. After serving in the army in World War I, he returned to Vienna and entered the Law Faculty of the University of Vienna, taking his *Dr. Juris* in 1921. Two years later, he obtained a second doctorate in economics. There followed a brief visit to America, attending courses at Columbia University and working as a research assistant to various American economists. Returning to Vienna in 1924, he and a number of other young promising economists (including G. Haberler, F. Machlup and O. Morgenstern) formed a circle under the watchful eye of Ludwig von Mises, whose own private seminar formed a fulcrum of economic discussion in Austria in the 1920s. In 1927, with Mises' support, Hayek became the director of the Austrian Institute for Business Cycle Research; two years later he was admitted as *Privatdozent* (lecturer) to the University of Vienna, the first rung on the ladder of academic success in the Austria of those days.

Shortly thereafter, Lionel Robbins invited him to give some lectures at the London School of Economics. Published under the title *Prices and Production* (Routledge & Kegan Paul, 1931; 2nd ed., Kelley, 1978), these lectures made a considerable stir in the English-speaking world and led to a professorship at the London School of Economics which lasted 18 years. According to *Prices and Production*, rising prices in a boom lead to a fall in real wages, which then induces the substitution of labour for machines and a general shortening of production periods; in consequence, interest rates rise, investment falls off and the economy turns down. Conversely, in a slump the rising level of real wages revives investment as labour is displaced and periods of production are lengthened. According to this argument, quite contrary to the usual Keynesian reasoning, a rising level of consumption after a certain point reduces rather than increases investment, and vice versa for a falling level of consumption.

Hayek wrote an unfavourable review of Keynes' *Treatise on Money* to which Keynes replied; Piero Sraffa on behalf of Keynes wrote an equally critical review of *Prices and Production* to which Hayek replied. The controversy was joined by every prominent monetary economist of the day and was only put to rest by Keynes' *General Theory* (1936) which totally altered the terms of the debate.

Hayek continued to work on a by-product of that debate as summed up in his *Profits, Interest and Investment* (Routledge & Kegan Paul, 1939; Kelley, 1978) and *The Pure Theory of Capital* (Macmillan, 1941; University of Chicago Press, 1975). He participated in another controversy, stemming from Mises' denial that a socialist economy could price its goods and services in accordance with the principles of relative scarcity, and edited a classic volume on *Collectivist Economic Planning: Critical Studies on the Possibilities of Socialism* (Routledge & Kegan Paul, 1935; Kelley, 1978). He had long shown expertise in the history of economic thought and now extended it to the history of political ideas: a series of articles on 'scientism', later to appear as *The Counter-Revolution of Science* (Free Press, 1952), traced modern collectivist beliefs in economic planning to the eighteenth-century theories of Saint-Simon and August Comte. In 1944, *The Road to Serfdom* won him momentary notoriety as a political thinker and marked the beginning of his later rise to leadership in the world-wide libertarian movement. After the war, he became a frequent visitor at American universities, founded and for 12 years headed the Mont Pelerin Society, a group of social scientists dedicated to defending the principles of the free market, and published a series of influential essays, appearing between hard covers in *Individualism and Economic Order* (Routledge & Kegan Paul, University of Chicago Press, 1948).

In 1950, he left Britain and became Professor of Social and Moral Sciences at the University of Chicago. Further works in the history of ideas, including a surprising treatise on psychology, *The Sensory Order: An Inquiry into the Foundations of Theoretical Psychology* (Routledge & Kegan Paul, University of Chicago Press, 1976), led in 1960 to the masterpiece of his 'middle years' – *The Constitution of Liberty* (Routledge & Kegan Paul, University of Chicago Press, 1960). This was a major statement of modern liberalism which shocked many readers by its effective criticism of inheritance taxation and high marginal rates of income tax. In 1962, Hayek returned to Europe as Professor of Economic Policy at the University of Freiburg in Breisgau, West Germany. After retirement from Freiburg in 1968, he spent a further nine years in Austria at the University of Salzburg before finally leaving academic life at the age of 78.

The Salzburg years witnessed the publication of his final major work, the three-volume study of *Law, Legislation and Liberty* (Routledge & Kegan Paul, University of Chicago Press, 1973, 1976, 1979), capping a career marked by 18 books, 15 pamphlets, 142 journal articles and chapters in books, not one of which is shallow or superficial. Some of his old papers, such as 'Economics and Knowledge' (*Economica*, February 1937) have recently been disinterred and found to open new vistas that should have been explored earlier; in this paper he argued, quite correctly, that economic theory had never actually demonstrated how the knowledge which economic agents require to achieve equilibrium is generated and communicated among each other by the process of competition.

At the heart of many of his later writings was the 'doctrine of unintended social consequences': most of the worthwhile institutions of modern society (markets, courts, the legal system and even the government itself) are the unintended by-products of individual actions taken for other reasons and never could have been deliberately and consciously created. It follows, according to Hayek, that the least interference with spontaneous individual action there is, the better. This is not an argument for doing nothing, but rather an argument for doing little and for doing it gradually. This doctrine of 'least interference' lends itself either to a traditional conservative or to a radical anarchist interpretation. There are young libertarians who would oppose all censorship or regulation of pornography in modern society on Hayekian grounds, and yet Hayek himself never went that far in opposing government intervention. Contrariwise, Hayek latterly extended his doctrine to central banking, thus clashing with traditional economic liberalism which always treated state monopoly of the issue of money as an exception to the general rule of laissez-faire. In short, everyone agrees with what Hayek meant in general but there is a large spectrum of opinion as to what he meant in many particulars.

It will take another generation fully to digest Hayek's many and multi-faceted contributions to economics and indeed to social science as a whole.

Allyn Young was highly regarded in his time but today is known chiefly for a devastating review of Pigou's *Wealth of Welfare* (1913) and a much-reprinted paper on 'Increasing Returns and Economic Progress' (1928). Considering that he wrote no books and only a few major articles, it is difficult to understand nowadays why his reputation should have stood so high in his own lifetime. In part, the answer is that many of his efforts went into applied economics that quickly dated; for the rest, he never stayed long enough in one place to consolidate his reputation. Although a child prodigy, graduating at the age of 17, lack of means held back his Ph.D. until the age of 26. His first teaching post was at Western Reserve University in Cleveland, which was followed in rapid succession by a year at Dartmouth College, a year at Wisconsin University, four years at Stanford University, one year at Harvard University, two years at Washington University, one year at Cornell University, nine years back at Harvard University, concluding with one year at the London School of Economics.

Ugo Mazzola was the discoverer of the concept of 'public goods' – goods whose indivisible benefits and non-rivalrous consumption inhibit provision by any market mechanism. Although the full significance of his discovery was not appreciated until fairly recently, he was widely recognized in his own day as a major fiscal theorist, applying the principles of the Marginal Revolution to questions of public finance.

Mazzola graduated from the University of Naples at the age of 20 in 1883. He pursued post-graduate studies at the University of Berlin with Adolf Wagner and returned to Italy in 1887 to take up a chair in public finance at the University of Pavia. In 1896, he banded together with other economists, bought up the *Giornale degli Economisti* and helped to transform it into a centre of liberal economic thought. In the next 20 years, the *Giornale* published articles from all the leading Italian economists including Pantaleoni, Pareto and De Viti de Marco. Mazzola's major work on public finance, entitled *I dati scientifici della finanza pubblica*, appeared in 1890.

Note

Several paragraphs in this Introduction were borrowed from my *Great Economists Before Keynes* (Wheatsheaf Books, 1986) and *Great Economists Since Keynes* (Wheatsheaf Books, 1985).

[1]

Irving Fisher, F. D. R., and the Great Depression

William R. Allen

> I am naturally a theorist. I love theorizing. But I'm always leery about it.
>
> . . . the evidence has seemed to me to point in that direction. I am ready, if and when evidence points the other way, to move back again; for my ideal is to have my opinion, like a steam gauge, register whatever the facts require.
>
> I am fundamentally a reformer . . . .
>
> —Letters from Irving Fisher to Irving Norton Fisher, March 17, 1944, and August 30, 1944 (Yale)

> As you must know, I am, in my aims, a conservative. But I believe we need some radical surgery to save our American system from radicalism.
>
> —Letter from Irving Fisher to Edwin W. Kemmerer, March 10, 1939 (Princeton)

> It used to irk me a little that you didn't seem to set more store by my brains. One reason I switched from Mathematics to Economics was because economics, being more human, would appeal to you more.
>
> —Letter from Irving Fisher to his wife, February 23, 1937 (Yale)

I

Schumpeter declined to grade Keynes' *General Theory* "as if it were a student's examination book." And it is understandable that he would be loath to rank major economists generally.[1] But we may be forgiven the minimal suggestion that, through his own era, Irving Fisher had no superiors in American economics. Indeed, Schumpeter himself did "grade" Fisher: he was probably his country's "greatest scientific economist."[2]

Long before the beginning of President Franklin D. Roosevelt's New Deal in 1933, Fisher had credentials in abundance which distinguished him as a genuine giant of the profession. Superb theorist,

WILLIAM R. ALLEN *is Professor of Economics at the University of California, Los Angeles.*

1. Joseph A. Schumpeter, *Ten Great Economists* (New York, 1951), p. 291; reprinting of "John Maynard Keynes," *American Economic Review* 36 (1946).

2. Ibid., p. 223; see also idem, *A History of Economic Analysis* (New York, 1954), p. 872.

mathematician, and econometrician, he had by then produced half a dozen monumental books, beginning with his dissertation, *Mathematical Investigations in the Theory of Value and Prices* in 1892, and culminating with *The Theory of Interest* in 1930. Walrasian architect in the large structure of price, interest, and monetary analysis, he was also a prodigious innovator in the particular detail and topic and in the integrated, synthesized application.

Remarkably, this magnificent scholar, on the Yale faculty from 1890 to 1935, was not widely and generally recognized during most of his career as "this country's greatest scientific economist," deserving to be ranked with the world's best of his time. Even now, while the word of his greatness spreads, it spreads but slowly.

A man of great energy and vast catholicity of interests, Fisher did not confine himself to esoteric matters of economic theory and technique. He was a man concerned with his world, and in this vale of tears and ignorance, there were many things to set right—things of health and of world peace and of economic equity and of governmental reform.[3]

Righting wrongs, it was clear to Fisher, entailed government policy—new, positive government actions in some instances, regulatory actions in other cases, and revised, reduced, or eliminated actions in still others. He was pleased to have consulted with five presidents before 1933[4] and to have participated in several political ventures. But it was in the late years of his life, after the beginning of the Great Depression and during the New Deal, that this gentle, generous, aristocratic scholar from New Haven—often dismissed as a mere reformist, crusading crank—dedicated himself to immediate public problems and policies.

Fisher apparently well realized that influencing major changes in politics during the New Deal required first influencing That Man in the White House. Indeed, Fisher reports that, in a conversation in 1933, he made the President smile by saying, "I keep forgetting that

3. For biographical information, see: Irving Fisher, *Stable Money: A History of the Movement* (New York, 1934), Appendix I, esp. pp. 374-89; Arthur D. Gayer, ed., *The Lessons of Monetary Experience* (New York, 1937), pp. 441-44; Joseph E. Reeve, *Monetary Reform Movements: A Survey of Recent Plans and Panaceas* (Washington, D.C., 1943), esp. pp. 162-69; Max Sasuly, "Irving Fisher and Social Science," *Econometrica* 15 (1947): 255-78; Irving Norton Fisher, *My Father, Irving Fisher* (New York, 1956); Maurice Allais, "Irving Fisher," *International Encyclopedia of the Social Sciences* (New York, 1968), vol. 5, esp. pp. 475-76.

4. Presidents Theodore Roosevelt, Taft, Wilson, Harding, and Hoover. See letter from Fisher to his wife on conversation with F. D. Roosevelt, August 9, 1933 (Yale).

you're not the whole government!"[5] Noting reports and fears of "revolution"—"probably no president since Lincoln inherited a more alarming situation because of the baffled rage of the unemployed and bankrupt and those who fear becoming so"[6]—he urged leadership on the President. His exhortation (and criticism) was vigorous and direct—at least three times, he found reason to sign letters, "your frank friend";[7] it was persistent and prolonged, taking the form of more than one hundred written messages from early 1933 through 1939 (with twenty-five from Roosevelt to Fisher) and another twenty-odd through November 1944 and also the form of personal conferences, there being at least four and possibly seven meetings of Roosevelt and Fisher between August 1933 and January 1936;[8] and it was expansive and generally optimistic—with adequate pursuit of proper goals, he assured the President, "centuries of future prosperity, free from great depressions, will be your monument."[9]

But the world was not to be saved by economic recovery and reform alone, even if that was of "first interest."[10] Fisher had made "intensive studies on several . . . problems besides those of money and unemployment."[11] There was the broad area of public health, including health insurance, a proposed Department of Health (or of General Welfare, or of Health and Welfare), narcotics, and eugenics.[12] This area provided probably "the best examples of the most appropriate form of governmental investments."[13] Public health

5. Loc. cit. "Today practically nothing can be done except through him or with his consent." Letter from Fisher to Orlando F. Weber, October 27, 1937 (Yale).

6. Letter from Fisher to FDR, February 25, 1933 (Yale). ". . . the emergency is the greatest in our financial history. . . ." Letter from Fisher to FDR, March 2, 1933 (Yale).

7. Letters from Fisher to FDR, March 18, 1933 (Yale), June 16, 1936 (Yale), and October 14, 1937 (FDR). Fisher left no room to doubt his intensity: "I urge you with more earnestness than I have ever urged anything in my life, to adopt, if you have not already, the money philosophy of [Benjamin] Strong [Governor of the Federal Reserve Bank of New York, 1914-1928]. . . . I cannot repress my earnestness. Were it necessary I believe I would be willing to die to secure from you the boon I believe you can deliver to your waiting fellow countrymen." Letter from Fisher to FDR, February 25, 1933 (Yale).

8. The clearly documented dates are August 9, 1933, September 6, 1934, July 11, 1935, and mid-January 1936; uncertain dates include January 9, 1935, October 1935, and about December 10, 1935. Fisher and Roosevelt first met "at the Murray Hill Hotel at the beginning of the Cox and Roosevelt campaign" [1920]. Letter from Fisher to FDR, November 22, 1934 (Yale).

9. Letter from Fisher to FDR, June 16, 1936 (Yale).

10. Letter from Fisher to FDR, December 13, 1934 (Yale).

11. Letter from Fisher to FDR, November 10, 1936 (FDR).

12. Letters from Fisher to FDR, June 11, 1934 (FDR), January 14, 1937 (FDR), and February 22, 1937 (FDR).

13. Letter from Fisher to FDR, December 13, 1934 (Yale). Such investments "re-

and hygiene included the "drug-craving" problem of alcohol; the professor told the President straightforwardly, "I regret the repeal of Prohibition and your part in it," and he advocated "the virtual suppression of advertising" even of beer and wine, consumption of which "tend[s] to lead, sooner or later, to spirits."[14] Presumably less pressing was "calendar reform."[15] But of growing urgency was "world peace," and Fisher evidently was hopeful before and during World War II that a second effort, with United States participation, would be successful in establishing an effective World Court and a League of Nations, based on "*collective international police action* . . . to *enforce* peace."[16]

II

For all his other interests—profound or quixotic—it was the problems of national income, employment, and price level on which Fisher wrote "furiously"[17] during the 1930's. Understandably, in his largely gratuitous, but sometimes requested, counsel to the President, Fisher did not provide elaborate, well-developed analyses. But in his cryptic reviews and summary assertions, several characteristics are conspicuous.

His fundamental premise and basis for all other analysis and policy prescription was this: money matters and matters most. He was, indeed, the first of the modern "monetarists," and much of the best current discussion has a decided Fisherine quality. The depression has been and the recovery will be (and, in due course, was) a monetary phenomenon: "the only sure and rapid recovery is through monetary means," and the President would do well to "anounce publicly and aggressively that, of all things tried, monetary policies have succeeded most."[18] More specifically, the money stock in the form of

turn far more than the ordinary rate of interest in economic benefits to the country but so diffuse the return that no private investor would get back enough benefits from his own investment to entice him." Loc. cit.

14. Letter from Fisher to FDR, November 12, 1933 (Yale).

15. Letter from Fisher to FDR, November 10, 1936 (FDR).

16. Letters from Fisher to FDR, June 11, 1934 (FDR), January 4, 1936 (Yale), July 20, 1937 (Yale), August 20, 1937 (FDR), October 6, 1937 (Yale), and November 22, 1944 (Yale) (emphases in original). In his 1934 and 1944 letters, Fisher notes having organized the "Pro-League Independents" in the Cox-and-Roosevelt campaign.

17. Letter from Fisher to William R. Foster, January 20, 1936 (Yale). His publications during this period include, along with *The Theory of Interest* (New York, 1930): *The Money Illusion* (New York, 1928, 1930), *The Stock Market Crash—and After* (New York, 1930), *Booms and Depressions* (New York, 1932), *Stamp Scrip* (New York, 1933), *Inflation?* (New York, 1933), *After Inflation, What?* (New York, 1933), *Stable Money: A History of the Movement* (New York, 1934), *100% Money* (New York, 1935, 1936, 1945), and *Constructive Income Taxation* (New York, 1942).

18. Letter from Fisher to Louis M. Howe, Secretary to the President, May 18,

"check-book money" had been permitted to fall from the 1929 level by over one-third, and it must be largely restored: "as the great depression was primarily monetary, the remedy must be largely monetary."[19] Massive changes in the money stock—"the chief direct cause of the depression and of the recovery"[20]—result in changes in the price level, and both theory and empirical evidence indicate that "deflation reduces employment and reflation restores it."[21] Our "one salvation . . . is to get us out of the depression—and not 'gradually' but at once and in the only way which has worked—monetary reflation."[22]

During the sharp recession of 1937–38, which greatly worried Fisher,[23] he concisely reviewed much of his basic position:

1934 (Yale). Also letters from Fisher to FDR, June 11, 1934 (FDR), December 18, 1934 (Yale), May 23, 1936 (Yale), June 16, 1936 (Yale), and October 23, 1937 (Yale).

19. Letter from Fisher to Henry A. Wallace, Secretary of Agriculture, November 26, 1937 (Yale).

20. Letter from Fisher to FDR, December 21, 1936 (Yale).

21. Letter from Fisher to FDR, September 11, 1933 (Yale). "I think the word 'reflation' is a good one because the prefix adds to its meaning a reference to recent history." Letter from Fisher to E. W. Kemmerer, February 3, 1933 (Princeton); see also letter from Fisher to Kemmerer, December 18, 1932 (Princeton). "Reflation" referred to correction—up or down—of an undesirable previous change in the price level. Letter from Fisher to Winthrop W. Aldrich, Chairman, Chase National Bank, January 6, 1936 (Yale). "Some day we may have to fight inflation again. I have all my life but Hoover and [Ogden L.] Mills [Secretary of the Treasury] have no real reason to fight it now unless it be 'politics.' What we are fighting now is deflation. It needs to be stopped and reversed just as in 1920 inflation needed to be stopped and reversed. The reversal in each case may well be called reflation." Letter from Fisher to FDR, February 25, 1933 (Yale).

To some, "reflation" was a term of intended camouflage. In February 1932, Wallace wrote to William Hirth, "The word inflation grates harshly on the ears of many bankers. Therefore, we speak of reflation and save their feelings." William E. Leuchtenburg, *Franklin D. Roosevelt and the New Deal, 1932-1940* (New York, 1963), p. 38.

22. Letter from Fisher to Marvin H. McIntyre, Assistant Secretary (later Secretary) to the President, May 12, 1934 (Yale). "I have never thought that money was the only factor in this, or any other depression. In fact, at the beginning of the depression I gave it much less of a role than now. The more I study the more I am convinced that it is the major factor. . . . There are, I realize, numerous other factors as explained in my book 'Booms and Depressions.' " Letter from Fisher to Fritz Lehmann, New School for Social Research, July 20, 1937 (Yale).

23. "Just now we are losing demand deposits fast. I am *very fearful*—more than ever before." Letter from Fisher to Ralph W. Manuel, bank president, Minneapolis, November 20, 1937 (Yale) (emphasis in original). "I fear we are now in as crucial a period as that of 1929/30 when deflation was permitted to destroy our wealth." Letter from Fisher to Senator Robert F. Wagner, November 24, 1937 (Yale). "Unless the present recession is checked it means another great depression." Letter from Fisher to Wallace, November 26, 1937 (Yale). "Just now I am a pessimist. I hope you can give me some hope that the country won't be allowed to go very much further toward Hades." Letter from Fisher to Lauchlin Currie, Federal Reserve, January 20, 1938 (Yale). See also letters from Fisher to Daniel C. Roper, Secretary of Commerce,

(1) This "recession" is very largely monetary.
(2) But I agree with you that it is not wholly monetary and that the "monopoly" price of labor is largely responsible for unemployment.
(3) I also agree that booms and depressions are to some extent unavoidable. But if monetary control were ideally exercised, booms and depressions would be far smaller than they are.
(4) Money management, under appropriate legislative authority, could do far more than it has and could control the volume of circulating medium within one percent of whatever standard is set up. . . .
(6) We do not need to subscribe to the naive versions of the "quantity theory of money" to admit that the volume of the circulating medium is an important factor in booms and depressions—both as a cause and as an effect. . . .
(8) Even if . . . our present recession in business can be attributed chiefly to a recession in velocity rather than volume, or even if the recession be entirely non-monetary, the remedy could still be an increase in volume.[24]

The asserted correlation of money stock with income and employment was found, Fisher contended, not only in the experience of

November 26, 1937 (Yale), and to Robert L. Owen, November 26, 1937 (Library of Congress—Owen).

24. Letter from Fisher to Marriner S. Eccles, Chairman, Board of Governors, Federal Reserve System, January 20, 1938 (Yale). Fisher "urged" the President to have measures taken "for increasing the circulating medium in order to promptly secure recovery. A quick recovery is entirely feasible." He warned that "we are on the verge of a big drop" and expressed "the desperate hope that you and your co-workers will take *immediate* action to increase the volume and flow of money, that is, of effective purchasing power." Letters from Fisher to FDR, December 20, 1937 (Yale), and February 9, 1938 (Yale) (emphasis in original); see also letter from Fisher to FDR, July 20, 1937 (Yale). But there was "an apparent lack of a proper monetary policy in Washington" (letter from Fisher to Francis L. Brown, insurance company president, Rockford, Illinois, November 19, 1937 [Yale]), although there was "in Washington . . . real knowledge of how to do this" (letter from Fisher to Orval W. Adams, President, American Bankers Association, December 19, 1937 [Yale]). Fisher was "disquieted by the reports of what Eccles has been saying. It seems to me that the control of money, the easiest of all controls and most incontestably proper for the government, is not being exercised nor even planned for fully." Letter from Fisher to Homer Cummings, Attorney General, December 10, 1937 (Yale). Fisher recommended to "Wallace's economists" that "they urge Wallace to urge the President" to increase money in circulation. Wallace "almost surely" did so. But then, "why hasn't President Roosevelt done something?" Letter from Fisher to his wife, December 16, 1937 (Yale). "I'm going to make a desperate effort to stick a pin in F.D.R. He could save the day. . . . Why couldn't I have influenced the President more and earlier! I suppose it's my shortcoming." Letter from Fisher to his wife, December 12, 1937 (Yale).

the United States but in foreign histories as well, particularly that of Sweden and, to a lesser extent, England. On several occasions he urged the President to learn from such interpreted history—sending him literature for that purpose and trying to arrange appointments with him for Eli Heckscher and Ragnar Frisch—and insisted that it adequately tested his hypothesis as to the primacy of money. "Deflation inevitably and inexorably causes depression in all places and times,"[25] wrote Fisher, and "every nation which has recovered has done so by monetary means."[26] But the purported lessons of foreign experience were not to be readily accepted by the President. In one of his few substantive responses to the professor, Roosevelt wrote: "My general thought is that our economic problems necessarily differ greatly from those of almost all European countries. For the same reason that British financial problems could only be compared with ours if Canada, Australia, and South Africa were tacked onto England and Scotland!"[27]

Why did "falling prices turn profit to loss and compel shutdowns"?[28] In a 1933 letter to Roosevelt one week before his Inauguration, Fisher provided a relatively elaborate analysis in terms of "real debt":

> The kernel of it all is that since the stock market crash we had had (1) over-indebtedness, (2) consequent distress selling to try to get out of debt, (3) consequent falling prices, deflation or a swelling dollar, (4) consequently *an increase in the real debt.*
>
> Though the debts payable in America were (according to my "Booms and Depressions") reduced in number of dollars from 234 billions in 1929 to 197 billions in 1932, the dollar was so swollen that the latter 197 was the equivalent (in terms of the original dollars of 1929) of 302 billions! Now the dollar is still bigger. Each dollar of debts is 81% more burdensome than before we started down hill. In other words the liquidation *has not really liquidated* but, on the contrary *has actually aggravated*, the debts. That is the main secret of the depression. . . .
>
> The idea that we already are "nearly through" is wrong, we have not made any net progress whatever but our flounderings to get out of the debt bog has only sunk us deeper and deeper in terms of real things, cotton, wheat, lumber, etc. Those who do

25. Letter from Fisher to FDR, February 25, 1933 (Yale).
26. Article by Fisher, written for Index Number Institute, to be released June 10, 1935, copy sent with covering letter to FDR, June 3, 1935 (FDR).
27. Letter from FDR to Fisher, June 8, 1934 (Yale).
28. Letter from Fisher to FDR, February 25, 1933 (Yale).

not see this are those who only count the dollars owed but do not *measure* each dollar. They have the "money illusion" that the dollar of 1933 is the same dollar as that of 1929.[29]

He felt he had "made a real contribution in linking up the 'debt disease' with the 'dollar disease' " in analysis of "such mock liquidation," and he was "naturally anxious" to "reach all serious students of so-called cycle theory." For "if the diagnosis is correct it seems to me we are still in danger of going down into an almost bottomless abyss unless either there is a thorough-going debt scaling or a thorough-going and purposive rise in the price level."[30] It was preferred "to reflate the price level, that is, deflate the dollar, and permit payment of commitments on something like the basis on which they were undertaken."[31]

While merely stopping the fall in prices was not sufficient and some restoration of the price level was vital, Fisher made it clear that he was "*against inflation* as well as against deflation."[32] Again and

29. Loc. cit. (emphases in original). ". . . the more people pay, the more they owe, because the mass stampede of payments enlarge[s] the dollar." ". . . only the stock market has been liquidated, and other debts have increased in burden." Letter from Fisher to Ray B. Westerfield, February 27, 1933 (Yale). Fisher anticipated the analysis in correspondence as early as 1931. See letters to John Dewey, December 18, 1931 (Yale), and to Prime Minister James Ramsay MacDonald, December 18, 1931 (Yale).

30. Letters from Fisher to Kemmerer, February 3, 1933 (Princeton), to Nicholas Murray Butler, February 27, 1933 (Columbia), and to William G. Eliot, Jr., November [no day], 1933 (Yale). Fisher's major publications on the subject are *Booms and Depressions* (1932) and "The Debt-Deflation Theory of Great Depressions," *Econometrica* 1 (1933): 337-57; see also *Inflation?* (1933), pp. 80-84. While drafting *Booms and Depressions*, he was "hoping that this book may, from a practical point of view, at least, be my chief contribution in this field." Letter from Fisher to James Harvey Rogers, April 12, 1932 (Yale).

31. Letter from Fisher to FDR, February 25, 1933 (Yale). Roosevelt cabled the London Economic Conference on July 3, 1933, that the United States "seeks the kind of a dollar which, a generation hence, will have the same purchasing power and debt-repaying power as the dollar value we hope to attain in the near future." And in conversation with Fisher a month later, "he repeated what he has said publicly re raising the price level to the average level at which debts were contracted." Letter from Fisher to his wife, August 9, 1933 (Yale). See also letter from Fisher to Jacob Viner, Treasury, September 28, 1934 (Yale). Changes in the price level are accompanied by relative changes in agricultural and industrial prices: "when prices in general fall, prices at the farm fall by a greater percentage than prices in the city, because the freight and other intervening costs keep constant and so constitute a fixed difference between farm and city prices. Reversely, a general rise in prices helps agricultural prices more than industrial; that is, a general rise in prices would itself largely remedy the maladjustment between agricultrual and industrial prices." Memorandum from Fisher to FDR, October 22, 1934 (Yale).

32. Letter from Fisher to FDR, December 1, 1933 (FDR) (emphasis in original). Fisher wrote to the President several times about the dangers and the possible control of inflation during the period, 1940–1944 (June 19, 1940 [Yale], June 4, 1941 [FDR],

again, especially during 1933, he urged all possible haste in reflating: "reflation . . . is the first essential . . . of recovery."[33] But he emphasized that the desired rise in prices was limited—specifically, "up at least to within 10% of the level of 1926 and not . . . above 1926."[34] There must be "neither inflation or deflation; . . . having restored our price level to the point of maximum equity attainable, and no more, we must thereafter hold it stable; . . . then our prosperity will also be stable and permanent and our people's money safe."[35]

April 14, 1942 [FDR], July 30, 1942 [FDR], December 28, 1942 [Yale], September 13, 1943 [Yale], November 22, 1944 [Yale]). After the war, Fisher "was quite shocked to see how ignorant" a certain senator was "as to how to combat inflation. It was the usual Hamlet with Hamlet left out—practically no mention of money." Letter from Fisher to Congressman Jerry Voorhis, November 7, 1946 (Voorhis).

33. Letter from Fisher to Raymond Moley, December 16, 1932 (Hoover).

34. Letter from Fisher to his wife, August 9, 1933 (Yale). In late 1931, Fisher doubted "that the price level ought to be raised *all* the way back to where we started from but only say half way back." Letter from Fisher to Kemmerer, November 6, 1931 (Princeton) (emphasis in original). Similarly, more than a year later, the reflation goal was "put at 80 on the basis of 1926 being 100. This would be about half way back from where the price level is today." Letter from Fisher to Moley, December 16, 1932 (Hoover). In February 1933, he was a bit more cautious: prices should not double (which would put the index some 12 percent above the 1926 level), with an increase to only 70–75 percent of 1926 being preferred. Letters of Fisher to Rev. Charles E. Coughlin, February 16, 1933 (Yale), and to James H. Rand, Jr., President, Remington Rand, February 28, 1933 (Yale). In March, a 15 percent increase (to 65 percent of 1926) was deemed much too little, and a level of 80 percent of 1926 was about right. Letter from Fisher to Garfield V. Cox, Aaron Director, Paul H. Douglas, Albert G. Hart, Frank H. Knight, Lloyd W. Mints, Henry Schultz, and Henry C. Simons, all of the University of Chicago, March 19, 1933 (Yale). Beginning in June, it was advocated that the index "approach" the 1926 level "or thereabouts" as "the upper limit," and by October 1934, the unqualified objective was 1926. Letters from Fisher to FDR, June 1, 1933 (Yale) (sent also to O. M. W. Sprague, Treasury), December 1, 1933 (FDR), and September 6, 1934 (FDR), and memorandum from Fisher to FDR, October 22, 1934 (FDR).

Fisher at one point explained his mode of deduction: "I think the price level should be raised from the present 56 to 80 (1926 = 100). I think the principle is . . . that reflation should take us back to the weighted average level at which contracts affected by the reflation were entered into. This will give us nearly as it is humanly possible the greatest justice to the greatest number. This center of gravity is different for debtors than for creditors because many debts, such as government debts, have changed by bond sales since they were originally entered into. I took the various classes of debts described in . . . 'Booms and Depressions' and guessed at the weights, that is the amounts under each class which are to be allocated to different years back to war days, with the result that the weighted index representing the average level at which the debtors would be affected by reflation at the time they contracted their debts was 88, while the average for the creditors came out 78. The average of these two averages is 83 which in round numbers I have called 80." Letter from Fisher to Cox, Director, Douglas, Hart, Knight, Mints, Schultz, and Simons, March 19, 1933 (Yale).

35. Letter from Fisher to FDR, March 2, 1933 (Yale). "The present situation in currency cries to heaven for reflation (up to a reasonable price level about half way back) and, after such reflation, for stabilization." Letter from Fisher to FDR, Feb-

Reflation and then stabilization made desirable, if it did not necessitate, "a purely managed currency, unbacked by metal," Fisher claimed:[36] "we must have a stable dollar first, last and all the time, and I am willing to have the dollar managed to make it stable."[37] Internal balance required a high degree of "independence" from foreign disruptive influences—"otherwise we shall again suffer deflation or inflation if they do."[38] It followed that the "unstable" international gold standard was an anathema. "It was the universal gold standard which made the depression universal, spreading the deflation infection from one country to another. Only countries not on the gold standard escaped."[39] The gold standard does stabilize exchange rates, but that does not imply stability of domestic price levels—and "internal stability is far more important than external for the United States."[40] Further, American "domestic monetary stability . . . would stabilize foreign exchange relative to half the world," including Sweden and England. The other half would soon follow. "Such world stabilization, based on each nation's internal stability, would indirectly but most powerfully restore political stability and world peace."[41] Fisher noted the possibility of pegging the dollar with the pound or the franc, but this was only a second-best objective—and the pegging should be done only after the United States and its finan-

ruary 25, 1933 (Yale). "Production, trade and employment are depressed by falling prices, restored by reflation, and further improved by stabilization." Letter from Fisher to FDR, December 18, 1934 (Yale). Fisher urged the President "to make clearer to the public the fundamental injustices flowing from changes in the purchasing power of money." Letter from Fisher to FDR, February 21, 1935 (Yale). The President should "not countenance uncontrolled inflation." Letter from Fisher to FDR, September 6, 1934 (FDR). And Fisher had little fear of "overdoing . . . the reflation. . . .we have no experience, so far as I know, showing that in trying to correct deflation we run into inflation." Letter from Fisher to Kemmerer, December 18, 1932 (Princeton).

36. Letter from Fisher to FDR, October 22, 1934 (Yale).

37. Letter from Fisher to unnamed correspondent, July 22, 1938 (Yale). See also article by Fisher, "The Money Planks," Index Number Institute, for release June 22, 1936, copy sent to FDR, June 18, 1936 (FDR).

38. Letter from Fisher to FDR, June 1, 1933 (Yale); see also letter from Fisher to FDR, April 30, 1933 (Yale).

39. Letter from Fisher to FDR, April 30, 1933 (Yale); article by Fisher, "The Money Planks," op. cit.

40. Letter from Fisher to Philip Cortney, July 9, 1945 (Yale). "Sweden is profoundly right in putting her internal stability above external stability. . . . Yet most people have the erroneous idea that the external stability is the more important. This doubtless because the evils of external instability are clearly perceived as such, while the evils of internal instability are always attributed to something else." Letter from Fisher to FDR, August 9, 1937 (FDR).

41. Letter from Fisher to William Allen White, June 6, 1936 (Library of Congress–White, series C, box 246).

cial partners had established their desired price levels.[42] Generally, those who plead for "the restoration of the old-fashioned 'automatic' gold standard" ignore the fact that "events have proven that all there is automatic about it is the certainty with which it promotes booms and depressions."[43]

In the interests of proper monetary management, Fisher volunteered numerous suggestions pertaining to substantive policy, administrative structure, and political tactics. The most important policy proposals include the following:

(i) Devalue the dollar, if there is to be a pegged price of gold at all.[44] Fisher suggested, at successive times, gold prices of $30, $38, and $41.34 per ounce.[45] The immediate basis for this recommendation evidently was a surprisingly ready acceptance of the doctrine advanced by George F. Warren and Frank A. Pearson that dollar commodity prices (and output) would move with the dollar gold price.[46]

42. Letter from Fisher to FDR, February 26, 1933 (Hoover); letter from Fisher to his wife, August 9, 1933 (Yale); memorandum from Fisher to FDR, October 22, 1934 (Yale); letter from Fisher to Cordell Hull, Secretary of State, March 6, 1936 (Yale). While Fisher favored abandonment of the gold standard, "I realize such a course, if openly avowed, would 'raise hell,' especially with the gold and silver interests." October 22, 1934, op. cit.

43. Letter from Fisher to unnamed correspondent, July 12, 1938 (Yale). "I feel a little ashamed of myself for not having really fought against the retention of the gold standard or the reversion to it after the World War. Cassel did speak out and so did Keynes. I did make some efforts but felt I was butting my head against a stone wall and soon desisted." Letter from Fisher to Kemmerer, April 17, 1936 (Princeton).

44. Letters from Fisher to FDR, October 3, 1933 (Yale), and December 1, 1933 (FDR). Fisher was "in favor of America *managing her own price level*," one possible means being "the compensated dollar plan to which devaluation is the natural introduction." Letter from Fisher to FDR, April 30, 1933 (Yale) (emphasis in original); see also letter from Fisher to Rand, February 28, 1933 (Yale): "A fixed weight gold dollar and a fixed price level cannot both be maintained forever." Apparently, Fisher gave the President no hint of what "the compensated dollar plan" was. Two years earlier, in contact with President Hoover, Fisher disavowed application of the plan: "On thinking over our talk of Wednesday, I wonder if, when you expressed the fear that stabilizing the purchasing power of money would change the basis of contracts, you thought I was pleading for support by you of my old 'Compensated Dollar Plan.' I was not. It became evident long ago that immediate, practical progress lay along other lines." Letter from Fisher to Herbert Hoover, July 10, 1931 (Yale).

45. Letters from Fisher to FDR, June 1, 1933 (Yale), and September 6, 1934 (FDR), letter from Fisher to his wife, August 9, 1933 (Yale), and letter from Fisher to Howe, May 18, 1934 (Yale). The first price was to be only a temporary selling price (with gold purchased at the market price). The latter two prices were recommended after the price had already—from October 1933 to January 1934—been raised from $20 per ounce to $35.

46. The President asked Fisher in conversation if he "agreed with Warren and [James Harvey] Rogers that if he [Roosevelt] got the Federal Reserve to buy newly mined gold at say $29 an ounce it would help raise commodity prices. I said I did." Letter from Fisher to his wife, August 9, 1933 (Yale); see also letter from Fisher to his wife, May 12, 1932 (Yale). "Warren and Pearson's work seems to me of a very

The "price index . . . for basic commodities in the United States has varied with the price of gold. . . . in all countries studied, the price index . . . fluctuates with the price of gold. . . . the countries which have most raised the price of gold have gained most in production."[47]

(ii) Fisher used less esoteric analysis in telling the President that "we need a rise in the price level by the only means it can be raised or ever has been raised, an increase in the quantity or velocity, or both, of the circulating medium."[48] And the quantity of money can be increased by selling government bonds to banks. Fisher recommended expansionary open-market operations, commended such activity in the early New Deal, and felt that it would be facilitated in later years by the Banking Act of 1935.[49] He seemed cautiously hope-

---

high order. Such a collection and analysis of facts can find few parallels. I cannot agree with you that his [sic] work is wrong or useless. It has been, I believe, convincing to those who have read it with an open mind." Letter from Fisher to Viner, September 28, 1934 (Yale). Fisher found the Warren and Pearson *Prices* (1933) to be "splendid," "admirable and comprehensive," "an important forward step" with its "striking" new evidence. *Inflation?*, pp. 7, 24; untitled memorandum, January 1934 (Yale).

47. Letter from Fisher to FDR, December 18, 1934 (Yale). Soon after the inauguration of the President, Warren wrote to him: "The mere issuance of paper money or expansion of credit, so long as each dollar is kept at par, will have very little influence on prices. The world determines the value of 23.22 grains of gold in terms of commodities. We determine the grains of gold in the dollar, and only by this means can we set our price level out of line with the world value of gold. . . . There is one and only one way to raise our commodity price level; that is, by reducing the amount of gold in the dollar." April 24, 1933 (FDR). Warren had written to Fisher in the same manner. November 18, 1932 (Yale). It appears that by mid-1936, Fisher's confidence in Warren's perspicacity had waned. See letter from Fisher to Warren, August 14, 1936 (Yale).

48. Letter from Fisher to FDR, February 25, 1933 (Yale). "Purchasing power" is increased by "increasing the volume or velocity of money." Letter from Fisher to FDR, October 24, 1937 (Yale).

49. ". . . what has done most to get us out of the depression is the virtual manufacture of new circulating medium in the form of bank credits incident to the purchase of government bonds." Letter from Fisher to FDR, May 23, 1936 (Yale); cf. memorandum from Fisher to FDR, October 22, 1934 (Yale), and letter from Fisher to FDR, October 24, 1937 (Yale).

Contrary to the belief of one historian that Fisher strongly disapproved of the banking bill (ultimately, the Act of 1935), drawn largely under the direction of M. S. Eccles, new Governor of the Federal Reserve Board (Leuchtenburg, p. 159), Fisher was generally enthusiastic about the legislation. It is "a great step forward—probably the greatest in your administration—if, as I anticipate, you appoint the best men on the new Federal Reserve Board." Letter from Fisher to FDR, July 2, 1935 (Yale); see also letter from Fisher to FDR and enclosed article, " 'Deflation' from Dissolution of N.R.A.," Index Number Institute, for release June 10, 1935, sent June 3, 1935 (FDR). Although the Act of 1935 was "the most promising thing in the Roosevelt administration . . . I greatly regret that the power to increase reserve requirements was curtailed through the influence of Senator Glass, supposedly the most fearful of inflation of all the Senators." Letter from Fisher to Aldrich, December 22, 1935 (Yale). "The Presi-

ful that the Federal Reserve would find the sense of direction and decisiveness in open-market policy which it tragically lost in 1928 with the death of Benjamin Strong, Governor of the Federal Reserve Bank of New York.[50]

(iii) At least partly in the context of increasing the money stock was Fisher's early advocacy of governmental guarantee of bank de-

dent now has the power to appoint all seven members of the Federal Reserve Board and, presumably, will appoint those who believe in this Eccles Act. This means a definitely managed currency in the United States." Letter from Fisher to Senator Elmer Thomas, September 5, 1935 (Yale).

Fisher very actively offered guidance in the making of Federal Reserve appointments. Letters from Fisher to FDR, July 2, 1935 (Yale), and December 21, 1936 (Yale). "As I told the President when I first talked with him about this, which was last October, these appointments seem to me quite as important as if he had to appoint all of the Supreme Court at the same time. . . . All who have been appointed on the Board were on the 'preferred' list which I gave the President." Letter from Fisher to Foster, January 20, 1936 (Yale); cf. letters from Fisher to FDR, July 2, 1935 (Yale), and to Rogers, February 21, 1936 (Yale).

50. In early 1933, Fisher complained to the President-elect that the "old controversy between Governor Strong and the Board is, somewhat transformed, still the great problem today. . . . I had told Governor Strong that his policies would, I feared, die with him unless enacted into law. . . . Strong's policies did nearly die with him. . . . Had he lived and his policies been followed, I believe we would have been spared 90% of this depression." Letter from Fisher to FDR, February 25, 1933 (Yale), cf. n. 7, above, and letter from Fisher to Aldrich, December 22, 1935 (Yale).

Fisher favored "a Stabilization Commission which, in a sense, would be superior to the Federal Reserve System. . . . I have more and more come to the conclusion not only that the Federal Reserve System has lamentably failed as a preventer of inflation and deflation but that it is destined to fail in the future if reliance is placed upon it for that function. It has the bankers' traditions and the bankers' control and bankers know so little about stabilization. . . . The Stabilization function is a relatively simple one but it requires highly specialized knowledge." Letter from Fisher to Cox, Director, Douglas, Hart, Knight, Mints, Schultz, and Simons, March 19, 1933 (Yale). In 1934, Fisher recommended to the President establishment of "a 'monetary authority' or 'currency commission' with the sole task of managing the dollar." Letter from Fisher to FDR, October 22, 1934 (Yale). And in 1935, he wrote for public distribution that "we still need to restore further our broken down monetary structure," and "the proposed omnibus banking bill, duly amended, is what will do this best." " 'Deflation' from Dissolution of N.R.A.," op. cit.; see also letter from Fisher to FDR, June 16, 1936 (Yale).

Fisher thought generally well of Eccles (but see n. 24, above). "Chairman Eccles, I believe, has much more understanding of the money problem than any of his predecessors." Letter from Fisher to FDR, October 24, 1937 (Yale); see also letters from Fisher to Aldrich, December 22, 1935 (Yale), Foster, January 20, 1936 (Yale), and FDR, November 24, 1937 (Yale). With respect to Fisher's proposal for 100 percent required reserves against demand deposits (discussed later), Roosevelt was early assured that "Mr. Eccles believes it sound." Letter from Fisher to FDR, December 12, 1934 (Yale). Ten years later, he again wrote the President about Eccles and the 100 percent reserve plan: "Mr. Eccles is, I believe, at heart for it; but would, I think, not touch it politically until assured of your backing." Letter from Fisher to FDR, November 22, 1944 (Yale). Fisher considered as his opponents Senator Carter Glass and "bankers as a group." Letters from Fisher to FDR, February 25, 1933 (Yale), March 2, 1933 (Yale), April 4, 1936 (Yale), and June 16, 1936 (Yale).

posits: "*with reflation*, the risk in such guarantee would be negligible. Also, with such guarantee, *much* less new credit or money would be required."[51] And he suggested either fully paying off frozen deposits or partially lending to depositors of closed banks.[52]

(iv) Still another proposal was the "monetization" of "float," i.e., requiring banks to give immediately available credit to the depositors of collection items. Fisher estimated that adoption of such practice would increase the "circulating medium" by possibly five billion dollars and would be a preferable alternative to lowering the required reserve ratio.[53] Roosevelt forwarded the proposal to the Federal Reserve, where it was vigorously and caustically rejected.[54]

51. Handwritten postscript in letter from Fisher to FDR, May 13, 1933 (FDR) (emphases in original); also letter from Fisher to FDR, February 26, 1933 (Hoover), draft of telegram for FDR, from Fisher to John R. Commons, March 5, 1933 (Yale), and letter from Fisher to Cox, Director, Douglas, Hart, Knight, Mints, Schultz, and Simons, March 19, 1933 (Yale). For Fisher, such insurance was to be an "emergency measure" and a "temporary expedient," which he had advocated "for over a year."

52. "Open closed banks, or at any rate give the depositors their money by buying preferred stock or buying the banks' frozen assets." Letter from Fisher to his wife, August 9, 1933 (Yale). "Lend depositors on their frozen deposits—up to 50% or 75%." Letter from Fisher to Howe, May 18, 1934 (Yale).

On behalf of the President, Fisher was asked, "who gets the difference," if the government pays seventy-five cents on the dollar to a depositor in a bank which can pay only ten cents. Letter from McIntyre to Fisher, May 3, 1934 (Yale). Fisher replied: "Why not simply lend the money, on long term, to depositors via the bank and with its endorsement?" If need be, it would "be worth losing the 65 cents to help that much toward getting us out of the depression. . . . We would expect some losses but would save indirectly in relief expense; and at least a part of the loss . . . would be reclaimed as the banks' assets improved under reflation." Letter from Fisher to McIntyre, May 12, 1934 (Yale).

53. In advocating "monetization" of "float," Fisher supported a plan of his friend, Robert H. Hemphill, which had been sent to the President. The measure would make "reduction in bank reserves unnecessary and would be far preferable because:

"(1) The addition of the 'float' to our circulating medium would come *overnight* . . . while any considerable additional circulation medium through lowered bank reserves will require months of time.

"(2) The 'float' addition would be positive and certain while the other might never materialize at all, to any worthwhile extent.

"(3) The reduction of the reserve requirements is a step backward toward the very instability which has been the fundamental trouble. . . .

"The 'float' monetization would have the virtue, as compared with any other form of reflation, of causing no public alarm. You could then and, I believe, should reduce the scale of the spending program, which *does* cause alarm." Letter from Fisher to FDR, April 15, 1938 (FDR) (emphases in the original).

54. Eccles wrote to the President that the Hemphill plan, in addition to having "serious legal and administrative" difficulties, was largely misdirected: "It seems doubtful to me that depositors would be induced by such a concession to increase their expenditures, which in the final analysis are determined by their incomes. The plan places undue emphasis on the effect of increasing the amount of deposits,

(v) With respect to increasing the velocity of money circulation, Fisher supported the use of "dated stamp scrip."[55] Under general central direction, localities would issue scrip to "be used for local relief, paying employees of city for new public works, lending to local concerns." The scrip was not to be accepted unless it bore purchased dated weekly stamps. Since the holder of the scrip had an incentive to spend it before the date of affixing the next stamp,[56] the scheme

---

whereas the more important elements in the business situation are those which determine how and at what rate available deposits are utilized. These latter elements are largely nonmonetary." Letter from Eccles to FDR, April 29, 1938 (FDR). Eccles sent with his letter a five-page memorandum on the Hemphill proposal, and the President forwarded a copy to Fisher. The bulk of the argument contended that "the amount of deferment [generally less than one billion dollars] is small relative to total volume of deposits subject to check." Thus, "there are relatively few occasions when the use of bank deposits is restricted by credit deferment on account of collection items. . . . [A]bandonment of deposit credit deferment would have an appreciable effect on expenditures in the long run only if it permitted the carrying of smaller balances. . . . In any event the effect would not be more than an initial and temporary bulge; it would not have a continuous effect in increasing the use of bank deposits."

Fisher replied to the President that "even if only one billion were the correct figure, it would turn over say twenty times a year, making that much more annual purchasing power and eventually making about three billions more annual money income. . . . And it would be a *permanent* addition and not a mere 'bulge.' " As with "your so-called spending policy, the chief virtue of which is not the mere amount the Government has spent, but the continued flow of . . . additional deposits created by the sale of Government bonds to the banks . . . , one (or more) billion obtainable out of the float . . . would be that much more *revolving fund* which is what our demand deposits really are." Letter from Fisher to FDR, May 17, 1938 (Yale) (emphases in original). More sharply worded letters were sent to the President and to McIntyre by Hemphill (May 15, 1938) (FDR), who charged that "the President is receiving something less than enthusiastic cooperation in some important quarters" and contended that "we have a total of 6 to 6½ billions of deposit currency which is constantly impounded."

In a final salvo, Eccles wished "that professed friends of the President would not waste his time by trying to force on him theories that the trouble with the economy is a shortage of money. . . . The problem is not now and never has been a shortage of money. . . . The problem is not to create more and more money but to put what we already have to productive use. That means putting money into the hands of people who will spend it, creating real wealth. . . . There is nothing the Federal Reserve could do to force private banks . . . to give immediate credit for checks." In any case, "it still would not amount to a drop in the bucket. Under our system the way that deposits should be created is for business to come to the banks and borrow . . . Fisher . . . is much more intelligent [than Hemphill] but certainly misled on this point." Eccles to McIntyre, June 2, 1938 (FDR).

55. To the President he first proposed the scheme—"postage stamps attached weekly on money"—as "a sales tax . . . which will accelerate instead of retard business." Letter from Fisher to FDR, May 13, 1933 (FDR). Then it was suggested as a way to "unfreeze deposits in closed banks" as well as a means of "velocity control." Letter from Fisher to FDR, June 1, 1933 (Yale). "Transaction-stamp scrip has often failed, but I know of no case of dated stamp scrip which has failed." Letter from Fisher to Viner, September 28, 1934 (Yale).

56. "The statistical fact is that anything held for interest does not circulate as fast as what bears no interest. In the case of stamp scrip the interest is negative and it is a

constituted "an anti-hoarding tax."[57] The President told the Secretary of the Treasury that "I honestly think" the Fisher proposal "is worth your looking over."[58]

(vi) A proposal persistently advanced by Fisher rather outside the realm of "monetary policy" called for governmental subsidization of firms[59]—as a gift, in the initial statement,[60] and then as a moderate-length loan at a low rate of interest, in later versions[61]—on the basis of their increased hiring of labor for a specified minimun period.[62]

---

goad to increase the velocity." Letter from Fisher to Simons, December 14, 1934 (Chicago).

57. Letter from Fisher to FDR, September 6, 1934 (FDR). This "self-liquidating currency," to be retired after a year, "has the additional advantage that it cannot well be hoarded, and is endowed, while it lasts, with more than normal velocity." Fisher, *Inflation?*, p. 92. See also memorandum from Fisher to FDR, October 22, 1934 (Yale). Fisher had endorsed the stamp scrip proposal as early as July 1932 and supported the idea in numerous publications, including a book, *Stamp Scrip* (1933); see Reeve, p. 165. Of at least "a score of methods" to achieve reflation and stabilization, "the one which I am now pressing most is the stamp scrip plan, whether locally adopted or nationally." Letter from Fisher to Coughlin, February 16, 1933 (Yale). It is a "really remarkable device" (letter from Fisher to Rand, February 28, 1933 [Yale]) and, if applied nationally, "would almost snap us out of the depression in a short time" (letter from Fisher to Rogers, February 6, 1933 [Yale]). Fisher tried to have the plan adopted by New Haven; see letter from Fisher to Mayor John W. Murphy, September 26, 1932 (Yale).

58. Memorandum from FDR to Henry Morgenthau, September 15, 1934 (FDR). "By the way, and confidentially," he added, Senator "Pat Harrison is really interested in the plan which Fisher also advocates." See also letter from Senator John H. Bankhead to FDR, April 7, 1933 (FDR).

59. "I had a long talk with J. Maynard Keynes and find myself substantially in agreement with him, but it should be noted that . . . 'loan expenditure' is really a *monetary* measure involving added (government) deposits and their use as purchasing power." Letter from Fisher to FDR, June 11, 1934 (FDR) (emphasis in original).

60. ". . . subsidize re-employed laborers (or their employers) by contributing $1 per employee a day for 100 days toward the wages of *additional* labor." Letter from Fisher to FDR, June 1, 1933 (Yale) (emphasis in original); also letter from Fisher to Sprague, June 1, 1933 (Yale).

61. Letter from Fisher to his wife, August 9, 1933 (Yale); letter from Fisher to Howe, May 18, 1934 (Yale), letters from Fisher to FDR, June 11, 1934 (FDR), September 6, 1934 (FDR), April 29, 1935 (Yale), and May 23, 1936 (Yale); memorandum from Fisher to FDR, October 22, 1934 (Yale).

62. The fullest general statement of the plan (although omitting reference to the length of the loan or to the rate of interest) is given in a letter from Fisher to FDR of September 6, 1934 (FDR), repeated in a memorandum of October 22, 1934 (Yale), and in a letter of April 29, 1935 (Yale) (emphases in original): "Let the R.F.C. lend to *any* responsible concern (i.e., any concern which, say, is now operating and has been operating, to *some* extent, during the preceding 12 months) $1.50 [$2, in the version of August 9, 1933] for each employee taken on (for each day employed up to 100 days), said employee to be counted as additional to the average employed by the firm for the last three months.

"Thus, if a firm has averaged 1,000 employees and should average 1,500 for the next 100 days, the additional employment would be 500 men × 100 days, which would entitle the firm to a loan of 500 × 100 × $1.50, or $75,000.

Fisher vastly preferred to "stimulate reemployment in private industry" over reliance on employment by government through public works, which are "slow, clumsy, inefficient and costly,"[63] involving the "wrench" of a "double shift from relief to public works and then from public works to normal jobs."[64] Although the President is reported to have labeled the scheme "a great idea" and to have "expressed special interest" in it in 1933,[65] he wrote to Fisher in 1935: "I fully appreciate that there is considerable merit in the suggestion . . . and have passed it along to the Reconstruction Finance Corporation for consideration. There is, however, a great difference in opinion as to the amount of permanent employment that could be created through loans of the character stated."[66]

For Fisher, then, monetary policy had been, and promised to be, relatively effective in dealing with problems of national income and employment in both this and other countries. And, in general, he was well pleased by the President's early orientation and actions in this area. Further, both here and abroad, he wrote to Roosevelt, "there is a growing realization of the soundness of your monetary aims."[67] The

---

"This system would so simplify the conditions for extending loans that no *time* need be wasted in detailed analysis of the concern's financial condition.

"The safe-guards against bad loans would be. (a) the fact that the concern has kept going. (b) the presumption that most such concerns would not borrow unless they would be able to pay. (c) the fact that such a concerted action would pull up the weak sufficiently to make them strong. There would, of course, be a residual of bad debts. But it would be worth this loss to get the quick and concerted action." In a conversation with Fisher, the President asked how the government "would get the money to lend to employers, " and there was "a long discussion. He seemed not to realize that the Federal Reserve could be forced to disgorge to [the] U.S. gold because its profits are limited to 6% and to have thought that the gold belonged to the banks." Letter from Fisher to his wife, August 9, 1933 (Yale).

63. Memorandum by Fisher to FDR, September 6, 1934 (FDR); see also letter from Fisher to FDR, June 16, 1936 (Yale).

64. Letters from Fisher to FDR, June 11, 1934 (FDR), and April 29, 1935 (Yale).

65. Letters from Fisher to FDR, June 11, 1934 (FDR), and April 29, 1935 (Yale).

66. Letter from FDR to Fisher, May 13, 1935 (Yale).

67. Letters from Fisher to FDR, December 18, 1934 (Yale), June 3, 1935 (FDR), and June 16, 1936 (Yale), and article by Fisher, "Is the Money Question in the Campaign?" Index Number Institute, for release March 30, 1936, copy sent to FDR, March 31, 1936 (FDR). But in 1936, Fisher noted that "for two years and more Mr. Roosevelt has been silent on this great [money] question, after then pronouncing in favor of a managed currency and stable money—stable in purchasing power." "Is the Money Question in the Campaign?" op. cit. "I . . . deplore the rigidity during the last two years of the price of gold." Letter from Fisher to Hull, March 6, 1936 (Yale).

". . . it was a 'proud moment' when the President signed the devaluation bill," he wrote in early 1934. "I often wonder how much he realizes that his monetary policy goes back to me in large part—through Warren and Rogers and Rand, as well as directly. And the public doesn't know it except here and there. But I take a lot of satisfaction in the mere *adoption* of the policy of course." Letter from Fisher to I. N. Fisher, February 4, 1934 (Yale) (emphasis in original). Similarly, in the recession four

record was worse in the area of fiscal policy, such policy being, at best, subsidiary to proper monetary actions. "It was not Government expenditure which pulled us out of the depression," he wrote to the President in late 1937, but rather the expansion of "check-book money which *turned over twenty times a year*."[68] Increase (and the threat of increase) in taxes in particular and balancing the budget (along with "the whole budget balancing ballyhoo") in general tend to preclude that increase in the money stock and to inhibit that brisk rate of its expenditure which are required for recovery.[69] Taxation policy was less interesting as a tool of "stabilization" than as an object of reform, Fisher's main target in this connection being the "vicious," "harmful," and "ridiculous" capital gains tax.[70]

---

years later: "Did I tell you I wrote the President a fortnight ago a warning? And that the next day after the letter must have arrived he had Morgenthau and Eccles confer? And that they agreed on a half-way or tenth-way program which has, I think, put off the evil day so far?" He added, "Evil days impend though—so it seems to me. . . . But . . . I did my best to get the country out . . . from under the sword." Letter from Fisher to his wife, February 28, 1938. (Cf. n.24, above.)

68. Letter from Fisher to FDR, October 24, 1937 (Yale) (emphasis in original); see also n.54, above. Fisher doubted that "money spent by the government coming to an individual as income" differed appreciably in effect "from what it is when it comes in some other way." "The important thing is the effect of increasing the quantity of money. The manner in which this money is first spent by the government is of very little importance since it is re-spent over twenty times a year . . . and no one can say in what way the other nineteen and more spendings will be made." Letter from Fisher to Lehmann, July 20, 1937 (Yale).

69. Letters from Fisher to FDR, February 25, 1933 (Yale), May 23, 1936 (Yale), and November 24, 1937 (Yale). "I think balancing the budget is impossible for the present and that the effort to do it has defeated itself, being deflationary." We should be "warning against taxation until we have increased our taxable resources." Letter from Fisher to Rand, February 28, 1933 (Yale). But while some had "done grave harm by spreading the idea that balancing the budget is a magic formula for getting out of the depression . . . even balancing the budget can be readily done as soon as reflation comes." Letter from Fisher to FDR, February 25, 1933 (Yale).

"Sound recovery" from the severe recession of 1937–38 required restoration of the money stock, not "reckless (and largely useless) Government spending" (letter from Fisher to Wagner, November 24, 1937 [Yale]), and "would make pump priming unnecessary" (letter from Fisher to Congressman Andrew J. Tansue, December 3, 1937 [Yale]). But while Fisher asserted to the President that the recession could be checked "without sacrificing a balanced budget" (letter from Fisher to FDR, December 12, 1937 [FDR]), he expressed "fear" to a Cabinet member that "this attempt to balance the budget may lead us back where we started if a substitute is not found for the money creation which was going on as a by-product of an unbalanced budget" (letter from Fisher to Roper, November 26, 1937 [Yale]).

70. Letters from Fisher to FDR, December 21, 1936 (Yale), January 7, 1937 (FDR), and February 12, 1937 (Yale). In possibly his last message to Roosevelt, Fisher advocated reform of "our terrible Federal Income taxation in a manner which will promote, and not retard, prosperity." Referring to his *Constructive Income Taxation*, he proposed "virtually to abolish the taxation of corporate income on the ground that such taxation is double taxation of its stockholders" and "to tax only that part of income which is spent and consumed, untaxing the part which is saved and

III

Although Fisher spoke at length about policy objectives, policy tools, and policy-making institutions, government action was to take place within an economic and societal context of private property, profit incentives, and price-directed free markets. Indeed, one specific goal urged on the President by Fisher over a period of ten years was "to convince the business world, by deed as well as by word, that you are loyal to the American System of Free Private Enterprise and profits as against Statism, whether of the Russian or the German variety."[71] Fisher eschewed doctrinaire support of "the profit system, so-called capitalism" and "laissez faire."[72] But it was "necessary . . . to assure business beyond a shadow of a doubt that it can make profits with impunity; otherwise it will not employ more labor but less."[73] Make it clear "that you aim to free business, not to fetter it," and "reduce, as fast as possible, governmental intervention and activity in commerce, industry, and agriculture."[74] "Open the door for private initiative in the restoration of business activity; remove

---

invested." Letter from Fisher to FDR, November 22, 1944 (Yale). A decade earlier he argued to Simons: "My fundamental objection to the capital gain tax is that it means double taxation, for the capital taxed is merely anticipation of income presumably to be realized later and which when taxed after it is received is all the tax that it deserves. Taxing its capitalization ahead of time, i.e., in anticipation as well as in realization, is double taxation. Taxing inheritance is the only kind of capital tax that I feel clear should be made ordinarily." Letter from Fisher to Simons, December 14, 1934 (Chicago).

71. Letter from Fisher to FDR, November 22, 1944 (Yale). "I think it would be wise to sit back and see for some years yet what comes out of Russia before following her any further than the New Deal has done. In fact, I think the New Deal has been rather rash in this way." Letter from Fisher to Richard A. Lester, November 23, 1936 (Yale).

72. "I am greatly interested and pleased to think that you are courageously reverting to the unpopular laissez faire [in reference to Simons' 1934 pamphlet, *A Positive Program for Laissez Faire*]. I was brought up under laissez faire and while I have partly repudiated it I think there is a lot of sense in it for the most part and it should be the basis for an economic system but with perhaps more exceptions than you would have." Letter from Fisher to Simons, December 14, 1934 (Chicago). "I am a good deal of a believer in the profit system, so-called capitalism, and think it would work if the Government would do its own job better, particularly the job of stabilizing the dollar. I am quite ready, however, to gradually increase Government functions in so far as cautiously we find the Government can do anything better than private individuals." Letter from Fisher to John Bauer, American Public Utilities Bureau, December 20, 1938 (Yale).

73. Letter from Fisher to FDR, November 24, 1937 (Yale). "Announce unequivocally . . . that honest profits will not be taboo, however high, except as just taxes necessarily make it so." Letter from Fisher to FDR, September 6, 1934 (FDR); see also letter from Fisher to FDR, August 30, 1934 (Yale).

74. Letter from Fisher to Howe, May 18, 1934 (Yale), and letter from Fisher to FDR, September 6, 1934 (FDR); see also memorandum from Fisher to FDR, October 22, 1934 (Yale).

restriction on production; re-establish competition—all in order that the business, capital, and brains of the country may be mobilized to employ the idle."[75]

It was not Fisher's contention that all direct government employment through public works was necessarily unfortunate: it could serve a useful, marginal purpose in "absorb[ing] any residual unemployed." But "suitable" forms of work should be thus provided: "Select especially projects which are good investments to the country as a whole but would never be suitable for private capital because the returns would come mostly to other people than those who put up the money." Public health,[76] road building, and conservation projects are among the most promising. "A *wise* combination of two classes of enterprise, (1) those best left to individual capitalists and (2) those for the General Welfare best conducted by the government, would in time work wonders for the nation, far beyond anything which Russia is ever likely to reach as long as private initiative and private profits are repressed."[77]

Meanwhile, to the extent that the government continues to employ persons for relief work, "pay wages below those paid by private industry, so that labor will not be tempted to refuse private jobs offered."[78] And "artificially high and unearned wages" in private business "spell unemployment and compel increased Governmental interference."[79] Wages, after all, "are merely the price of labor" and, "like any other price, if higher than the market will bear, reduce the amount sold." In particular, "wages rest on productivity of labor,"[80] and boosting wages far above market-clearing levels will increase unemployment rather than purchasing power.[81]

75. Memorandum, unaddressed, evidently by Fisher, October 31, 1934 (Yale). One of the inevitable concommitants of such things as "processing taxes and price-fixing agreements" is "an ever-increasing army of supervisors, inspectors, and administrators." Loc. cit.

76. Examples are "expenditures securing pure water (e.g., waterworks), pure air (e.g., from installing smoke consumers, cleaner streets, air conditioning of occupied buildings), eliminating malaria bearing mosquitoes (as at Panama under Taft), typhoid bearing flies, and other insects." Letter from Fisher to FDR, October 22, 1934 (Yale).

77. Memorandum from Fisher to FDR, October 22, 1934 (Yale) (emphasis in original).

78. Letter from Fisher to FDR, September 6, 1934 (FDR); also memorandum from Fisher to FDR, October 22, 1934 (Yale).

79. Letter from Fisher to Howe, May 18, 1934 (Yale). "Employers, employees, and labor unions" must be persuaded "in the interest of re-employment to desist holding wages artificially high, and allowing them to fall enough to absorb the unemployed." Letter from Fisher to FDR, May 23, 1936 (Yale).

80. " 'Deflation' from Dissolution of N.R.A.," op. cit.

81. "If the NRA codes had set minimum wages at $1000 an hour . . . there could be practically no employment whatever." Loc. cit.; see also memorandum and letter

The observed unfortunate developments and proposals relating to terms of labor employment[82] illustrated a wider confusion and inconsistency in analyzing and prescribing for the depression. While the President's expansionary monetary policy had "been the chief cause of getting us out of the depression," Fisher wrote in mid-1936, recovery had been delayed by "your 'economy of scarcity' . . . based on the incorrect diagnosis of 'overproduction' ":[83]

> We need more reflation—raising the price level *through monetary means* but not by *making goods scarce*. The two have been confused. The first is merely *reducing to normal the unit for measuring income*. The second is *reducing the incomes* themselves; for real incomes are goods. We want, not to decrease but to increase incomes, by getting men and machines, now idle, to produce again; and that, indirectly is the result of reflation.[84]

Fisher objected "most violently" to "the philosophy of wealth destruction and limitation as a means of enhancing the money values for certain classes at the expense of the nation as a whole. On this matter some of the 'brains trust' do not seem to have brains to

---

from Fisher to FDR, October 22, 1934 (Yale), and December 18, 1934 (Yale). However, "William Greene can get a big following among workingmen who can be made to see that the minimum wages in the NRA codes will lose in purchasing power with every advance in the cost of living," so it would be well to "amend every code minimum by inserting a provision that said minimum is to be increased in proportion to the increase in" prices. Letter from Fisher to FDR, October 3, 1933 (Yale). "I infer from some of your remarks that some of your advisers have the same purchasing-power fallacy as did Dr. Townsend and as does Henry Ford. You cannot increase purchasing power by marking up wages. You can by increasing the volume or velocity of money." Letter from Fisher to FDR, October 24, 1937 (Yale).

82. Fisher asked the President to "drop or, at any rate, very greatly tone down your proposed legislation on minimum wages and maximum hours," which "threatens to decrease productivity and to intensify unemployment. I feel convinced that is where you are unintentionally leading the way." Letter from Fisher to FDR, October 14, 1937 (FDR).

83. Letter from Fisher to FDR, June 16, 1936 (Yale).

84. Letter from Fisher to McIntyre, May 12, 1934 (Yale) (emphases in original); cf. letter from Fisher to I. N. Fisher, August 15, 1933 (Yale). ". . . what we need is more money not less goods. Higher prices due to more money to buy with create employment by making profits possible." Memorandum from Fisher to FDR, October 22, 1934 (Yale). If proper policies had been more vigorously implemented and improper policies eschewed, "I am convinced we might and should have gotten out of the depression six months ago." Letter from Fisher to McIntyre, May 12, 1934 (Yale). (Key portions of this letter were retyped by White House staff, evidently for distribution among selected members of the Administration.) Had it not been for "employers' and investors' fears, due to parts of the New Deal," especially the N.R.A., "we could, I think, have been practically out of the depression many months ago and there would be no demand now for an Upton Sinclair." Letter from Fisher to FDR, August 30, 1934 (Yale).

trust."[85] "I most earnestly hope," Fisher told the President near the beginning of the 1936 campaign, "you will not try to defend the indefensible."[86]

It clearly followed, in Fisher's view, that certain conspicuous features of the New Deal—most notably, the NRA and the AAA—had "actually retarded recovery."[87] While not entirely "out of sympathy" with such programs,[88] he concluded that in general they undesirably obstructed the working of the free market, pegging prices above equilibrium levels, directly and indirectly curtailing production and thus employment, and restricting anticipated profits. "Capitalism, if it is to be retained, must have the lure of real profits, to justify its either seeking or getting the financing needed for normal reemployment of labor."[89] In early 1934, Fisher warned the President

85. Article by Fisher, "Is the New Deal a Consistent Whole?" for release June 11, 1934, copy sent to FDR, June 4, 1934 (FDR). See also letter from Fisher to Howe, May 18, 1934 (Yale); memorandum from Fisher to FDR, October 22, 1934 (Yale); articles by Fisher for Index Number Institute, " 'Deflation' from Dissolution of N.R.A.," op. cit., "Is the Money Question in the Campaign?" op. cit., "The Money Planks," for release June 22, 1936, copy sent to FDR, June 18, 1936 (FDR); letter from Fisher to FDR, October 14, 1937 (FDR).

86. Letter from Fisher to FDR, June 16, 1936 (Yale).

87. Letters from Fisher to FDR, March 18, 1934 (Yale), August 30, 1934 (Yale), October 22, 1934 (Yale), December 18, 1934 (Yale), June 3, 1935 (FDR), and January 4, 1936 (Yale); letter from Fisher to Hull, March 6, 1936 (Yale). Fisher was not entirely gentle in publicly criticizing the President, who "once said that if he found that his plans along these lines [of controlling and restricting production and decreasing real wealth in order to increase the monetary value of what is left], as exemplified in the N.R.A. and the A.A.A., should fail to yield their intended benefits, he would be the first to admit it. He has not, however, been the first, by any means. From many parts of the country now are coming facts and testimonies showing that this policy has been extremely disappointing. Let us hope that the President will, at least, give heed to these evidences." "Is the New Deal a Consistent Whole?" op. cit. But he also privately suggested that Roosevelt had been badly informed and advised: ". . . may I suggest that you check up the reports to you from General [Hugh] Johnson, Mr. [Donald] Richberg and others inside your organization, by getting outside and totally disinterested reports made direct to you?" Letter from Fisher to FDR, August 30, 1934 (Yale). At any rate, "the N.R.A. was hastily conceived, hastily formulated, and hastily organized and its collapse is the logical result. So far as I know, no economists originally recommended, or later reviewed or approved the N.R.A. And, so far as I know, all economists who have studied it believe, with Professor W. I. King, that the middle letter in 'NRA' could more properly stand for 'Retardation' than for 'Recovery.' " " 'Deflation' from Dissolution of N.R.A.," op. cit.; cf. letter from Fisher to I. N. Fisher, March 8, 1934 (Yale).

88. "I was glad to see it [N.R.A.] abolish child labor and the sweat shop, combat cut-throat competition and give promise of an ultimate 'get-together' of employers and employees. I even favored the *principle* of minimum wages and maximum hours, though not all the applications made of this principle." " 'Deflation' from Dissolution of N.R.A.," op. cit. (emphasis in original); see also letter from Fisher to FDR, March 18, 1934 (Yale).

89. Letter from Fisher to FDR, March 18, 1934 (Yale). "In a capitalistic economy,

that "you may soon have to choose between the regimentalists and the money-stabilizers";[90] in mid-1935, he urged the President to "go slow in resurrecting the NRA";[91] and in early 1937, he wrote unequivocally that "I am opposed to the renewal of the old NRA and AAA, as restricting the production of wealth."[92]

IV

While directing the bulk of his attention and advice, especially during the first two years of the New Deal, to short-run matters of income "recovery," Fisher never put far aside major interest in monetary "reform." Surely, the reform measure most generally associated with him is the proposal for 100 percent reserves against demand deposits in commercial banks.[93]

The essential effect of imposing 100 percent reserves would be to separate the *lending* function of financial institutions—along with money-holding, money-shifting, and currency-deposit convertibility functions—from *money creation*, control of the size of the money stock then being solely a governmental function.

---

employment depends on the employer, lured by the prospect of high profits. When, as now, he fears he won't be allowed more than say 6% or 7% profit but runs the risk of 100% losses, he doesn't dare extend himself and employ labor as he would if reassured." Letter from Fisher to FDR, August 30, 1934 (Yale).

90. Letter from Fisher to FDR, March 18, 1934 (Yale). One early reason given by Fisher for a vigorously expansive monetary policy was that "a prompt resumption of rapid reflation will help enormously to make the NRA a success." Letter from Fisher to FDR, September 11, 1933 (Yale).

91. Letter from Fisher to FDR, June 3, 1935 (FDR).

92. Letter from Fisher to FDR, February 8, 1937 (FDR). In a blunt, if not bitter, public statement early in the 1940 campaign, Fisher asserted that the American depression "record is the worst in the world"—and "the chief reason for our failure to cope more successfully with the depression and its unemployment was the New Deal, with its N.R.A., . . . with its A.A.A. and wealth-destruction policies. . . . Mr. Roosevelt . . . has experimented on, and impoverished, his country." Statement by Fisher for release July 20, 1940 (Princeton). See also letter from Fisher to Kemmerer, April 17, 1936 (Yale).

93. Fisher's publications on the subject include: *100% Money* (New York, 1935, 1936, 1945); "100% Money and the Public Debt," *Economic Forum* 3 (1936): 406–20; "100% Money Again," *Social Research* 3 (1936): 236–44; "The Bankers' Interest in 100% Money," *Bankers Magazine* (1936): 285–88; "100% Reserves: An Old System Adapted to Modern Needs," *Searchlight* (Newark), February, March 1937, reprinted in *Commercial and Financial Digest* (Los Angeles), June 1937; "100% Money—and Branch Banking," *Northwestern Banker* (Des Moines), March 1937; "Note Suggested by Review of '100 Per Cent Money,' " *Journal of the Royal Statistical Society* 100 (1937), Part II: 296–98; "The Principle of 100% Reserves," *Dynamic America*, 1938: 13–17; "Why Banks Could Make More Money Under 100% Reserve System," *American Banker* 108 (1943).

The 100 percent reserve proposal hardly originated with Fisher. The actual practice of seventeenth-century goldsmiths,[94] statements of Hume and of Ricardo,[95] the position of the nineteenth-century Currency School, the Peel Bank Act of 1844,[96] and more[97] can be cited as evidence of early concern with full-reserve requirements, although, of course, the ancient emphasis was on reserves for currency instead of reserves for demand deposits. In the 1920's, the 100 percent proposal was revived by Frederick Soddy, a Nobel Laureate in chemistry at Cambridge University.[98] In 1933 the plan was sponsored in a privately circulated statement by Henry C. Simons and several of his University of Chicago colleagues.[99] Other leading economists of the 1930's—including Lauchlin Currie, A. G. Hart, James Angell, and Frank Graham, as well as Simons[100]—sympathetically analyzed the suggested reform. Still, with Fisher's conspicuousness in the debate, it can reasonably be labeled "the Fisher plan."

94. Fisher, "100% Money and the Public Debt," op. cit., p. 409; James W. Angell, "The 100 Per Cent Reserve Plan," *Quarterly Journal of Economics* 50 (1935): 5–6.

95. Lloyd W. Mints, *A History of Banking Theory in Great Britain and the United States* (Chicago, 1945), p. 23; Leonard L. Watkins, *Commercial Banking Reform in the United States* (Ann Arbor, Michigan Business Studies, VIII, 1938), p. 16.

96. Mints, esp. pp. 75–77; Jacob Viner, *Studies in the Theory of International Trade* (New York, 1937), esp. pp. 220–34. "The 100% reserve plan would merely be finishing the job which Sir Robert Peel intended to do through the Bank of England Act of 1844, for it would extend to deposits his principle of covering all additional notes of the Bank of England by a reserve of 100% in government money. He simply did not foresee that deposits would become circulating medium and so would, in a few years, make the very same troubles—depressions and booms—that bank notes formerly made." Letter from Fisher to FDR, December 21, 1936 (Yale).

97. See, e.g., Benjamin Bromberg, "Two Neglected Twentieth Century 100 Per Cent Reserve Economists," *American Economic Review* 29 (1939): 553; the two in question are W. E. Brooks and J. R. Cummings.

98. See Frederick Soddy, *Wealth, Virtual Wealth and Debt* (New York, 1926, 1933), pp. 197–98, 298; idem, *Money versus Man* (London, 1931), pp. 95–96; idem, *The Role of Money* (London, 1934), pp. 67–69, 211. See also Watkins, pp. 16–19, and Margaret G. Myers, *Monetary Proposals for Social Reform* (New York, 1940), ch. 3, esp. pp. 95–101.

99. The others included G. V. Cox, Aaron Director, P. H. Douglas, A. G. Hart, F. H. Knight, L. W. Mints, and Henry Schultz. Fisher, *100% Money*, p. xiii.

100. Albert G. Hart, "The 'Chicago Plan' of Banking Reform: A Proposal for Making Monetary Management Effective in the United States," *Review of Economic Studies* 2 (1935): 104–16; Lauchlin Currie, *The Supply and Control of Money in the United States* (1934; New York, 1968), pp. 151–56 (also a reprinted memorandum, "A Proposed Revision of the Monetary System of the United States," submitted to the Secretary of the Treasury in September 1934, pp. 187–226); Angell, pp. 1–35; Frank D. Graham, "Partial Reserve Money and the 100 Per Cent Proposal," *American Economic Review* 26 (1936): 428–40; Henry C. Simons, "A Positive Program for Laissez Faire: Some Proposals for a Liberal Economic Policy" (1934), reprinted in his *Economic Policy for a Free Society* (Chicago, 1948), pp. 62–65.

Fisher proclaimed with little inhibition the advantages of the plan. The subtitle of his 1935 book *100% Money* is, "Designed to keep checking banks 100% liquid; to prevent inflation and deflation; largely to cure or prevent depressions; and to wipe out much of the National Debt." He was no more reticent in his letters to the President. In a relatively full summary, he wrote:

> This plan divorces "check-book money" completely from banking and makes it a government function, as it should be and as was intended . . . .
>
> The 100% plan would obliterate the present distinction between real money ("pocket-book money") and credit money ("check-book money"). . . .
>
> Bankers could then be left freer than now from any government interference with their proper business—lending money, as distinct from creating money or destroying it.
>
> The 100% plan would automatically *insure all* checking deposits so that any other sort of insurance would be rendered superfluous.
>
> The plan would weaken the arguments for branch banking now so greatly feared by thousands of small individual banks.[101]

Fisher left no room for doubt that the central purpose and inevitable consequence of the scheme was to enable monetary authorities "absolutely to control the volume of money";[102] further, it was "the *only* practicable plan proposed for transferring completely all control over our chief circulating medium from the banks to the Government";[103] and the plan entailed a reserve requirement of a full 100

101. Letter from Fisher to FDR, December 21, 1936 (Yale) (emphasis in original); see also "Outline of Proposed New Monetary Legislation," attached to letter from Fisher to FDR, October 24, 1937 (Yale). "One special reason for adopting the plan at this time is that it would reduce the national debt which is reaching alarming figures . . . . It seems . . . certain to become a leading topic in the next session of Congress and . . . it is more than possible that it will be adopted." Letter from Fisher to Rogers, July 16, 1934 (Yale).

102. Letter from Fisher to FDR, October 24, 1937 (Yale). He added: "As to its velocity, you personally can by a change in attitude do much, as you did when you announced the 'breathing spell.' " See also letter from Fisher to FDR, December 21, 1936 (Yale). By "taking away all money-creation from the 'money changers'—the real economic royalists—. . . you will have accomplished, I believe, more for posterity than by all your other cherished proposals put together." Letter from Fisher to FDR, May 14, 1937 (FDR).

103. Letter from Fisher to FDR, November 10, 1936 (FDR) (emphasis in original); the adoption of this proposal, "as a part of a managed currency plan, would, I am sure, go down in history with the emancipation of the slaves." See also letter from Fisher to FDR, April 23, 1935 (Yale).

percent, not 99 or other smaller percentage.[104] The "main point" of the plan was that it "would prevent a boom, but by the same token . . . , it would prevent a depression."[105]

Fisher first broached the idea to the President no later than January 1934,[106] and through 1937 he often returned to support of the proposal.[107] Apparently, the President responded only once, then noting simply that the plan, while having "many elements of attractiveness . . . , involves a number of complex considerations," and it had been referred for study to the Treasury and to the Federal Reserve.[108]

In 1939, Fisher tried again, this time with the support of Paul Douglas, Frank Graham, Earl Hamilton, Willford King, and Charles Whittlesey. They sent to the President "A Program for Monetary Reform," a five-page mimeographed statement. The "Program," reportedly approved by nearly two hundred other economists, called for "certain definite criteria for money management," sufficiently well defined "as to leave only a minimum of discretion to the Monetary Authority";[109] and the power of commercial banks to change the size of the money stock by lending and investing was to be eliminated by requiring 100 percent reserves.[110] The President only acknowledged

104. Not only would a reserve requirement of less than 100 percent fall quantitatively short of the desired reform, "but a full 100% reserve, as compared with even a 99% reserve, makes a qualitative change. For the reserve then becomes the property of the depositor instead of the banks, while the bank becomes a mere trustee." Letter from Fisher to FDR, December 21, 1936 (Yale).

105. Letter from Fisher to Willford I. King, March 17, 1935 (Oregon).

106. "In accordance with your request, through Mr. McIntyre, Mr. Hemphill and I had a talk with Secretary Morgenthau last week in regard to the '100%' idea in money in relation to banking." Letter from Fisher to FDR, January 13, 1934 (FDR).

107. Letter from Fisher to Howe, May 18, 1934 (Yale); letters from Fisher to FDR, June 11, 1934 (FDR), September 6, 1934 (FDR), October 22, 1934 (Yale), December 12, 1934 (Yale), December 18, 1934 (Yale), April 23, 1935 (Yale), December 21, 1936 (Yale), October 24, 1937 (Yale), November 4, 1937 (FDR), and December 19, 1937 (Yale). "Frankly, I am terribly disappointed at the slowness of your monetary policies. . . . [T]he 100% money plan could get us out of the depression *far faster* and keep us out with far greater certainty than any other plan, to say nothing of getting the government largely out of debt to boot. Incidentally it would solve your major political problems and bring Father Coughlin into camp again. To my mind, it would be the master stroke of your administration." Letter from Fisher to FDR, April 23, 1935 (Yale) (emphasis in original).

108. Letter from FDR (prepared by Wayne C. Taylor, Assistant Secretary of the Treasury) to Fisher, March 23, 1937 (Yale).

109. "Among the possible standards to which the dollar could be made to conform . . . : (a) Establish a constant average per capita supply . . . of the circulating medium. . . . One great advantage of this 'constant-per-capita-money' standard is that it would require a minimum of discretion on the part of the Monetary Authority. (b) Keep the dollar equivalent to an ideal 'market basket dollar' . . . a representative assortment of consumer goods . . . 'constant-cost-of-living' standard."

110. The "Program" is dated February 1939; a copy was sent to Roosevelt, with a

receipt of the material.[111] Two years later, the group, now joined by John Commons and "in behalf of some 400 economists (85% of those expressing an opinion)," submitted to the President almost identically the same "Program."[112] The President responded that the statement "will receive careful study."[113]

In the dark winter of 1940-41 and in many anxious months to come, presumably radical banking reform was not in the forefront of the President's concerns. And in April 1945, before the tasks of peace were again the predominant concern, President Roosevelt left the scene. In that same month, Fisher announced that he was "resuming the effort" of banking reform.[114] But two years later, in April 1947, Professor Fisher was lost as well.

---

covering letter from Fisher and another letter from all six economists, March 15, 1939. The joint letter begins (emphasis in original): "The newspapers report a statement just issued by the Federal Reserve Board that it 'does not favor the enactment of any bill based on the assumption that the Federal Reserve System or any other agency of the Government can control the volume of money and credit . . . .' This statement is, to say the least, open to serious doubt. Moreover, it evidently contradicts your own repeated statements that we are seeking to establish and maintain a dollar of constant purchasing and debt paying power.

"We can see little difference between this statement of the Board and the statements former Federal Reserve officials made in 1926 and 1928 in opposition to legislation which, if adopted, would have forced the Board to combat the depression from 1929 on. As there was no law to compel them to take action, they did practically nothing.

"On the other hand, an ever increasing number of economists favor legislation which, while giving the Board or other Monetary Authority more power, would take from it its present discretion in determining policy (or issuing policy-making statements), but instead prescribe as narrowly as possible *how* the Board or other agency shall contribute towards the prevention of both booms and depressions."

111. Letter from FDR (prepared by the Treasury) to Fisher, April 21, 1939 (FDR). Fisher had written March 9 that he and the others were sending the document, and the President replied March 13 that he would look forward to receiving it. "A program formulated by such outstanding economists as yourself and your associates ought to be a distinct contribution to the subject of monetary reform."

112. The "Program," along with a brief "Memorial to Congress" and a covering letter from Fisher, was sent to FDR January 27, 1941 (FDR).

113. Letter from FDR to Fisher, February 13, 1941 (FDR).

114. Form letter from Fisher to "Dear Colleague," April 1945 (Oregon).

This paper is part of a project generously supported by the Earhart Foundation; supplemental assistance has been provided by the U.C.L.A. Research Committee. The bulk of the citations are to archival materials, primarily in Manuscripts and Archives, Yale University Library (Irving Fisher papers). Other collections include Franklin D. Roosevelt Library (Hyde Park), mainly President's Personal File 431; Law School Library, University of Chicago (Henry C. Simons papers); Manuscripts, Princeton University Library (Edwin W. Kemmerer papers); Special Collections, University of Oregon Library (Willford I. King papers); Manuscript Division, Library of Congress

(Robert L. Owen and William Allen White papers); Rare Book and Manuscript Library, Columbia University Libraries (Nicholas Murray Butler papers); Hoover Institution on War, Revolution and Peace, Stanford University (Raymond Moley papers); H. Jerry Voorhis personal files (Irving Fisher file). When a given document is known by me to be found in both the Yale collection and another collection, only Yale is noted in the citations. (Evidently, most of the Fisher material that is in the Roosevelt Library now has copies in the Yale Library.) The splendid cooperation of the several librarians and others with custody of the materials used here is greatly appreciated.

[2]

History of Political Economy 12:1

Irving Fisher on the financial economics of uncertainty

John H. Crockett, Jr., University of Houston

I. *Introduction*

Many of the contributions of Irving Fisher to financial economics are well known. As presented by Jack Hirshleifer (1965), for example, the established theories of the asset-acquisition decision process represent extensions of the basic theory developed by Fisher to analyze the microeconomic factors leading to the determination of the rate of interest in a riskless world. Fisher's choice-theoretic framework has provided the foundation for the multi-period approach required to deal with the time dimension embodied in long-lived real and financial assets.

The other essential feature associated with these assets is the uncertainty which characterizes the returns they generate, a factor which gives rise to substantive analytical difficulties that await a completely satisfactory resolution. Fisher also undertook pioneering theoretical investigations into the effect that uncertainty has on the valuation of risk assets. This work has not been widely recognized. For example, Black (p. 249) has written:

> Irving Fisher developed in great detail a theory of the determination of the rate of interest and of aggregate investment and consumption in the case of certainty. . . . He considered the problem of the determination of these quantities under uncertainty but did not have the tools available to deal with the problem. . . . Fisher also failed to realize that dealing adequately with uncertainty required two prices, rather than just one. In place of the rate of interest alone we have the rate of interest and the price of risk.

In fact, Fisher dealt explicitly with the pricing and the allocation of risk in the capital markets. The failure of Black and others to recognize Fisher's efforts to deal with uncertainty stems from the fact

A preliminary version of this article was read at the 1977 Conference of the Western Economic Association, Anaheim. The comments of Rich Pettit and Meyer Ungar are gratefully acknowledged.

that this issue was treated in Fisher's *The Nature of Capital and Income*, the 1906 companion volume to the original edition of the work on interest determination, which appeared in 1907 as *The Rate of Interest*. The most commonly referenced work of Fisher, *The Theory of Interest* (1930), constitutes a revision of the 1907 book. It is apparent that Fisher viewed both the 1906 and the 1907 volumes as components of the same piece; in *The Theory of Interest* (p. 3n.) he wrote:

> *The Nature of Capital and Income* (first published in 1906) was primarily intended to serve as a foundation for *The Rate of Interest* which immediately followed it. It was my expectation that the student would read the former before reading the latter. But now, for the convenience of those who do not wish to take the time to read *The Nature of Capital and Income*, I have written this first chapter summarizing it. . . . I hope also that some who have not read it may be moved, after reading this chapter, to read *The Nature of Capital and Income* in full.

Unfortunately, *The Nature of Capital and Income* has been neglected in recent years. The primary objective of that work was to provide a systematic treatment of the fundamental concepts of capital and income, laying to rest metaphysical debates about their character by establishing for them a sound theoretical and empirical basis. This approach was dictated by Fisher's belief that the elimination of the confusion surrounding income and capital was a prerequisite for understanding the nature and the determination of interest, the topic he turned to in *The Rate of Interest*.

Fisher recognized that the presence of uncertainty would materially influence the determination of the capital values of income streams. As a result, the treatment of uncertainty was an integral component of his work. The purpose of the present article is to explore Fisher's treatment of uncertainty as it influences financial decisionmaking. Such an enterprise is useful both for the insights it provides into the history of economic analysis and for the perspective it furnishes from which to investigate issues which remain controversial.

The body of the article is divided into three sections. In Section II, Fisher's conceptual approach to uncertainty is reviewed. Section III takes up Fisher's framework for analyzing the influence of uncertainty, including his approach to quantifying subjective attitudes toward risk. Section IV summarizes Fisher's approach to risk management and compares his scheme with modern ideas on this topic. Finally, some concluding comments are offered in Section V.

II. *Fisher's Conceptualization of Uncertainty*

Because of the complexities the admission of uncertainty introduces for economic analysis, it is not uncommon initially to ignore the problem by assuming that transactors possess complete information about relevant magnitudes in all states of nature and in all time periods. Once it is decided to allow for the presence of uncertainty, there is an obvious need for the adoption of a conceptual approach to the problem which serves to define issues appropriate for analysis. For example, it is usually assumed that even in an uncertain world, transactors have full knowledge of their utility functions; this assumption makes possible an analysis in terms of optimizing, rather than adaptive, behavior. The purpose of this section is to outline the major components of Fisher's conceptual approach.[1]

In developing his theory of interest, Fisher found it convenient initially to assume complete certainty, but he was aware of the costs of this assumption in terms of the applicability of the theory. In *The Rate of Interest* (p. 207), he put the problem this way:

> Up to this point we have ignored the element of chance, by assuming that the entire future income-stream, or at any rate, such portions of it as needed to influence present choice, are foreknown and mapped out in advance. . . . This assumption, like the assumption that bodies fall *in vacuo*, in the ordinary presentation of the theory of gravitation, has enabled us to complete our formal statement of the theory more easily, although at the expense of exact conformity to actual historical fact; for, in the concrete world, the most conspicuous characteristic of the future is its uncertainty.

Realizing the limitations of a certainty-based theory, Fisher went on to explore the complications introduced into his interest theory by the presence of uncertainty. His basic conclusion was that uncertainty introduced what he termed "disturbances" into the factors which determined the rate of interest, or more accurately, the multiple rates of interest present under uncertainty. Since these disturbances add an element of indeterminacy to the explanation of interest, Fisher dealt with the influence of uncertainty in a qualitative fashion, indicating the direction of departures from that which would hold in the absence of risk.

1. Throughout the article, no distinction will be made between *risk* and *uncertainty*. The terms will be used interchangeably, as Fisher used them, in referring to situations where future outcomes cannot be forecast with complete reliability.

Given the influence of uncertainty, some attempt to express the nature of uncertainty rigorously was clearly necessary as a prelude to dealing with it analytically. Here, one of Fisher's contributions was to stress the subjective nature of uncertainty from the point of view of economic transactors. Fisher argued in the following way (*The Nature of Capital and Income*, p. 266):

> Some persons will estimate more highly than others the risks taken. From this fact it might seem that there is a distinction between the actual risk incurred and the estimate which individuals put upon it. But a little consideration will show that this distinction is spurious; for, by the nature of the case, *chance is always an estimate*. Chance is subjective. . . . In the actual world of events, there is no uncertainty.

Emphasizing the subjective dimension of uncertainty is useful as a means for focusing on what may be the inappropriate assumption that objective, i.e., external, probability distributions are provided for transactors. Although, as will be seen shortly, Fisher himself advocated the use of mathematical probability in dealing with uncertainty, he was mindful of the limitations of such an approach. In particular, he wrote (*The Nature of Capital and Income*, p. 268):

> Of course the actual statistical record may afford an important and sometimes the only basis for our degree of knowledge and ignorance. Practically it therefore often happens that we derive our estimate of chances from the behavior of events "in the long run." . . . But while statistics supply data for the forming of subjective estimates of chance, they do not, themselves, constitute chances.

Fisher's approach here is useful in calling attention to the inherently subjective nature of probability-based specifications of uncertainty. In the modern theory of asset valuation under uncertainty, it is common to assume that all decisionmakers share identical estimates of all relevant probability distributions of outcomes. Fisher's emphasis on the subjective nature of uncertainty makes evident the particularity of the assumption of homogeneous expectations. More generally, Fisher's treatment makes apparent the complexity involved in generating appropriate estimates of the expectations of transactors which are required to develop complete solutions to valuation problems. For example, models of the process by which expectations are formed which depend on an extrapolation of observed historical variability ignore the dynamic character of subjective uncertainty. Finally, a Fisherian approach involving subjective probabilities has proved to be quite useful in a number of applications. For instance, Yaari's analysis (1965) of the Friedman-Savage paradox (1948), where an individual simultaneously exhibits apparently conflicting attitudes toward risk, stressed the subjective aspects.

In considering the effects of uncertainty on the problem of evaluating streams of payments, Fisher explicitly called attention to the importance of expectations in explaining fluctuations in the prices of risky assets. For example, he argued (*The Nature of Capital and Income*, p. 265):

> The introduction of the element of *chance* will bring other and even more important changes in capital value. If we take the history of the prices of stocks and bonds, we shall find it chiefly to consist of a record of changing estimates of futurity, due to what is called chance. . . .

Fisher here expressed a view later stated forcefully by Keynes in analyzing the importance of expectations about an uncertain future as determinants of economic activity, an influence heightened by the inherent volatility of these expectations.[2] Again, the subjective or psychological component of the process by which expectations are formed is a critical element which may be overlooked by an extrapolation technique or by some other objective approach to modeling this process.

As already mentioned, Fisher presumed that probability theory provides a useful framework for organizing decision problems under uncertainty. Although not developing the idea in a thorough fashion, Fisher indicated an understanding of the need for formulating an empirically based axiomatic structure for these problems. In his words (*The Nature of Capital and Income*, p. 269):

2. Fisher's views on the importance of expectations may partially explain his expressions of optimism after the crash of 1929 which proved so costly to his professional reputation. In this light, his professed optimism can be interpreted as an attempt to stimulate confidence which, had it been forthcoming, would have been self-fulfilling. On this point, see Irving Norton Fisher 1956.

Fisher explicitly expressed his understanding of this phenomenon in *The Nature of Capital and Income*, pp. 88–89: "Failures are sometimes due to a false fear of calamity, a shock to business confidence. This will cause a shrinkage of value in several ways. For instance it will induce creditors to demand payment and refuse renewals of bills. Forced liquidation and contraction of credit are the result. No physical capital is destroyed, but the form of ownership is disturbed, and often the management, being transferred from stockholders to bondholders, is turned from competent to incompetent hands. Above all, the expectations of the future are changed and confused. Plans are given up, orders are countermanded, and trade is stopped. Assets, representing as they do the value of future expectations, suffer sudden and heavy reductions." For a full development of these ideas, see Fisher's *Booms and Depressions*, where his cycle theory is systematically presented.

> But, in showing that chance is purely a psychological and not an objective magnitude, we are still far from defining chance as a mathematical magnitude. In order to measure chance, it is necessary to state (1) when two chances are equal or unequal; and (2) when one chance bears any given ratio to the other.

Although Fisher cast his discussion in terms of the analysis of risky prospects themselves, it appears that he was aware of the importance of behavioral rules which allow the consistent ordering of these prospects. Thus, his work anticipated the conceptual approach of Ramsey (1931) and Von Neumann and Morgenstern (1953) which has proved to be so fruitful in investigating choice behavior under uncertainty.

For purposes of evaluating streams of payments under uncertainty, Fisher distinguished between two sources of variability in capital values—uncertainty about future elements in the payments stream and uncertainty about future rates of interest which influence valuation through the discounting process. Variations in the income stream will be discussed in Section III below; the importance of interest rate fluctuations in Fisher's scheme will be outlined here.

Fisher pointed out that unanticipated changes in interest rates could influence valuation in two distinct ways. In the first place, Fisher noted, changes in interest rates implied changes in market values of outstanding securities, leading to capital gains or losses for the holders of these securities. Fisher was of the opinion that since fluctuations in interest rates were normally small and gradual, this was not likely to be a significant element. Of course the behavior of interest rates is an empirical issue; the increased volatility of interest-rate movements in the recent past might well have led Fisher to reappraise the relative importance of this aspect of interest-rate uncertainty.

The second source of uncertainty flowing from interest rate fluctuations was thought to be considerably more important as a practical matter; it is also more interesting because of its novelty. Fisher recognized that interest rate changes would lead to changes in the opportunity rate at which intermediate cash flows could be reinvested, thereby influencing the ultimate terminal value of risky prospects. In Fisher's words (*The Nature of Capital and Income*, pp. 273–74):

> If the intention in advance is to reinvest it becomes important not simply to know the present rate of interest, but to forecast the future rate. . . . Although the bond represents nominally a fixed and certain series of income items, yet, in view of the intention to reinvest, it actually represents an income which is quite uncertain . . . because of the uncertainty in the future rate of interest.

Thus, the appraisal of a stream of payments, even if the payments themselves are riskless, involves the implicit forecasting of the term structure of interest rates if the maturity of the payments stream is different from the anticipated holding period. Recognition of the importance of the reinvestment rate represents a significant insight into the subleties of the process by which streams of payments are evaluated. In fact, the reinvestment rate and its influence on valuation have continued to generate controversy in spite of Fisher's explicit attention to the issue. For example, differences in implicit assumptions about this rate have been a long-standing source of confusion in the capital-budgeting literature.[3]

From this discussion it is apparent that Fisher was aware at the conceptual level of the complexities introduced into financial decisionmaking by the existence of uncertainty. Moreover, he was clear in emphasizing the critical role played by the simplifying assumption of certainty when he invoked this assumption. For instance, he wrote (*The Nature or Capital and Income*, p. 202):

> The rate of interest acts as a link between income-value and capital-value, and by means of this link it is possible to derive from any given income-value, its capital-value, i.e., to "capitalize" income. To do this we assume that the expected income is foreknown with certainty, and that the rate of interest (in the sense of an annual premium) is foreknown, and also that it is constant during successive years.

This passage makes obvious Fisher's understanding of the role of the rate of interest in reflecting the time value of money, a role completely distinct from embodying considerations of uncertainty. To see how Fisher approached this issue, we turn next to a review of his framework for rigorously evaluating the impacts of risk.

III. *Risk Quantification and Analysis*

To deal successfully with risk in decision situations requires that two distinct problems be solved. Some specification of risk must be developed so that alternatives can be compactly summarized. In addition, a theory of choice behavior under risk consistent with this specification must be postulated so that alternatives can be evaluated. Although Fisher did not provide a solution to these problems sufficiently powerful to yield closed-form valuations of risky prospects, his analysis resulted in substantive contributions to the understanding of each of these dimensions.

3. For a recent discussion of this issue, see Dudley 1972.

As has been previously pointed out, Fisher advocated a probabilistic approach for specifying the relevant outcomes in chance situations. His discussion of the details of such a procedure indicates that he envisioned a two-parameter, mean-variance approach to summarizing the information contained in the probability distributions characterizing streams of payments. In such a framework, transactors have utility-of-wealth functions which are defined over the expected value and the variance of terminal wealth, and wealth-increasing prospects are described in terms of these same characteristics. Thus, his work represents an initial representation of the approach which is embodied in the modern portfolio theory of Harry Markowitz (1952).

In treating subjective probability distributions, Fisher focused on their expected values, or what he called their mathematical values. In an appendix contained in *The Nature of Capital and Income*, however, he developed in some detail the idea that the standard deviation of a distribution was a suitable measure of risk. In his words (pp. 406–7):

> For a more minute analysis of the bearing of chance it is preferable to measure the variability with reference to the mean. . . . A simple measure of the extent of variability displayed by such a series of deviations from the mean is what is called the "standard deviation."

Turning to the behavioral aspects, Fisher not only recognized that risk aversion was dominant for most individuals, he also endorsed that fact. The following passage provides an example of the way in which he combined the roles of scientific economist and moralist (*The Nature of Capital and Income*, pp. 275–76):

> If a professional gambler should always pay the mathematical value of the chances, he would in the long run, probably come out about even, as is well known from "Bernoulli's Theorem." . . . But the actual price which one will pay is not necessarily the mathematical value of the chance. It may be higher; it is usually lower. The gambler is usually a person who will pay more than the mathematical value of the chance. At Monte Carlo, the "bank" makes its profit in this way, although its victims know full well that they are paying more than the mathematical value of their chances. The consequence, of course, is ruin to most of them. Fortunately, persons who deliberately gamble are in most communities in the minority. The ordinary man is unwilling to pay even the full mathematical value of the chance. He is reluctant to assume any risks, and is, on the contrary, willing to make sacrifices in order to rid himself of them.

While suggesting that risk aversion is predominant, Fisher recognized the existence of differing levels of risk aversion among individuals. To develop this point, he introduced two other characteristics of risky prospects in addition to their mathematical values. He described these elements in this way (*The Nature of Capital and Income*, p. 276):

> There are three values which apply to an uncertain return: (1) the value which that return would have if the uncertainty could be eliminated, or its *riskless* value; (2) the value which would be attached to it if the investor were willing to pay the product of the income by the chance of obtaining it, or the *mathematical* value; (3) the value which he is actually willing to pay, or the *commercial* value.

Of these three dimensions, the riskless value is the only unclear one. As an example of the riskless value, in the case of a lottery ticket entitling the holder to a chance at a $100 prize, the riskless value would be $100 regardless of the odds of winning. Fisher's concept of the riskless value of an uncertain prospect may appear to be inappropriate. In situations where several outcomes are feasible, it is incorrect to impute any particular significance to a single outcome in isolation; this point is obscured in the case of the simple two-outcome lotteries described by Fisher as examples. As used by Fisher, however, the idea of the riskless value of a prospect is straightforward; he simply used it as a way of expressing the odds of a specific outcome's occurring.

This point is clarified in Fisher's further discussion of the three values characterizing a risky prospect and the relationship among them (*The Nature of Capital and Income*, pp. 276–77):

> The ratio of the mathematical to the riskless value may be called the "coefficient of probability." . . . The ratio of the commercial to the mathematical—a ratio which will vary according to the temperament of the individual—may be called the "coefficient of caution." Given these ratios, we can for a given individual derive the commercial value from the riskless value by multiplying the riskless value by the coefficient of probability and the result by the coefficient of caution. . . . The product of these two ratios is the ratio of the commercial value to the riskless value . . . and may be called the *coefficient of risk*.

The concepts introduced here embody the essence of Fisher's contribution to the behavioral aspects of decisionmaking under risk. He devised this approach to emphasize the two conceptually distinct modifications which the presence of uncertainty introduced into a valuation problem. At one level there is the change in the nature of opportunities themselves, which Fisher represents in the distinction between riskless and mathematical values. Then, there is the fact that because of subjective differences in risk tolerance, individuals will make the distinction between mathematical and commercial value.

Fisher's coefficient of caution and commercial value are widely recommended as being appropriate for organizing the problem of evaluating an uncertain prospect, although modern usage is framed in somewhat different terms. The analysis in terms of certainty equivalents, suggested by the Lutzes (1951), for instance, is in effect the same as that presented by Fisher. What the Lutzes call a "correction factor" serves the same function as Fisher's coefficient of caution in summarizing subjective attitudes about risk tolerance.

In view of the important role of the coefficient of caution, it is natural to investigate it further. In Fisher's words (*The Nature of Capital and Income*, p. 277):

> The coefficient of caution expresses a feature of individual character as determined partly by nature and partly by environment. In times like the colonial period when lotteries were common, or in places like Monte Carlo, where gamblers congregate, the coefficient of caution is such as to represent an abnormal lack of caution. The opposite extreme is found in the timid investor who hoards money rather than risk its investment in any form. The coefficient of caution also varies with the same individual under different circumstances. Chief among these varying circumstances, as Professor Norton has pointed out, is the amount of capital of which the individual is possessed. The more capital a man possesses, the less is his chance of serious loss in any enterprise involving risk; and for this reason a rich man finds it possible to grow still richer.[4]

Again from this passage Fisher's belief that risk preference is almost a pathological pattern is evident. Here also Fisher presented an interesting explanation for decreasing absolute risk aversion in the sense of Arrow and Pratt (1971). Fisher's explanation, expanded in an appendix in *The Nature of Capital and Income*, is that as one's wealth increases, the boundaries of tolerable outcomes widen; there is less chance of ruinous consequences from assuming a particular risk. As Fisher put it (pp. 408–9):

4. The Professor Norton referred to is cited for personal correspondence with Fisher and for "Theory of Loan Credit," *Publications of the American Economic Association*, 1904.

> The wider the range of deviation considered, the less the chance that the actual dividends in any year will fall outside that range. Moreover, the chance decreases *far faster* than the range increases. This relation, which follows from the theory of probability, has very important consequences in the theory of distribution. From it follows as a corollary that the richer an individual, the less risk in *taking* risks. Being possessed of capital, he has a wider range within which he can safely afford to operate, and therefore he has a far greater probability of keeping within these limits of safety than his less fortunate competitors.

In discussing the implementation of his approach to valuation, Fisher was brief. From an example which he provided, it is clear that he intended for the commercial values of the elements in a stream of payments to be discounted at a riskless rate in order to determine the present value of the prospect. Beyond this he made no suggestions about sources of the information which would be required to implement the technique. However, he acknowledged this problem, writing (*The Nature of Capital and Income*, pp. 282–83):

> Usually, however, the chances involved are so indefinite that the reckoning is made only by rule of thumb. Any further attempt to apply the theory of probability would therefore outrun the exigencies of practice. Nevertheless it is more than conceivable that the time may come when practical brokers will make use of probability computations in the same way that they now make use of bond tables.

Fisher's comment here is of particular interest because it reflects his concern over the practicality of putting into operation theoretical contributions. It is important to recall that Fisher at this stage of his career was a leading theorist. Although accessible to the informed non-specialist, his work was breaking new ground in theoretical economics. The contrast between Fisher's concern over the practicality of theoretical developments and contemporary attitudes which assign little significance to this aspect suggests how changing professional norms can shape the development of a discipline by providing criteria for determining the professional worth of a contribution.

Fisher also pointed out an alternative method of evaluating uncertain income streams, what is called in finance texts the risk-adjusted discount rate technique. Fisher described the technique in these words (*The Nature of Capital and Income*, pp. 279–80):

> There is another way, and one which conforms more to ordinary usage, in which the commercial value of the bond may be derived

> from the riskless value. While the price of the bond will vary inversely with the risk, the rate of interest varies directly with the risk; so that as the value of the bond descends, the corresponding rate of interest will ascend. . . . Were it possible, it would be simpler to confine the application of the phrase "rate of interest" to an exchange between present and future riskless income. But in this case, it is always exceedingly difficult to state what the riskless rate of interest is, since some slight risk attaches to almost every investment. Accordingly it is usual to regard the commercial rate as a true "rate of interest."

The problem of isolating the risk premium impounded in observed market rates cited by Fisher continues to characterize modern presentations of the risk-adjusted discount rate approach, as is evidenced by the discussion of Robichek and Myers (1965), for example. Although the risk-adjusted discount rate may be more appealing on intuitive grounds, it is ultimately no easier to implement empirically than the certainty-equivalent technique. This fact is clearly reflected in Fisher's analysis.

From this review of Fisher's approach to the problem of valuation under uncertainty, it should be apparent that his contribution was a significant one. He clearly recognized the basic elements of the problem, and he proposed an analytical framework for dealing with these elements which resembles in many ways the one used in present textbook discussions, such as Van Horne's (1977). In fact, there is little of significance which Fisher did not treat, a conclusion supported by his comprehensive approach to the management of risk.

IV. *Fisher on Risk Management*

One of Fisher's characteristics, shared with other eminent economists of his day, was the way in which he integrated theoretical contributions with practical applications. Thus, in treating financial decisionmaking under uncertainty, after having developed a conceptual framework of admittedly limited practicality, he went on to analyze various techniques which men of affairs might use in dealing with uncertainty. To one who reviews Fisher's contribution here, it is striking that his recommendations encompass much of what is found in current formulations of the same material.

For purposes of evaluating uncertain streams of payments, Fisher emphasized the importance of accurate forecasting in a comprehensive sense. He described the forecasting process in this way (*The Nature of Capital and Income*, p. 284):

> In forecasting the income from capital, it is necessary to forecast all the elements which may influence it and also their variability. These elements are sometimes exceedingly numerous. A stockholder in a railroad, in order to obtain a true idea of the value of his property, must look forward to the traffic of the road, the price which can be charged for this traffic, the cost of operation, involving the amount of labor, fuel and materials, the prices paid for these items, etc. To forecast any one of these involves, in turn, some knowledge of outside conditions, as the outlook for crops, prices of agricultural products, probabilities of increased trade through connecting lines, increased density of population, possible competition, possible adverse legislation, etc.

This catalogue of relevant factors still provides a useful set of guidelines for a security analyst. Fisher was aware of the complexities involved in a comprehensive forecasting scheme such as the one outlined, but he was also optimistic about the ultimate reduction in much of this uncertainty as a consequence of technological progress. As he put it (*The Nature of Capital and Income*, p. 291): "It has been seen that risk is nothing but an expression of ignorance, and decreases with the progress of science. It may be said that the chief progress now being made industrially consists in lifting the veil which hides the future." Specific developments cited by Fisher for their effect in reducing uncertainty include the growth of trade journals which expedite the flow of information, advances in technical education, and applications of scientific methods in fields such as mining and agriculture. No doubt Fisher the visionary would be disappointed by the fact that although impressive progress has been made in areas such as these, uncertainty about future prospects remains a major source of economic instability.

Fisher also provided useful insights into the analysis of fixed-income securities, where the primary risk to the holder involves the possibility that periodic interest payments will not be made. Fisher's technique for evaluating this possibility is as follows (*The Nature of Capital and Income*, pp. 409–10):

> An important application of these models is to the calculation of the chance that earnings should fall below the amount required to pay interest on bonds. This chance is found from the probability table. It is the probability corresponding to that relative deviation obtained by dividing the difference between the *mean* expected earnings and the interest by two thirds of the standard deviation. . . . Merely to glance over past earnings and receive an impres-

> sion is not a very scientific mode of utilizing the facts which those earnings display. To average them is not of much more value. While it is important to know the mean, it is also important to know the dispersion about the mean. . . . The best procedure would therefore seem to be to calculate first the mean of past experience as to earnings; secondly, the standard deviation from that mean; thirdly, the chances of fluctuations thus displayed (e.g., the chance of earnings falling below the interest-paying line); and fourthly, to correct the results thus obtained by taking into account the degree in which it is believed that the future will not follow in the footsteps of the past. Only the last of these four operations need be done by the rule of thumb. But at present all but the first and often even that are left to the merest impression.

Again Fisher's approach is virtually identical to modern textbook analysis of the problem of estimating the adequacy of interest coverage for bonds.[5]

The analysis of the riskiness of debt securities was important in Fisher's scheme of risk management, for it functioned to emphasize that "the creditor is a risk-taker" (p. 83) and that "the distinction between stockholders and bondholders is chiefly one of degree, and may be bridged over by intermediate forms" (p. 85). Nonetheless, Fisher argued that the creation of a variety of financial claims with differing risk characteristics, along with the process of collateralization, was an important technique for managing risk in that it made possible transactions motivated by divergencies in subjective attitudes toward the exposure to risk. Fisher called this approach the method of guarantees, where "it is possible by a division of the ownership of capital wealth, for one class of property holders to assume the burden of risks and to *guarantee* to another class a fixed income" (p. 288).

Rather than eliminating risk, the method of guaranties is a technique for shifting risks, a fact which Fisher noted. In contrast, he cited a number of techniques for actually reducing risk by what he termed "specific safeguards." Included in this category were inventories of raw materials and finished products and precautionary cash balances. In discussing the holding of these assets, Fisher called attention to the fact that sacrifices in nominal returns were required in

5. As a part of his theory of economic fluctuations, Fisher stressed the impact that financial distress arising from the aggressive employment of financial leverage might have on business activity. See *Booms and Depressions*, pp. 8–11.

order to gain the benefits of risk reduction, suggesting insight into the functioning of the capital markets.

Fisher devoted considerable attention to developing the rationale for, in his words (*The Nature of Capital and Income*, p. 291) "that important means of avoiding and shifting risks, called insurance. Insurance involves the offsetting of one risk by another; that is, the consolidation of a large number of chances whereby relative certainty is, as it were, manufactured out of uncertainty." Fisher recognized that "insurance" could be obtained through diversification by holding numerous similar real assets in a portfolio, where the chances of a disastrous outcome for any single asset are largely independent of the outcomes of the other assets, the ultimate effect being to reduce overall variability in income, or "to steady the income" (p. 293).

Fisher explained that the realization of this benefit of diversification among real assets depended on the scale of holdings. To the extent that it was impossible for individuals to achieve this scale, as for instance, in housing, there was an incentive for the market to provide insurance explicitly. It is interesting to note Fisher's comment about one potential difficulty when diversification takes place through insurance, the so-called moral hazard (*The Nature of Capital and Income*, pp. 294–95):

> Thus, if a person insures the life of someone in whom he has no financial interest, he is merely gambling on that person's life. Some years ago in Michigan there was an abuse of this type called "graveyard insurance." Speculators went through the form of insuring the lives of certain old persons, in other words of betting on their deaths, a procedure not only vicious as gambling but calculated also to lead to crime. The same considerations apply to fire insurance, where a person insures a building in which he is not financially interested, or over-insures one in which he is.

Finally, Fisher discussed the important role played by speculators in managing risk. As he put it (*The Nature of Capital and Income*, p. 295): "Where risks cannot be reduced to a statistical basis, and therefore cannot be insured against, recourse is often had to the shifting of the risk into the hands of those who are willing to take it. Such persons are speculators."

Following in the classical tradition of the analysis of speculation, Fisher argued that a speculator could be distinguished from a mere gambler by "special knowledge, so that the risk to *him*, owing to superior foresight, is at the outset less than it would be to others" (p.

295).[6] He went on to emphasize the dangers which arise from speculation where this special insight is not present. As he expressed it (*The Nature of Capital and Income*, pp. 295–96):

> The chief evils of speculation flow from the participation of the general public, who lack the special knowledge, and enter the market in a purely gambling spirit. In addition to suffering the usual evil consequences of gambling, they produce evil consequences for the non-participating public by causing factitious fluctuations in the values of the products or property in which they speculate. The evils of speculation are particularly acute when, as generally happens with the investing public, the forecasts are not made independently. Were it true that each individual speculator made up his mind independently of every other as to the future course of events, the errors of some would probably be offset by those of others. But as a matter of fact, the mistakes of the common herd are usually in the same direction. Like sheep, they follow a single leader.

This passage illustrates Fisher's attitude toward the problems potentially arising from speculative excesses associated with mass psychological factors. Fisher had a great faith in the perfectibility of human nature, however, and by exposing this problem, he hoped to point the way toward an improved environment.

Fisher closed out his discussion of techniques for risk management with a lucid explanation of the way hedging can be used to reallocate risk, provided that arrangements exist for entering into futures transactions. He emphasized that the benefits potentially resulting from hedging would be widely distributed in a competitive system by lowering costs of production and, in turn, prices.

Fisher went to such lengths in discussing practical ways of dealing with uncertainty in an attempt to explain to a wide audience the essential aspects of a complex topic. In his words (*The Nature of Capital and Income*, p. 300), "Risk is one of the direst economic evils and all of the devices which aid in overcoming it—whether increased guaranties, safeguards, foresight, insurance, or legitimate speculation—represent a great boon to humanity." Basic to the utilization of

6. In an early discussion of the effects of uncertainty, Fisher argued that superior forecasting ability was an important characteristic of successful entrepreneurs. In particular, he pointed out that correct anticipation of price-level movements would make consistent gains possible on borrowing and lending transactions in a market where only partially accurate anticipations were reflected in nominal interest rates. See his *Appreciation and Interest*, pp. 76–80.

any of these techniques is an educational process; this was the thrust of Fisher's treatment of risk management.

V. *Concluding Comments*

An investigation like this one is useful for two reasons. It is always fruitful to review the ground covered by an intellectual pioneer like Fisher because of what we learn about him and his contributions. Ultimately more significant, however, is what we learn about the present status of the discipline in the light of the historical perspective provided. In the case of the financial economics of uncertainty, dramatic analytical progress has been made since Fisher's time in dealing with the normative aspects of decisionmaking. From this review of Fisher's work, however, it should be apparent that these developments have taken place from a much less primitive point of departure than is frequently presumed.

Combining as it does the theoretical with the practical, Fisher's mode of analysis underscores the inherent shortcoming of much of the modern theory, which is virtually incomprehensible to the non-specialist. Fisher's work also calls attention to the fact that limited progress has been made in modifying institutional arrangements for dealing with uncertainty. In spite of reforms such as the movement toward comprehensive disclosure, and in spite of technological innovations which expedite the processing of information, the financial markets, and by extension, the real sector, are subject to fluctuations generated by varying estimates of uncertainty.

REFERENCES

Arrow, Kenneth J. "The Theory of Risk Aversion." Reprinted in *Essays in the Theory of Risk-Bearing*. Chicago, 1971.

Black, Fisher. "Equilibrium in the Creation of Investment Goods Under Uncertainty." In Michael C. Jensen, ed., *Studies in the Theory of Capital Markets* (New York, 1972), pp. 249–65.

Dudley, Carlton L. "A Note on Reinvestment Assumptions in Choosing Between Net Present Value and Internal Rate of Return." *Journal of Finance* 27 (Sept. 1972): 907–15.

Fisher, Irving. *Appreciation and Interest*. New York, 1896. Reprinted, New York, 1965.

———. *Booms and Depression*. New York, 1932.

———. *The Nature of Capital and Income*. New York, 1906.

———. *The Rate of Interest*. New York, 1907.

———. *The Theory of Interest*. New York, 1930.

Fisher, Irving Norton. *My Father Irving Fisher*. New York, 1956.

Friedman, Milton, and Leonard J. Savage. "The Utility Analysis of Choice Involving Risk." *Journal of Political Economy* 56 (Aug. 1948): 279–304.

Hirshleifer, Jack. "Investment Decisions Under Uncertainty: Choice-Theoretic Approaches." *Quarterly Journal of Economics* 79 (Nov. 1965):509–36.

Lutz, Friedrich, and Vera Lutz. *The Theory of Investment of the Firm*. Princeton, 1951.

Markowitz, Harry. "Portfolio Selection." *Journal of Finance* 7 (March 1952):77–91.

Pratt, John W. "Risk Aversion in the Small and in the Large." *Econometrica* 32 (Jan.–April, 1964):122–36.

Ramsey, F. P. "Truth and Probability." In his *The Foundations of Mathematics and Other Logical Essays*. London, 1931.

Robichek, Alexander A., and Stewart C. Myers. *Optimal Financing Decisions*. Englewood Cliffs, N.J., 1965.

Van Horne, James C. *Financial Management and Policy*, 4th ed. Englewood Cliffs, N.J., 1977.

von Neumann, John, and Oskar Morgenstern. *Theory of Games and Economic Behavior*. 3d ed. Princeton, 1953.

Yaari, Menahem E. "Convexity in the Theory of Choice Under Risk." *Quarterly Journal of Economics* 79 (May 1965): 278–90.

[3]

History of Political Economy 12:2

A. T. Hadley on monopoly theory and railway regulation: an American contribution to economic analysis and policy

Melvin Cross, Dalhousie University, and *Robert B. Ekelund, Jr.*, Auburn University
and Texas A & M University

I. *Introduction*

The development of the railroad in the nineteenth century and its subsequent effects upon economic development in Western nations has been for decades a much-discussed topic among economic historians. More recently historians of economic thought have begun to relate microanalytic contributions to the peculiar industrial characteristics of railroads and to the pricing structures which mirrored them.[1] The purpose of this article is to focus upon the contributions of an American—Arthur Twining Hadley—to this literature.

Hadley (1856–1930) was not an engineer, unlike some of his important predecessors dealing with railway economics and 'public goods,' but was in turn a tutor of Greek logic and Roman law (at Yale from 1879–1883), a free-lance writer and lecturer on railway economics, and ultimately President of Yale University for over twenty years (1899–1921). The bulk of his economic writing was completed before the turn of the century, principally in *Railway Transportation* (1885), *Economics* (1896), and several contributions to the *Quarterly Journal*

1. These characteristics are tractable enough and consist mainly in the existence of high fixed costs and specialized equipment which were the foundation of all sorts of pricing and competitive problems to thoughtful observers and railway management. Non-assignable costs, both 'common' and joint, led to speculation about pricing structures related to monopoly, price discrimination, marginal cost pricing and joint cost equilibria (later to become 'peak-load' pricing theory). Long-period 'short runs' in the presence of specialized plant and equipment offered a unique glimpse into the nature of competition and market periods. It has even been suggested that railway economics may have led to marginalism itself. But the interesting feature of this development for historians of thought is that cost and pricing structures of the firm in imperfect competition, including location analysis and important observations relating to industrial organization, were discussed and even modeled by transport specialists long before they became an object of concerted interest in the discipline's mainstream.

of Economics, though his interest in rail questions persisted through his career as an educator and public servant.[2]

Hadley's training in economics was eclectic and, if all available materials are to be believed, largely self-acquired. In addition to his undergraduate training at Yale (between 1872 and 1876) and his study of German historicism at Berlin, Hadley was a close friend of Irving Fisher during his professorship of Political Economy at Yale (1891–1899). His citations, especially in *Economics*, reveal a clear familiarity with the growing 'scientific literature' of the discipline. Cournot, Jevons, Walras, writers in the tradition of the Ecole des Ponts et Chaussées, Kleinwächter (a German writer on cartels), in addition to Mill, Sidgwick, Marshall, and a large number of American economists, are all given prominent reference. He is listed by Schumpeter, along with Dunbar, Newcomb, Sumner, Walker, and Wells, as one "who prepared the ground" for American achievements in economics, but the nature of his training set him apart from these contemporaries. Though Schumpeter hints at his achievements in the theory of the monopoly firm and, with respect to Hadley's *Economics*, adjures scholars "to really look at it" (1954), p. 866), he gives no clue to the nature of Hadley's contributions. Indeed, Hadley regarded Marshall's *Principles* (in its third edition by 1896) as "incomplete" and needful of "an account of the Relations between Private Property and Public Welfare" (the subtitle of his 1896 work).

The purpose of the present article is to discuss Hadley's view of industrial competition and his underlying theory of the monopoly firm. Utilizing his own framework, we wish to show that Hadley (i) formalized a theory of monopoly-price discrimination in a manner superior to

2. A bibliography of Hadley's prolific output appears in the posthumously published *Education and Government* (1934), presumably gathered by his son Morris Hadley; also see Fisher 1930 and *Dictionary* 1932. Though his interest in economics was not lessened by the advent of his administrative career, his related publications were motivated more by 'economic education' in the popular press than by serious scholarship. Political science and education (1901) received the lion's share of his attention. A popular lecturer, Hadley delivered papers at a large number of American universities (including the universities of Virginia and North Carolina and Harvard University). In 1907–8 he was Roosevelt Professor of American History at the University of Berlin, and during the spring of 1914 he lectured at Oxford University. In 1910 and 1911 Hadley was appointed by President Taft to serve as Chairman of the Railroad Securities Commission. The Hadley Commission report filed in 1911 recommended greater profits for the American railroads and I.C.C. valuation of physical property (Kolko 1965, p. 203). Late in life Hadley was considered as a possible candidate for the U.S. Senate and for the Presidency. A world traveler, he died aboard ship in Kobe harbor in 1930 shortly after visiting Peking. A planned *magnum opus*, tentatively entitled "Principles of Industrial Economy and Their Application to Current Political Problems" was interrupted by his death.

previous and, to some extent, future writers on the topic, (ii) contributed to marginalism directly in depicting the marginal cost–marginal revenue rule as the operational principle of the firm, (iii) anticipated the period analysis of Marshall by examining the firm's short-run loss minimization strategy, a quasi-rent concept, and industrial market periods, and (iv) utilized this theory and a theory of cartels to correctly identify emergent market structures in the 1880's, a characterization which led him to judge the Interstate Commerce Commission as unnecessary if not harmful, and cost-plus regulation as inherently inefficient (this latter conclusion has been supported in recent historical studies of the period: Spann and Erikson 1970; Kolko 1965). We consider these topics *seriatim*, contrasting (where appropriate) Hadley's achievement with those of earlier and later contributors in these areas.

II. *Discriminating Monopoly and Marginalism in the Firm*

In 1885 the theory of discriminating monopoly—indeed, the whole microanalytic approach to the firm—was hardly a standard topic in the growing discipline of economics. Despite increasing professionalism of the discipline, analytical contributions in the mainstream, especially to firm theory, were still relatively isolated, although Walras, Jevons, and the Austrians, as well as Marshall, had gotten the marginal utility theory of value and exchange (and in Marshall's case, supply and demand theory) off to a running start. A good case may be made for the fact that nonprofessional economists of many nations had already traveled much further in the area of 'the neoclassical' theory of the firm, and with the exception of Cournot, these advances were made in connection with railroad capital and pricing problems.[3]

3. A partial listing of these contributors and their achievements reveals how very far they had gotten: (1) Augustin Cournot by developing, in 1838, the marginalist theory of the firm and the theory of duopoly and the rudiments of 'game theory'; (2) Charles Ellet (1839, 1840a, 1840b) in establishing a mathematical theory of the monopoly railroad firm where location served as a parameter of the rates charged (Ekelund and Hooks; Calasoyas); (3) Jules Dupuit (1844, 1849) and a host of members of the Ecole des Ponts et Chaussées such as Emile Cheysson (1887) who established the basis for the modern approach to monopoly demand theory, price discrimination, cost-benefit and welfare economics, and the theory of public goods (Ekelund 1968, 1970; Ekelund and Hebert, 1978); Dionysius Lardner (1850) who developed a theory of the railway firm, *sans* marginalism, much admired but largely ignored by Jevons (Hooks 1971): Fleeming Jenkin (1870), whose clear graphical exposition of supply and demand functions with hints of an elasticity formulation paved the way for the English achievements in these areas; (6) Carl Friedrich Wilhelm Launhardt (1872, 1882), whose excursions into location theory and market area analysis along with those of Ellet and Cheysson (Hebert 1972), were pathbreaking achievements. A. T. Hadley was most certainly aware of some of these writers in addition to major writers of the neoclassical age. In constructing his chapter on "Railway Policy in France" (1885, pp. 187–202) Hadley cites his reliance on the *Annales des Ponts et Chaussées* and on A. Picard's work on French

Exempting the obscure work of Charles Ellet, the American scene was practically devoid of microanalytical work (of the neoclassical variety) in the nineteenth century. In 1885 the influence of the German Historical School and the lingering debates over facets of classical doctrine (e.g., F. A. Walker's assault on the wages fund; Henry George's preoccupation with Ricardian rent theory) occupied the energies of most of the best minds in America. An exception was A. T. Hadley, who, following the tradition of Ellet, advanced to the formal analysis of the firm and the theory of price discrimination, a performance which, Schumpeter argued (1954, p. 978), was superior to Pigou's.

It is now known that two conditions are necessary for successful price discrimination among different markets. The first is an element of monopoly power, and the second is an ability to separate markets. Under such circumstances a profit-maximizing firm will equate, in each market, marginal cost with marginal revenue. Markets with relatively inelastic demands will be discriminated against. This common practice had been discussed in the context of railway rates before. Dupuit, Ellet, and Dionysius Lardner had all come up with methods of separating markets in order to discriminate against strong demanders of passenger or freight service. Dupuit had emphasized the effects of doing so upon total welfare produced by railway firms, whereas Ellet, and to a much lesser extent Lardner, illustrated the principle only in a locational context. Notions of elasticity were prerequisite to these arguments, but it was left to Hadley to link all of these discriminatory methods with a simple elasticity specification.

Hadley's model of short-run profit maximization

Hadley, like all economists dealing with railway problems, was acutely aware of the distinction between fixed and variable costs and the fact that the portion of fixed costs borne by any class of traffic is price-determined rather than price-determining.[4] He incorporated

railroad policy (1884), but he argues that few members of the Ecole "were men of genius or originality in the highest sense of the word" (1885, p. 190), betraying a lack of familiarity with the important work done there in the nineteenth century. By 1896 Hadley was assuredly acquainted with the work of Cournot (1896, p. v) and in 1885, in constructing his appendix on the theory of railroad rates (which we analyze in the text), Hadley cited Lardner's rate analysis (1885, p. 261 n. 1) and noted that his own was different. The impact of Hadley's very close friend Irving Fisher on his work may only be guessed at, though he may have learned of Cournot from Fisher. It is the case, however, that Fisher regarded Hadley's work as highly original, lamenting the fact that Hadley's serious writing was cut short by an administrative career (1930).

4. Hadley showed that the relevant considerations in rate making are marginal costs and marginal revenues. If a particular rate is lowered, for example, railroad management can expect traffic and hence both gross revenues and expenses to increase. The relevant question then becomes "will net earnings increase? That is to say will gross

these short-run cost considerations into a model of price discrimination, and his theory of railroad rates included both a traffic demand curve and a mathematical statement of the relationship between traffic carried and the rate charged. Hadley's curve is shown in Figure 1. Price, the independent variable, is plotted on the horizontal axis while the quantity of traffic is plotted on the vertical axis. The curve thus shows an inverse functional relationship between rate and quantity of traffic. Hadley called his curve, represented by *tt* in Figure 1, a *traffic*

Figure 1. Traffic Demand Curve. From Hadley 1885, p. 262.

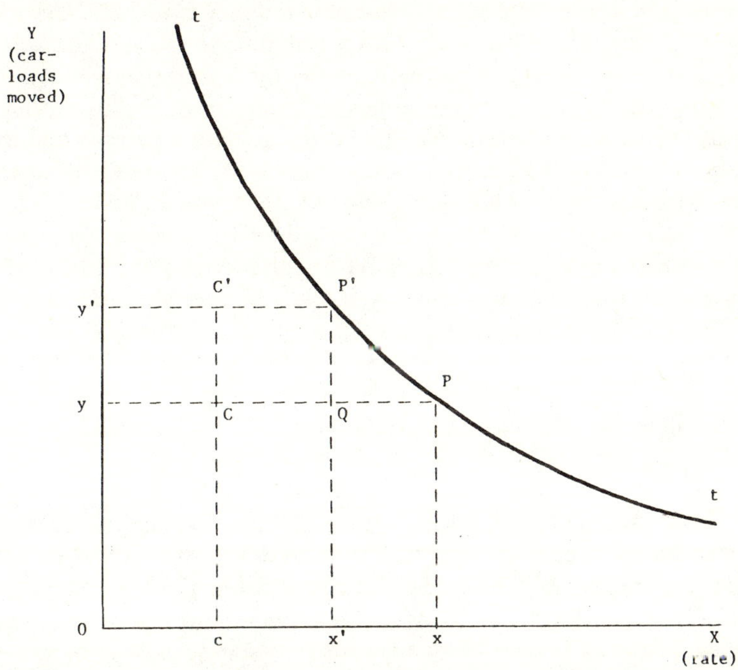

earnings increase faster than operating expenses?" Since a large part of railroad expenses are fixed, the revenues generated by the increased traffic following a rate reduction are usually the most important consideration. Hadley accordingly said that for a road developing new business, "Any rate which will more than cover the expense of moving the cars and handling the goods is a paying rate, *provided the business can be had on no other terms*." Both the distinction between fixed and variable costs and the fact that the portion of fixed costs born by any class of traffic is price-determined rather than price-determining are thus recognized. As Hadley put it, railroads will "try to get all they can above operating expenses"; therefore, "Railroad profits are to a large extent of the nature of rent rather than interest. They represent excess of market value above operating expenses." Fixed charges are not taken into account in rate making, but of course it is important to consider "prospective traffic and rates . . . before incurring fixed charges" (1885, pp. 109–12, 123, n. 1, 265). An implicit assumption of elastic demand is carried throughout Hadley's discussion.

curve. The variable X, plotted on the horizontal axis, represents rate per carload for some given distance, and Y represents carloads moved. Under Hadley's assumption of profit maximization, "The manager [will lower] rates until the differential of gross earnings on a particular line of traffic ceases to be greater than (i.e., becomes equal to) the differential of the operating expenses" (Hadley 1885, pp. 261–62).

To proceed with the analysis, we consider rate x in Figure 1. Carloads of traffic moved would then be y and the total revenue generated by that branch of traffic would be $OxPy$. If we treat c, the cost of moving each additional carload, as constant, part of total revenue $OxPy$ can be described as the "special expense of handling y carloads." The variable c of Figure 1 is accordingly the cost of moving each additional carload, and $OcCy$ is the cost directly attributable to the movement of y carloads. This means $cxPC$ becomes "the share which this particular line of business can contribute toward the general expenses and dividends. It is this rectangle which the manager tries to make as large as possible in each particular case" (Hadley 1885, pp. 262–63).

We now move to the effect of a rate reduction. Suppose the carload rate is reduced to x' in Figure 1, increasing the volume of traffic to y'. It is assumed gross revenues will rise to $Ox'P'y'$ and gross expenses to $Oy'C'c$. The increase in gross earnings can be expressed as

$$yy'P'Q - x'xPQ = x'\Delta y - y\Delta x. \qquad (1)$$

and the increase in operating expenses as

$$yCC'y' = c\Delta y. \qquad (2)$$

Operating under an implicit assumption of elastic demand, Hadley recognized that as long as the increase in revenues brought about by additional traffic exceeds the increase in cost, it is justifiable to seek new traffic. He accordingly said, "At the point where the [increase in gross earnings] ceases to exceed the [increase in operating expenses], the differentials must be equal. Then

$$xdy - ydx = cdy; \qquad (3)$$

or

$$(x-c)\,dy = ydx \qquad (4)$$

[1885, pp. 262–63]."[5]

At this point in his analysis Hadley had determined that profits would be maximized at the point where marginal revenue equals mar-

5. Hadley used very clear, discrete examples of the marginal cost–marginal revenue rule to improve the reader's understanding of marginalism as applied to firm behavior (1885, p. 110 for example).

ginal cost, though he did not carry out simple (and tautological) manipulation to make a forceful point of the matter. If both sides of equation (4) are divided by dy and multiplied by x/x the following result can be achieved:

$$x\left(1 + \frac{1}{\epsilon}\right) = c \qquad (5)$$

where

$$\epsilon = \frac{dy}{dx}\,\frac{x}{y}\,.$$

Since ϵ represents price elasticity of demand, the left-hand side of (5) is the standard algebraic statement of marginal revenue. Because c represents constant marginal cost, equation (5) provides the ubiquitous marginal-revenue-equals-marginal-cost rule. Equations (3) and (4) are simply variants of the same rule. Equation (3) requires the net change in total revenues to be set equal at the margin to the change in total cost where both changes are induced by a rate adjustment. For the same rate adjustment, equation (4) requires the net change in total contribution to fixed cost and profit to be set equal at the margin to the change in total revenues stemming from only the rate change itself. The right-hand side of (4) does not include the effect of the induced traffic change caused by the rate adjustment. Equation (4) can also be obtained by maximizing $cxPC$ of Figure 1, the net revenue rectangle.[6]

Two points concerning Hadley's contribution and of his development of the marginal conditions are important here. First, since Hadley (1885, p. 263) explicitly stated that each type of traffic would have its own demand curve, he had, in effect, presented the theory of third-degree price discrimination. His reference to a demand curve for each item of traffic clearly defined the separate markets of a monopolist. (In the railroad case these markets could be separated by the identifiable characteristics, i.e., by freight classifications or by distances, e.g., long and short haul discrimination). Hadley's comparison of railroad profits and rents together with a simple manipulation of his equations shows that prices in the separate markets are directly related to the demand elasticities of each market. Indeed, since equation (5) requires marginal revenue to equal marginal costs, we can use it to write:

$$\text{marginal revenue} = \text{price}\left(1 + \frac{1}{\epsilon}\right) \qquad (6a)$$

$$\text{price} = \frac{\text{marginal revenue}}{\left(1 + \frac{1}{\epsilon}\right)} \qquad (6b)$$

6. The net revenue rectangle is represented by $cxPC = (x - c)y$. Maximization requires that $(x - c)dy - ydx = 0$ which is easily rearranged to produce equation (4) See Hadley 1885, pp. 262–63.

where x in equation (5) has been replaced with "price" in equations (6). An examination of Pigou's 1932 edition of the *Economics of Welfare* shows that he had not yet discovered this relationship. According to Pigou, the monopolist would, in effect, set marginal revenue equal to marginal cost in each of his markets. Pigou also said that should the monopolist do this, the relative rate charged in each market would not depend solely on the demand elasticity of that market. All of the conditions influencing demand in each market had to be considered (Pigou 1932, p. 302). One year later, Joan Robinson (pp. 36, 187 n. 2) responded by producing equation (6b), but a different arrangement of it[7] had appeared almost fifty years earlier in Hadley's work.[8]

7. The plus sign in the denominator of (6b) is replaced with a minus sign in Robinson's analysis because she treated ϵ as a positive coefficient. The negative sign of dy/dx in the treatment here makes these two versions compatible.

8. At this point a summary of future developments is useful in placing Hadley's achievements. Though described by Adam Smith (p. 683) and analyzed by many individuals (see above, n. 3), the understanding of price discrimination by the economics profession was, in 1891, sufficiently imprecise to warrant an article by Taussig (1891) that was designed to set the issue straight but which did not. The article did mark the beginning of formal academic concern for the *theory* of monopoly price discrimination, though it remained encased in the theory of railway rates and in international trade theory until Robinson's classic treatment. Following Taussig's treatment, Pigou (1904, 1912, 1932) and F. Y. Edgeworth (1910, 1911, 1912) advanced the analysis of price discrimination, but neither produced a simple relationship that linked price, marginal revenue, and demand elasticity. Advances in the theory of discrimination were also made in connection with dumping—see Hobson 1904 or Culbertson and Ekelund 1977, Viner 1923, and Yntema 1929; and Hotelling looked at the concept in a locational in 1929. With the exception of Yntema, however, the simple relationships eluded even these writers. The analysis of the output effects of price discrimination was also incomplete. Robinson removed both of these shortcomings in 1933, but Hadley already had traveled partway to this goal. Equation (5) shows that the concept of price elasticity of demand is fundamental to Hadley's analysis. In fact, elasticity of demand at the profit-maximizing point can easily be derived from his equations. Consider equation (4). It can be rewritten as

$$\frac{dy}{dx}\frac{(x-c)}{y} = 1 \tag{7}$$

or

$$\frac{dy}{dx}\frac{x}{y} = 1 + \frac{dy}{dx}\frac{c}{y}. \tag{8}$$

Equation (8) tells us elasticity of demand at the profit-maximizing point. If cost c is zero, we get the familiar result:

$$\frac{dy}{dx}\frac{x}{y} = 1. \tag{9}$$

Equation (9) is simply the elasticity condition for maximum total revenue and hence maximum profits when costs are zero. A comparison of equations (7) and (9) reveals that the only difference between them is that x in (9) is simply replaced by $(x - c)$ in (7). The term $(x - c)/y$ represents per carload net contribution to profit, and dy/dx represents the incremental adjustment in traffic stemming from an incremental rate change. Equation (7) thus requires profit elasticity of demand to equal 1 if a maximum

Secondly, price elasticity of demand was an integral part of Hadley's specifications. While he did not examine the concept separately, he clearly recognized that different demand curves would have different elasticities and used the words *sensitive* and *insensitive* respectively in place of the words elastic and inelastic. Furthermore, factors affecting the demand for transport—a derived demand—with specific reference to value of the commodity, distance transported, and the possibility of lower rates opening new sources of both demand and supply (Hadley 1885, pp. 263–65; 1896, pp. 166, 326–27 n.1) were discussed. In addition, the assumption of constant costs was released, allowing Hadley to determine the effect of reduced handling costs on the optimum rate.[9]

Railway applications

Railway management utilized the apparatus Hadley described to implement all sorts of profit-maximizing discrimination. These types include (i) class (classification) discrimination, where different *commodities* transported were charged rates based upon differences in demand elasticities, (ii) personal discrimination—discrimination between individuals in similar pricing situations, and (iii) the famous 'long and the short haul discrimination,' which is self-explanatory. As a policy matter, as we will see, Hadley disapproved only type (ii) discriminations, and then not all of them, arguing that the financial health of the railroad and especially its ability to expand service to new markets and to lower the average price of transport (thanks to decreasing cost conditions) required 'competitive' price discrimination. Discrimination could 'fill out' capacity by adding new markets, in other words, and, for substantial ranges of output, at decreasing costs. Discrimination on long-haul rates, which was part of the *competitive process*, could have this effect.[10]

---

is to occur. The establishment of these relationships appears to be the basis for Schumpeter's suggestion that Hadley's progress did not compare unfavorably with Pigou's (Schumpeter, p. 949).

9. After determining the profit-maximizing conditions, Hadley modified his assumption that the cost of hauling each additional carload was constant. This allowed him to determine the effect of a reduction in handling cost on the optimum rate: "Any thing which diminishes the expense of handling additional traffic makes it advantageous to reduce rates lower than would otherwise be the case. For if, previously, $xdy - ydx = cdy$, any thing which diminishes c without changing general business conditions will make $xdy - ydx > cdy$; that is, it will place us at a point where further reductions in rates increase gross earnings faster than they increase operating expenses" (1885, p. 264).

10. Hadley also correctly assessed the effects of differential charging in the 'back haul' as contributing to an extension of railway service and a decrease in average rates. Though r t a case of price discrimination, but rather one of joint supply (Locklin 1933, 1966, pp. 142–43; Ekelund and Hulett 1973), Hadley noted that the back-haul example

The 'necessary case' for discrimination—oysters

At other times discrimination was necessary to get any service supplied at all. In the so-called 'necessary case' or 'all or none' case for discrimination Hadley came up with the most famous example in the literature—the case of oyster transport from Delaware to Philadelphia where *all* parties to the discrimination benefited. Although the example was widely criticized, it remains a classic in railway rate theory.

This simple case concerned a point X on the coast of Delaware that was found to be good for oyster production. The maximum rate that could be charged on oysters shipped from X to Philadelphia without eliminating production was $1 per 100 pounds. Production would stop at any higher rate. If a carload could be moved daily at the dollar rate, shipment of the oysters would be profitable. The service was inaugurated only to find that point X could generate only one-half carload daily. Furthermore, it was found that any rate reduction would not increase the oyster traffic from X, since production was limited by the physical capacity of the oyster bed. Revenues were thus only half as much as had been anticipated, while expenses were almost as great as they would have been for a full carload. The service was unprofitable, and the car appeared slated for elimination, when an alternative presented itself.

At point Y beyond X was a much larger oyster bed. The fishermen on this bed shipped their oysters to market over a different line that also charged a rate of $1 per 100 pounds. Thus, if the railroad operating the car from X charged the fishermen at Y 75 cents per 100 pounds for shipment to Philadelphia, the car would be filled. The cost incurred by moving the oysters from Y to X was only 25 cents. The railroad consequently decided to take a half carload from X at $1 and fill the remaining half with oysters from Y at 75 cents. The fishermen at X naturally protested. Nevertheless, a rate of $1 per 100 pounds would not generate a paying quantity of traffic, and a uniform charge of 75 cents was not sufficient to pay variable costs. When the oyster growers at X realized this, they went along with the discriminatory rate rather than lose the service. Everyone, including those discriminated against, was made better off (Hadley 1885, pp. 116–18; Schumpeter, pp. 949, 978 n. 20).[11]

---

showed how "railroad charges [had] been so much reduced during the past fifteen years. It also [explained] how some goods [could] be profitably carried at rates which [seemed] utterly unprofitable" (1885, pp. 107–8). By-products, as examples of joint-supply pricing techniques, were similarly analyzed (1885, p. 113 n. 1).

11. Not until Robinson's analytical work was this possibility raised again. In addition to the 'necessary case,' the possibility that all might benefit from discrimination is raised whenever the introduction of discrimination increases output over what it would

The oyster example may be interpreted in two ways, both of them correct: (i) as an example of the necessary use for price discrimination, and (ii) as a case where all parties benefit from discrimination. Hadley's oyster example did not remain unchallenged, however. Pigou (1932, pp. 308–9) agreed that price discrimination might allow some output to be produced when a single price would not, but he quarreled with an assumption (which he erroneously attributed to Hadley) that the situation was a general one for railroads. While it is correct that Hadley encountered the 'all or nothing' case at several points in this analysis of discrimination, he did not use the case as a defense of all railway discriminations. In the long and short haul case (such as the oyster example) Hadley envisioned discrimination as primarily a competitive means to *add* markets while protecting revenues by discriminating against the more inelastic short-haul traffic (1885, p. 118). Classification discrimination, which Hadley analyzed at length (1885, pp. 112–14 for example), had the same effects. Other comment, on the oyster example in particular and on Hadley's argument for discrimination in general, principally by W. Z. Ripley and J. M. Clark, was based upon the distributional effects of discrimination and upon the efficacy of Hadley's assumption of rail competition.[12] They failed, we be-

---

be at simple monopoly price. Whenever the latter situation exists (with linear or non-linear curves) and is combined with *decreasing* marginal costs, all parties benefit from discrimination (Robinson 1933, ch. 15).

12. The reaction to Hadley's defense of discrimination was interesting but, we argue, all of his critics ignored his wider analysis of the effects of statutory regulation in the control of competition. W. Z. Ripley (1920, pp. 164–65) regarded the example where two loss-minimizing railroads competed price to the level of variable cost as beyond improvement, but he was not so uncritical of the oyster example. Discrimination against an intermediate point on a direct route would, he said, involve an attempt to extract higher revenues from existing traffic, and not an attempt to generate new traffic. Ripley advocated "standards of reasonableness" imposed by a regulatory commission on discrimination of this kind (1920, pp. 216–26). J. M. Clark (1923, p. 214 n. 1) also criticized the oyster example, arguing that it was a special case because discrimination generated exactly one-half carload of business and no more. Traffic ordinarily grows with time, making it unnecessary to solicit business with special pricing. Pigou (1932, pp. 311–13) made a similar point, but neither of these criticisms view long-haul discriminations as an instrument of competition in what was essentially a competitive market. Schumpeter hints at this interpretation when he notes that "It is characteristic of a comparatively backward state of analysis that this case [Hadley's oyster case] was treated like a curious exception instead of being made to follow from a more general set-up in which absence of discrimination would constitute a special (or limiting) case" (1954, p. 949). Clark's attack on Hadley's position hinged upon the former's strong belief that railroads were 'natural monopolies,' a belief which, we will show, was challenged by Hadley. Clark did not think that market forces would limit the use of monopoly power, but noted that the problem of allocating overhead costs remained. This could be done with discriminatory pricing, but not without opening the problem of favoritism in price setting (Clark 1923, pp. 1, 11, 23–24). In 1910 Clark discussed "standards of reasonableness" for price discriminations, thus indicating a belief in the necessity of statute-legislative control (Clark 1910, pp. 74–75, 111–13, 125, 155). An implied confidence in

lieve, to consider Hadley's analysis of the effects of statutory regulation on the railway industry, a subject which we will discuss shortly.

III. *Short-Run Loss Minimization: Market Periods, Price Oscillations and Competition Between 'Partial Monopolies'*

Hadley's analysis of short-run minimization, which caught the fancy of Irving Fisher, provided the basis for an interesting and original analysis of competition between 'monopolies.' In developing his argument, Hadley first considered Ricardo's concept of competition. In the Ricardian model high prices attracted resources to an industry, while low prices caused exit. Prices adjusted to some natural level. If price fell below production cost, output would not be forthcoming. Hadley felt that in many of the businesses of his time, this did not apply. To demonstrate his point he hypothesized a railroad connecting two points between which it carried 100,000 tons of freight at 25 cents per ton. Total revenue was then $25,000 of which "$10,000 [was] paid out for the actual expenses of running the trains and loading or unloading the cars, $5,000 for repairs and general expenses, the remaining $10,000 [paying] the interest on the cost of construction." If a parallel line were built and a rate war ensued, rates would drop to 10 cents a ton. That is, only the $10,000 cost directly attributable to movement of the 100,000 tons would be charged out in freight tolls. Any rate over 10 cents would help to defray overhead and hence would result in a smaller loss than would shutdown. Thus capital would not exit and production would continue. Hadley concluded:

> Ricardo's theory was based upon the assumption that when payment fell below cost of service, active competition would cease. His theory fails because, far below the point where it pays to do your own business, it pays to steal business from another man. The influx of new capital [would] cease; but the fight [would] go on, either until the old investment and machinery [were] worn out, or until a pool of some sort [was] arranged [Hadley 1885, p. 72].

This argument was supported with other examples in which the case of high fixed costs was contrasted with the case where fixed costs were a relatively small proportion of total costs. With the smaller ratio of fixed to total costs, relatively small downward price movements would cause short-run shutdown to occur, and conversely (Hadley 1885, pp. 69–73). Hadley noted that loss minimization could become important in *any* industry with large amounts of fixed cost, though he did not be-

---

the efficiency and effectiveness of such control is found in most American writers of the period, but not in Hadley.

lieve that large fixed costs automatically created a natural monopoly demanding regulation.

Hadley went on to say that Ricardo's analysis was developed in a time when industries were much more atomized; furthermore, Ricardo "assumes that there may be a permanent profit due to monopoly of location while any permanent loss will be avoided by withdrawal of capital." However, Ricardo's "theory of rent represents essentially a banker's view of farming, which, like a farmer's view of banking, takes much more account of the profits than of the losses" (Hadley 1896, pp. 290–91). Hadley believed banking capital to be the most mobile of any industry. He suggested that Ricardo, being a banker, gave to economics the idea that capital could be easily shifted (Hadley 1885, p. 41). If this were the case, high profits in any industry "could last but a few weeks. But it takes time to build a successful furnace, factory, or railroad" (Hadley 1885, p. 51). Quick entry of capital therefore could not be expected in heavy industry. With this in mind, Hadley said: "The years of expansion [are] years of large return to the owners of old investment" (Hadley 1885, p. 51). If business decisionmakers were to misjudge, however, plant expansion could cause problems: "Mere over-production can be remedied in a few months. Over-investment means lasting over-production till the investment itself is worn out, or till the business of the country slowly grows to a higher point" (Hadley 1885, p. 54).

Hadley obviously thought capital reallocation was more difficult than Ricardo had assumed. This, said Hadley, combined with the tendency of an individual firm to have substantial control of prices, caused a situation in which prices would oscillate from a high extreme to a low extreme. At the high extreme, one firm might receive handsome profits, causing entry. This in turn would cause negative profits followed by exit and a return to the high price levels. There would be no tendency toward a stable price with normal profit levels; in this sense competition would be ruinous. This form of competition was linked to the phenomena of business cycles, and in the process, both underconsumption and overproduction were described (Hadley 1885, pp. 69–74, 289–94).[13]

13. We do not investigate the macro issues which Hadley's microanalysis of industrial organization suggests, except to note that he linked fixed-capital characteristics to an insufficiency of aggregate demand and subsequent economic downturns. Here his writings take on a distinct Keynesian flavor—"The modern civilized world is in a perpetual danger of under-consumption" (1896, p. 148)—and there are even overtones of Austrian business cycle theory (1896, pp. 147–58).

IV. *Competition, Regulation and the Interstate Commerce Commission*

One of the most interesting aspects of Hadley's work was the nature of his participation in the debate over one of the most significant and far-reaching economic policy events of his day, the institution of federal regulation of the railroads. Railroad problems of the 1870's and 1880's very probably led Hadley to an *analysis* of railway economics, and the latter outfitted him well for the heated debate which followed.

Certain questions are raised in Hadley's analysis which are germane to the formation of the I.C.C. Were railroads of that day 'natural monopolies' in the sense that monopoly pricing and the emergence of a single firm were the logical or actual outcomes of competition in the market? Or was a form of competition viable in these markets? Further, what was the actual role of class and distance discrimination in the competitive process? And, most fundamentally, what was the nature of the political-economic relationship which developed between the railroad and the I.C.C. in the opening years, and what was its effect on general economic welfare? Hadley's assessment of these issues presages a very modern view of the problem of regulation.

In common with virtually all other writers on railway questions, Hadley thought railroads to be characterized by decreasing costs due to the high component of overhead (fixed) costs. But unlike so many of the others he did not believe them to be 'natural monopolies.' If the latter were the case, we would expect to observe much merger activity and a dearth of new entrants. Neither was observed, however, since the railroad costs were not *perpetually* declining. The railroads along with water, electric, and telephone 'monopolies' (1896, pp. 170) were what Hadley called "particular monopolies" (1885, p. 63) with peculiar short-run problems due to high fixed costs and limited ability to discriminate. Competition in these circumstances would cause oscillating rates between those based on short-run variable costs and the monopoly rate. Although some consolidation took place (Hadley 1886, p. 360), as a result of declining costs, Hadley argued that the nonregulated market solution was pooling via cartels.[14]

More important, Hadley described a *theory* of cartel agreements: "This agreement may take any one of four forms; (1) Agreement to maintain rates; (2) To divide the field; (3) To divide the traffic; (4) To

14. Analysis of railway conditions in England, France, Germany, and virtually all other nations with railroads led Hadley to conclude that "competitive discrimination" necessitated pooling. It was a ubiquitous phenomenon sanctioned by law or practiced by public management of all railway systems in the world except that of the United States.

divide the earnings. The last three are commonly known as pools" (1885, p. 74). The first kind of agreement, though common in most "organized industry," was difficult to enforce (i.e., "easy to violate the agreement indirectly, and so hard to detect any such violation"), and "It is for the interest of all that rates in general should be maintained; but it is for the interest of each concern to secure business for itself by not quite maintaining them. This constitutes a great temptation to depart from schedule prices" (1885, p. 75).

Recourse is then had to the other forms of agreement, which have varying advantages and policing costs associated with them. Most important, private pooling lent stability to railroad rates, while actual and potential competition from new entrants *strictly* limited monopoly profits. In general, and with specific reference to railroads, Hadley argued:

> Combination does not produce arbitrary results any more than competition produces uniformly beneficent ones. . . . Our railroad management has many faults and abuses in detail; but, taking its work as a whole, it has brought down rates to a cheapness which is unequalled elsewhere, and has developed the business of the country on a scale which would have been impossible under any system of rates based on cost of service. Nor does it [pooling and price discrimination] leave the door open for inordinate profits. The moment a combination places its figures so high as to do this, other capital will seek investment in the same line; and though these new investments are apt, before long, to come into the pool at the old rates, yet they have cut down the profits by their entrance. . . . It is usually far-sighted policy for a combination to put its rates so low as not to tempt new capital too rapidly into the field. If that lesson is learned, the public gets the benefits of competition without its disadvantages [1885, pp. 76–77].

Nevertheless, entry combined with other inherent instabilities in cartel arrangements led to breakdowns and rate wars in the railway industry. Hadley correctly noted that these features precipitated railroad crises in 1857–59, 1873–77, and 1884–85 (1886, p. 34), and he produced convincing statistical evidence on the matter (1890, pp. 161–62). But, he believed, these breakdowns led to the 'capture' of regulation by railroads, so that the industry managed to obtain *legal* rate stability (1888, p. 184).[15]

15. According to Hadley, the railroads "were tired of fighting, and were glad to make the law for the time being a pretext for the cessation of rate wars. The danger of disobeying the law was greater than the danger of suffering from the cut rates of a rival" (1888, p. 184). Hadley's view is consistent with the modern 'capture' theory of

Hadley was worried that the industry's 'capture' of regulation might (i) not produce rate stability, owing to the prohibition against pooling contained in the provisions of the Act, and (ii) that, of crucial importance, the I.C.C. or *any* similar regulation of *any* industry would create massive allocative distortions. On the first count, Hadley had underestimated the ability of the railroads, with the approbation of the I.C.C., to quote differential rates which in effect 'pooled traffic.' He also ignored the increased costs imposed by the I.C.C. for 'cutthroat competition,' i.e., rate reduction on long-haul traffic had to be assumed (and could be met by all competitors), and it had to be extended to all traffic. The I.C.C. had, in effect, increased the cost of cartel violations (Spann and Erickson, p. 237).[16] A "protective stance" toward the industry had already begun, as Hadley noted.[17]

The second of Hadley's predictions is even more interesting. Hadley developed an idea which was virtually unknown then—that railroads and other 'utilities' may be constrained by many forces, the most important of which is potential market competition. The effectiveness of rivalrous competition, in other words, may have *no relation* to *market structure*. Hadley believed that potential competition, bankruptcies of customers, substitute products, and so on, would limit the exercise of monopoly powers (Hadley 1885, pp. 76–77; 1886, pp. 43–44; 1888, pp. 175–76; 1896, pp. 164–65). Those dependent on the monopoly might be severely damaged before these forces took effect, but Hadley nevertheless thought government regulation a poor alternative to competitive market forces. Discrimination, if tampered with, would redirect market forces from optimal societal investment.[18]

---

regulation (Stiger 1971; Posner 1974) and his application of it to railroads antedates similar historically and empirically supported arguments (Kolko, pp. 26–29, 24–41; Spann and Erickson) by over 85 years.

16. Hadley did not see that the structure of the I.C.C.'s control over rebates and other regulations may have been sufficient to prevent seriously deleterious rate wars and lower profits. There were in fact rate outbreaks, such as in the dressed-meat business (Hadley 1888, p. 184), but while acknowledging these, Spann and Erickson concluded that market shares remained fairly constant in spite of these "wars" and that railroad profits rose between 1887 and 1893 (1970, pp. 237–38). Kolko and MacAvoy (1965) concur in the latter conclusions, although Hadley does note selective bankruptcies of local carriers caused by a scaling down of short-haul rates (1889, pp. 172–76). By 1890 Hadley had observed a new consolidation movement in response to the prohibition against pooling. Thus, in this view, the I.C.C. was contributing to the monopolization of the railroads (i) by promoting consolidation and the legal fixing of rates and (ii) by legal restrictions on entry.

17. Early on, Hadley noted the protective attitude taken by the I.C.C. towards the industry vis-à-vis suspensions (1888, pp. 164–65) and water and foreign competition (1888, p. 182).

18. Spann and Erickson, with estimated elasticities, calculated the welfare effect of the decrease in short-term rates and the increase in the more competitive long-haul sector for 1890 showing a significant net loss (1970, pp. 241–42).

Profit regulation would introduce allocative distortions, and Hadley referred to an official of the British Board of Trade who remarked on the "maze of absurdities" produced by British profit limitation (Hadley 1885, pp. 111–15, 120–22, 126; 1896, pp. 165–168). Limiting profits for the purpose of lowering railroad rates defeated its own end, "but the temptation to save at the spigot and waste at the bunghole is almost irresistible when the public eye is fixed exclusively on the spigot" (Hadley 1928, p. 178). Profit limitations on 'utilities' were characterized as leading to intransigence in management, i.e., cost increases and not rate reductions follow profit restrictions (1896, pp. 166–67).[19] Managers of public corporations or publicly regulated business would maximize their own present value rather than that of the firm (1896, p. 179). Not the least of the problems of commission regulation, according to Hadley, was the *inherent* tendency for such bureaucracies to expand.[20]

In sum, regulation of railroads or other industries of like kind was unnecessary, in Hadley's view, and in the long term disastrous for the welfare of society. Hadley wanted a judicial solution of clearly defined property rights; (a) legalizing pools, (b) preventing a modicum of personal discrimination (but not other kinds), and (c) legally requiring the publication of activities (1885, p. 80). Such a solution would promote some 'stability' without prohibiting competitive entry and the market imposed limitations that the limitation implied. In fact, Hadley believed that the effect of monopoly was to retard but not destroy the forces of industrial competition. Regulation, he thought, would further retard them. Neither price-discriminating monopoly nor regulation was envisioned as a perfect solution to the American railway question, and Hadley did not defend monopoly. As he pointed out, "We are not arguing in favour of this system, but against the popular remedy—a statute" (1885, p. 115).

19. Hadley thus anticipated the x-inefficiency problem in regulation: see Peacock and Rowley 1972 and Davies 1971 for modern formulations.

20. Consider the following: "Again, a commission with judicial powers is almost certain to magnify its own office. This danger made itself strongly felt in England, where the English Commission constantly undertakes more than it can accomplish. The United States Commission [as yet unformed] might decide a few cases; but its authority would be evaded in a hundred times as many more. The worst evil which could possibly befall us, would be the attempt to apply a great deal of regulation somewhere, by an agency which was not strong enough to enforce such regulation everywhere" (1885, p. 144–45). The view further implies that profit maximization through competition may survive the institution of regulation. Competitive forces are merely redirected while regulation causes and creates more problems than it solves (e.g., the Averech-Johnson effect).

VI. *Conclusions*

We have shown in this article that Schumpeter's assessment of A. T. Hadley as one of the Americans who "prepared the ground" for later achievements in economics is somewhat less than totally accurate. His contributions to economic analysis, and specifically to the theory of price discrimination, were original from the point of view of previous contributors and, in its implicit specification of elasticity, even of later contributors in that branch of microanalysis. And more, his characterization of short-run profit maximization and cartel theory and its application to railroads and of the effects of regulatory and entry controls upon the industry was unique and anticipatory of recent studies of the period. Most important, however, a fresh and original approach to questions of public economic intervention emerges from Hadley's work. Far from being simply 'a writer on railway topics,' then, Hadley's contribution spans important areas of concern in modern economics, especially those dealing with regulation and competitive organization. As such he deserves more recognition in the development of American economics than he has received.

REFERENCES

C. D. Calasoyas. "The Mathematical Theory of Monopoly in 1839: Charles Ellet, Jr." *Journal of Political Economy* 58 (1950): 162–70.

E. Cheysson. "La Statistique géometrique: ses applications industrielles et commerciales." *Le Génie Civil* 10 (1887): 206–10, 224–28.

J. M. Clark. "Standards of Reasonableness in Local Freight Discriminations." *Studies in History, Economics, and Public Law* 37 (1910), no. 1.

———*Studies in the Economics of Overhead Costs*. Chicago, 1923.

A. A. Cournot. *Researches into the Mathematical Principles of the Theory of Wealth*. Translated by N. T. Bacon, New York, 1960 [1838].

W. P. Culbertson, Jr., and R. B. Ekelund, Jr. "John A. Hobson and the Theory of Discriminating Monopoly." *History of Political Economy* 9 (1977): 273–82.

D. Davies. "The Efficiency of Public versus Private Firms: The Case of Australia's Two Airlines." *Journal of Law and Economics* 14 (1971): 149–65.

Dictionary of American Biography. New York, 1932, pp. 77–80.

J. Dupuit. "On the Measurement of the Utility of Public Works." Translated by R. H. Barback in *International Economic Papers*, no. 2 (London, 1952), pp. 38–110 [1844].

———. "On Tolls and Transport Charges." Translated by E. Henderson in *International Economic Papers*, no. 11 (London, 1962), pp. 7–31 [1849].

F. Y. Edgeworth. "Applications of Probabilities to Economics." *Economic Journal* 20 (June, Sept. 1910): 284–304, 441–65.

———. "Monopoly and Differential Prices." *Economic Journal* 21 (1911): 143–48.

———"Contribution to the Theory of Railway Rates." *Economic Journal* 22 (1912): 198–218; 23 (1913): 206–26.

R. B. Ekelund, Jr. "Jules Dupuit and the Early Theory of Marginal Cost Pricing." *Journal of Political Economy* 76 (1968): 462–71.

———. "Price Discrimination and Product Differentiation in Economic Theory: An Early Analysis." *Quarterly Journal of Economics* 84 (1970): 268–78.

——— and R. Hebert. "French Engineers, Welfare Economics, and Public Finance in the Nineteenth Century." *History of Political Economy* 10 (1978): 636–668.

——— and D. Hooks. "Joint Demand, Discriminating Two Part Tariffs and Location Theory: An Early American Contribution." *Western Economic Journal* 10 (1972): 84–94.

——— and J. R. Hulett. "Joint Supply, the Taussig-Pigou Controversy, and the Competitive Provision of Public Goods." *Journal of Law and Economics* 16 (1973): 369–87.

C. Ellet, Jr. *An Essay on the Laws of Trade in Reference to the Works of Internal Improvement of the United States*. New York, 1966 [1839].

———. "A Popular Exposition of the Incorrectness of the Tariffs of Tolls in Use of the Public Improvements of the United States." *Journal of the Franklin Institute, Philadelphia* (1840a) 29: 167–72, 225–32.

———. "The Laws of Trade Applied to the Determination of the Most Advantageous Fare for Passengers on Railroads." *Journal of the Franklin Institute, Philadelphia* (1840b) 30: 369–79.

I. Fisher. "Obituary: Arthur Twining Hadley." *Economic Journal* 40 (1930): 525–33.

A. T. Hadley. *Railroad Transportation: Its History and Its Laws*. New York, 1885.

———. "Private Monopolies and Public Rights." *Quarterly Journal of Economics* 1 (1886): 28–44.

———. "The Workings of the Interstate Commerce Law." *Quarterly Journal of Economics* 2 (1888): 162–87.

———. "Railroad Business Under the Interstate Commerce Act." *Quarterly Journal of Economics* 3 (1899): 170–87.

———. "The Prohibition of Railroad Pools." *Quarterly Journal of Economics* 4 (1890): 158–71.

———. "Population and Capital." *Publications of the American Economic Association* 9 (1894): 557–66.

———. *Economics: An Account of the Relations Between Private Property and Public Welfare*. New York, 1896.

———. *The Education of the American Citizen*. New York, 1901.

———. "The Meaning of Valuation." *American Economic Review* 18 (1928) supp.: 173–80.

———. *Education and Government*. Edited by Morris Hadley. New Haven, 1934.

R. F. Hebert. "A Note of the Historical Development of the Economic Law of Market Areas." *Quarterly Journal of Economics* 86 (1972): 563–71.

J. A. Hobson. "The Mystery of Dumping." *Contemporary Review* 85 (1904): 186–97.

D. L. Hooks. "Monopoly Price Discrimination in 1850: Dionysius Lardner." *History of Political Economy* 3 (1971): 208–23.

H. Hotelling. "Stability in Competition." *Economic Journal* 39 (1929): 41–57.

F. Jenkin. "The Graphic Representation of the Laws of Supply and Demand, and Their Application to Labour." *The Graphic Representation of the Laws of Supply and Demand, and Other Essays on Political Economy*, 1868–1884. London, 1931 [1870].

G. Kolko, *Railroads and Regulation, 1877–1916*. Princeton, 1965.

D. Lardner. *Railway Economy*. New York, 1968 [1850].

W. Launhardt. "Kommerzielle Tracierung der Verkehrswege." *Zeitschrift für Architektur und Igenieurswesen* 18, no. 4 (1972): 515–34.

———. "Die Bestimmung des zweckmässigsten Standortes einer gewerblichen Anlage." *Zeitschrift des Vereines Deutscher Ingenieure* 26 (1882): 106–15.

D. P. Locklin. "The Literature on Railway Rate Theory." *Quarterly Journal of Economics* 47 (1933): 167–230.

———. *Economics of Transportation*. Homewood, Ill., 1966.

P. W. MacAvoy. *The Economic Effects of Regulation—The Trunkline Railroad Cartels and the Interstate Commerce Commission Before 1900*. Cambridge, Mass., 1965.

A. T. Peacock and C. K. Rowley. "Welfare Economics and the Public Regulation of Natural Monopoly." *Journal of Public Economics* 1 (1972): 227–44.

A. Picard. *Les Chemins de fer français*, 5 vols. Paris, 1884.

A. C. Pigou. "Monopoly and the Consumers' Surplus." *Economic Journal* 14 (1904): 388–94.

———. *Wealth and Welfare*. London, 1912.

———. *The Economics of Welfare*. London, 1932.

R. Posner. "Theories of Economic Regulation." *Bell Journal of Economics* 5 (1974): 335–58.

W.Z. Ripley. *Railroads, Rates, and Regulation*. New York, 1920.

J. Robinson. *The Economics of Imperfect Competition*. London, 1969 [1933].

J. A. Schumpeter. *History of Economic Analysis*. New York, 1954.

A. Smith. *An Inquiry into the Nature and Causes of the Wealth of Nations*. New York, 1965.

R. Spann and E. Erickson. "The Economics of Railroading: The Beginning of Cartelization and Regulation." *Bell Journal of Economics and Management Science* 1 (1970): 227–44.

G. J. Stigler. "The Theory of Economic Regulation." *Bell Journal of Economics and Management Science* 2 (1971): 3–21.

F. W. Taussig. "A Contribution to the Theory of Railway Rates." *Quarterly Journal of Economics* 5 (1891): 438–65.

J. Viner. *Dumping: A Problem in International Trade*. New York, 1966 [1923].

T. O. Yntema. "The Influence of Dumping on Monopoly Price." *Journal of Political Economy* 36 (1928): 686–98.

[4]

History of Political Economy 13:4

Ragnar Frisch and business cycle research during the interwar years

Jens Christopher Andvig, Institute of Economics, University of Oslo

I. *Introduction*

Most of the interest in the development of early modern macroeconomics has been concentrated around the so-called Keynesian Revolution. The development has been seen primarily as a succession of macroeconomic models. In the fifties history writing was extremely simple. Earlier thinkers could be evaluated against the standard IS-LM model and receive high grades if they had constructed models similar in structure. They were then precursors of Keynes. With A. Leijonhufvud's contributions, the picture of 'what Keynes really said' became more blurred. One lost the simple key to the period. However, it is still usual to describe the history of early modern macroeconomics as consisting of a succession of or a competition between several more or less specified sets of macroeconomic models.

This way of writing the history of economics is valuable in many cases, and probably the most interesting way when trying to incorporate the insights achieved during the early period into today's theory. At the same time one loses sight of many of the important historical processes which shaped the actual research procedures current today. When we look back and observe the kind of research into macroeconomic problems—like unemployment and inflation—that was actually done in the 1920s, the gap between the empirical and the theoretical approach seems to have been even greater than it is today. The tension between the empirical business cycle research exemplified by W. C. Mitchell and strict theoretical research like D. Robertson's *Banking Policy and the Price Level* may explain some of the later developments in macroeconomic research—and perhaps not only in macroeconomics. The conflict was an important motivating force in the early

Correspondence for the author may be sent to Mr. J. C. Andvig, Institute of Economics, University of Oslo, Blindern, Box 1095, Oslo 3, NORWAY.

econometric movement. One reason why this conflict has not received greater attention is that in a way it was resolved at about the same time as the Keynesian Revolution occurred, with the development of modern econometrics. The pattern of alliances for and against econometrics was complex. Keynes, for example, was on the 'wrong' and Schumpeter on the 'right' side of the fence.

The econometric program as developed by Frisch and others was directed not only against institutionalistic business cycle research, as asserted by Gunnar Myrdal (1973, p. 18), but against much of the theoretical approach as well. In order to understand the econometric program as applied to the macroeconomic field, the older conflict between business cycle research and 'monetary theory' (the most common name for the theoretical approaches) should be kept in mind. This is at least essential to any evaluation of Ragnar Frisch's contribution to macroeconomics.

II. *The Theoretical Approaches*

Unlike the empirical business cycle research approach, the theoretical attack on the problem of economic fluctuations was performed by several 'schools.' One had, for example, the Cambridge school with Keynes and Robertson, the Austrians with von Mises and Hayek, and the Swedish school with Gunnar Myrdal and Erik Lindahl. The schools disagreed, of course, on many important questions. From our point of view, however, it is of greater interest to stress what they had in common. Most important was perhaps the conviction that any real understanding of the phenomena could be gained only by developing an appropriate theory. Theoretical understanding demanded rigorous conceptual experiments. The starting point was in most cases some kind of economic equilibrium situation in which the plans of the different economic agents were reconciled. The equilibrium situation pictured could be somewhat different, with the English authors having a tendency to start from Marshall, the rest from Walras and Wicksell. In any case the theoreticians were committed to explaining economic fluctuations by means of forces which made sense within an economic equilibrium framework. At the time one was not aware of how ambitious this program had to be, how many restraints one had to put on the agents' behavior in order to make them behave in a consistent way—behavior patterns which could not easily be transformed into 'disequilibrium' situations.

From the theoretical point of view of a general-equilibrium model, the existence of business cycles was interesting only for the theoretical questions it posed. Any real explanation of the cycles had to be related to the main core of economic theory. Hayek expressed the attitude of most theoreticians when he wrote:

> We cannot superimpose upon the system of fundamental propositions comprised in the theory of equilibrium, a Trade Cycle theory rested on unrelated logical foundations. All the phenomena observed in cyclic fluctuations . . . have already been explained by the theory of economic equilibrium; they can only be integrated as an explanation of the totality of economic events by means of fundamentally similar constructions [1933, pp. 28–29].

The problem with equilibrium theory was that "this logic, properly followed through, can do no more than demonstrate that such disturbances of equilibrium can only come from outside" (Hayek, pp. 42–43). Thus it could hardly give a sufficient explanation of a business cycle. The way Hayek tried to 'save' the general-equilibrium theory by connecting it to an unstable monetary system was interesting; however, from our point of view his perception of the business cycle as a core-threatening phenomenon is more important.

Other theoreticians were seldom so explicit, but they probably shared his view. These theoreticians constructed many conceptual experiments which in a certain sense could simulate a kind of disequilibrium behavior, while at the same time they used as much of the statical reasoning apparatus as possible. They did so partly because they did not know any alternative apparatus, and partly because statics was easier to use in making sense of the individual's behavior. Some started consciously to develop the static approach simply as a tool for analyzing phenomena which seemed to demand strictly dynamic tools. For example, the 'temporary equilibrium' method of Lindahl was developed in the twenties.

The theoreticians attempted of course to construct logically rigorous models. The models were usually based on the assumption of some kind of rational individual behavior. An important question, then, was whether the model made sense as simulating the result of such behavior. The frame of reference for many of the models was not any potential empirically observable set of variables, but a set of variables constructed in the conceptual experiment having a more or less clear intuitive meaning for the economist who constructed it and members of his school. The final means of verification of a theory was often rather that it made intuitive sense than that it was consistent with empirical facts—but it should not, of course, be contradicted by facts.

Such intuition was not easy to communicate when conceptual systems were different, and was not easily connected to any kind of observable events. It was characteristic that Frisch's main direct scientific response to these schools of theoretical economics was to attempt to construct a conceptual system which should be able both to translate the different 'languages' into each other and at the same time to relate them to observable phenomena.[1] Mathematics was only sparsely used. This feature together with attempts to keep the analysis of the essentially dynamic phenomena within the straitjacket of statical reasoning methods, and the scanty reference to observable phenomena, may account for much of the obscurity within the different theoretical schools.

Attitudes toward empirical work differed both in theory and in practice. While, for example, Pigou's *Industrial Fluctuations* contained a wealth of empirical information, more strict theoretical works like Myrdal's *Monetary Equilibrium* and Robertson's *Banking Policy and the Price Level* contained hardly any reference to the empirical world at all. The basic point is, however, that not even Pigou made much systematic use of refined statistical methods in order to make the empirical observations relevant for his theoretical explanation of the cycle. It is also characteristic that a theoretician like Ohlin (Ohlin 1931) relied only on the simple empirical method of "journalism," as Frisch branded it. The theoreticians could not of course deny that empirical investigations were necessary and useful. However, they believed them to be of very narrow theoretical significance. This attitude was clearly expressed by Hayek:

> Even as a means of verification, the statistical examination of the cycles has only a very limited value for Trade Cycle theory. For the latter—as for any other economic theory—there are only two criteria of correctness. Firstly, it must be deduced with unexceptionable logic from the fundamental notions of the theoretical system; and secondly, it must explain by a purely deductive method those phenomena with all their peculiarities which we observe in the actual cycles [Hayek 1933, pp. 32–33].

To understand why Hayek stressed the limited usefulness of statistical studies, we have to take a look at the other approach to the study of business cycles dominant in the 1920s, the empirical approach. This was also the school Frisch became most directly involved with and attempted to reform.

1. It proved to be an almost impossible task, and Frisch worked on it for many years. He published only one mimeographed work in this field, in Norwegian: Ragnar Frisch 1935b. This work cleared the ground for his later national-income accounting system.

III. *Empirical Business Cycle Research*

While the theoretical approach represented a kind of progress in the scientific analysis of economic fluctuations in the sense that it developed more rigorous explanations of cyclical phenomena, the empirical inductionist school as represented by W. C. Mitchell also made several important contributions to the field compared with the pre-World War I situation. The progress here was a greater degree of systematization in the collection and empirical analysis of data. Theory construction remained loose.

The development of empirical business cycle research in the 1920s was a rather dramatic episode in the historical development of modern economics. Seldom has a research field increased so fast and apparently become so like a mature science—not so advanced as physics perhaps, but at least something like botany or zoology.

After a beginning in the United States, which continued to be the stronghold, the number of business cycle research institutes increased rapidly in Europe too. Although this type of research demanded much more by way of resources than the theoreticians needed, the empirical research groups seemed to have easier access to money. This was noted by Hayek, himself leader of the business cycle research institute in Vienna: "whether the money and labor so freely expended on statistical research in late years will be repaid by the expected success depends primarily on whether the theoretical understanding keeps pace with the exploration of the facts" (Hayek 1933, p. 39).

The degree of agreement between the practitioners was surprising, especially when we consider the potential political dynamite in this field. Even the Conjuncture Institute in Moscow was on everybody's mailing list. Peaceful coexistence here contrasted favorably with all the disagreements and discussions among the theoreticians. How could this come about?

The most important factor here, I believe, was precisely the lack of theories. This did not mean that the different researchers were without strong beliefs about what was 'really going on,' but their beliefs were not important for their research. The only basic idea really needed was of a mechanical character: the idea of the business cycle itself, the idea that for whatever reason a great number of economic variables moved up and down together in a rather regular wavelike pattern.

This idea was seldom questioned. The most famous exception was Irving Fisher's article of June 1925, "Our Unstable Dollar and the So-Called Business Cycle." Fisher was not himself a business cycle researcher in the narrow sense but a monetary theorist, and his criticism did not at first make much impact.[2]

The hard core of the empirical research program consisted in the collection and manipulation of a large number of economic time series. The manipulation was necessary in order to highlight the 'real' cyclical component in any given series.

A usual procedure was to fit a trend to the data and then observe the difference between the trend and the observed value. When this was done, one had a new time series which should be cleaned for the seasonal component. The remaining time series then consisted of the 'real' cyclical component plus an erratic factor which was both conceptually and practically troublesome. Mitchell had to admit that "it is clear that the ambition to isolate cyclical fluctuations has not been attained—thus statistical technique in its present state enables us to picture cyclical fluctuations only in a distorting combination with irregular fluctuations which we cannot measure" (Mitchell 1927, p. 257).

The notion of a business cycle could not be pictured by the time series of a single economic variable. The business cycle actually consisted of a nest of economic variables moving more or less simultaneously in the same direction. How could one get a more adequate picture of this complex movement, which at the same time could average out the erratic component? It may have been with such questions in the back of his mind that Warren M. Persons started to construct his famous A-B-C curves which were primarily intended to be a forecasting device.[3] Many other business barometers were also constructed. Several sets of weighting the variables in order to construct an index were tried. The weights were not ordinarily supplied with any theoretical foundation, but were based only on observed mechanical characteristics of the variables.

An important point about these business indexes was that their construction made it possible to allow for the fact that business cycles actually consisted of simultaneous variation of a great number of varia-

2. Fisher is one of the cases which do not fit our Manichean picture of the research situation in the twenties, as he was a monetary theorist who worked seriously with empirical problems. Fisher's example was important for Frisch and the early econometric movement. Schumpeter is another example. His empirical program, however, was founded on a theory which demanded detailed analysis of industrial structures and attracted few followers among economists. Among historians it was to become more popular.

3. The A-index was an aggregate of variables "leading" the business cycle. The "speculative curve," the B-index was the "main troop" and included variables like the aggregate price level and the unemployment rate. The C-curve included the "lagging" variables such as the discount rate. The choice of the variables included in each group was based on a great number of correlation coefficients between the different variables measured at different timepoints.

bles, while one could at the same time use the statistical techniques appropriate for a single variable time series. However, the extreme level of aggregation of economic variables, with few economic characteristics in common besides the mechanical character of their movements, made it difficult to study their interrelations. This may have reinforced the tendency to neglect economic theory. Instead of a definite structure of aggregated variables, Mitchell and others perceived the business cycles as vague "congeries of cyclical fluctuations in a large number of economic activities" (Mitchell 1927, p. 309).

The hard core of business cycle research consisted of a set of manipulative statistical techniques. It was thus more *directly* vulnerable to attacks made by theoretical statisticians on the method used than from the theoretical economists criticizing the inductionists for their lack of theoretical understanding. Attacks were made especially from the late twenties on. The development of probability theory in theoretical statistics in Europe, with the accompanying conceptual approach, was very important. Americans supporting the conceptual approach were, however, probably most directly influential at an early stage, Harold Hotelling in particular. The problem associated with Slutsky, that the manipulative techniques performed on a time series might create regular cycles not present in the data, dramatized the criticism.

Another important event, which paradoxically caused empirical business cycle research to stagnate, was the Great Depression of the thirties. One effect was obvious. Empirical business cycle research was to a higher degree than other types of economic research financed by businessmen, and philanthropy must have been one of the first items to be cut. Furthermore, the problem of the regular 3.5-year cycle must have seemed trivial in the context of the severe depression. According to Schumpeter (1954, p. 1165) the business barometers forecasted the depression. The fact remained, however, that the interpreters, the business cycle researchers, did not forecast it, and this further weakened the belief in (and the financial support of) the empirical program.

The last major factor, I will argue, was the fact that by the beginning of the 1930s, Ragnar Frisch and others, Jan Tinbergen in particular, had constructed an alternative *empirical* program for analyzing and describing business cycles which was able to put the adding and multiplying calculator machines to alternative uses. Frisch defined his position in relation to both the theoretical and the inductionist approach:

> Neither the classical nor the neoclassical school sought in any particular degree to verify the theoretical results by statistical observations. This was, in part, because such exact and complete obser-

> vations as would have been necessary for a proper verification were not available, and partly because the theoretical system itself was not adapted for such verification. The consequences of this did not fail to make their appearance. Anti-theoretical schools arose [Frisch 1932b].
>
> During the last ten years or so a bulky literature has arisen that characterizes itself as "quantitative economics." In the U.S. the movement is particularly dominant. I had the chance to attend a meeting . . . where the Americans' points of view were clearly expressed. I was struck by the fact that the people who participated used the expression quantitative economics merely as synonymous with economic statistics.
>
> This is in my opinion a complete misunderstanding of the essence and goals of quantitative economics. Quantitative economics is something different and more than the empirical manipulation of numerical data reflecting economic phenomena. The industrious collector and estimator of correlations can only supply a meager contribution to the analysis of economic phenomena as long as he works without the kind of plan and understanding only an economic theoretical scheme of thought can give. The economic statistics tells us nothing if not illuminated by theoretical analysis.[4]

To judge by these quotations, Frisch seems to have had most sympathy with the theoretical approach, although it had to be modified in order to open it up for empirical investigations. We will see, however, that in his actual research practice Frisch was more interested in and shared more of the attitudes held by the empirically oriented researchers.

IV. *Ragnar Frisch's Early Econometric Research Program*

Frisch's early academic training in Norway was in economics, which was then a short and rather superficial study.[5] Upon graduating in Oslo in 1919 he went to Paris, after some hesitation. He needed some time to make up his mind whether he should prepare for taking over his father's goldsmith store or should take the plunge into an academic ca-

4. Frisch 1931b. The translation from this and all other references where the source is written in Norwegian or any of the other Scandinavian languages is my responsibility, if not otherwise indicated.

5. The most important teachers in economics in Oslo at that time combined in a sensible and eclectic way ideas from the German Historical School, the neoclassical teaching of Jevons, Marshall, and the Austrians and even ideas from the older British classical economists. None of them made any important original contributions, and they did not influence Frisch to any great extent.

reer. In Paris he became a competent mathematician, specializing in mathematical statistics, and his first publications were in this field. He kept in touch with economics, however, and still considered himself an economist. "Sur une problème d'économie pure" from 1926 was his first really important publication in economics and it signaled how he considered that theoretical and empirical work should be integrated.

By the mid-twenties Frisch had already formulated an ambitious research program for himself which was to extend over the whole field of economics, ranging from the history of the discipline to general methodology to detailed problems in the theory of production and consumer behavior.[6]

The plan was permeated by an optimistic spirit. Earlier, mathematically inclined economists always had to defend themselves. The time had come for an attack, since "during the last generation, the resistance to introduction of mathematical methods in economics has been broken," he said in the plan. Although the mathematical methods could not be used in all fields of economics, they could be used much more extensively than most economists believed. Frisch labeled mathematical economic research 'econometrics.'

Frisch believed that 'econometric' research should put three tasks on the agenda:

> 1. To continue the work established by Cournot, Jevons, Walras, Fisher, Pareto and others; that is, to construct a general mathematical analysis of the statical phenomena, without specifying the relevant functions or achieving numerical results.
> 2. Extend the analysis by using this method to dynamic phenomena.
> 3. The statistical-econometric task: to specify the relevant functions and to determine the values of the parameters by a rational use of economic statistics, thereby gaining numerical results. [Cited from his unpublished plan.]

This program—today so commonly accepted that one seldom questions it—demanded active use of theory which had to be constructed and specified beforehand. At the same time, it was empirically oriented and implied a certain criticism of pure theoretical approaches. Frisch expressed his attitude in his inaugural lecture as professor in 1932:

6. He did not publish his ambitions, but typed them down in Norwegian in an undated plan which can be found in archive box 34 in the collection of Frisch's papers in Oslo. The plan was probably written in 1925 or 1926, and Frisch even tried to follow it, at least partially, for almost a decade.

> As long as the analyses remain purely qualitative and it is considered sufficient to prove that a certain measure produces effects in such and such definite *directions*, there is little prospect of truly elucidating matters. Practically all economic phenomena are related to each other. Economics resemble a tangled skein of interactive conditions which spread in all directions. If we satisfy ourselves with proving qualitatively the existence of the relationship between this factor and that, economics will be a sphere in which practically every assertion can be defended as long as it is defended with sufficient intelligence. A weighing of the relative proportion of strength between various pressures and counterpressures in economics is, naturally, not possible until a quantitative formulation can be given of the economic laws. The usefulness of economics in administrative and social respects will, therefore, essentially depend upon the extent to which its laws can be successfully quantified.[7]

Regarding point 2 of the program, it is interesting to note that Frisch at this early date had perhaps not yet reached his important conceptual distinction between statics and dynamics as two different ways of analyzing a problem, and not something inherent in the phenomena studied. However, he must have clarified his views on dynamics versus statics as early as 1928. They were published in 1929. His clear conceptualization of the dynamics/statics distinction was obviously an important part of his analytical equipment when he turned to business cycle research.

V. *Frisch's Early Ideas on Business Cycle Research*

Frisch at first regarded the field of business cycle research as an interesting field of application for theoretical statistics. For years it was his major research interest to develop a more flexible technique than harmonic analysis for decomposing time series into cyclical components. His first major publication in this field was the mimeographed "The Analysis of Statistical Time Series" from 1927, which also represented a kind of breakthrough for Frisch into the front ranks of mathematically inclined economists. Schumpeter later declared the technique Frisch then developed "to be a stroke of genius" (1939, p. 208). However, it was soon forgotten, partly because Wiener had developed an alternative method, partly because the interest in decomposing time series declined together with the business cycle research program itself. Frisch's method was a way of making harmonic analysis more

7. Frisch 1932b. The last idea, that economics had to be quantitative in order to be politically useful, has been extremely important in the development of the economist profession in Norway since World War II.

flexible by not assuming strict periodicity and not demanding such long time series in order to be able to detect different cyclical components.

Like the inductionist school, Frisch strongly believed that most economic time series really consisted of cyclical components which could be discovered by empirical analysis when using sufficiently refined statistical tools. He did, however, conceive the mechanical movements as somewhat more complex than most other researchers did. Instead of one business cycle, Frisch believed that the observable series was created by the interference between different waves of different periodicity and amplitude. How many, could be determined only by statistical scrutiny, but he suggested Kondriatievs, 'super'-Kondriatievs, Juglars, Kitchins, 2.2-year cycles, and so on. This idea was not so original as Frisch seems to have believed.

Considering how strongly Frisch had urged the active use of economic theory to guide research, it was somewhat paradoxical that he worked at least three years with his empirical decomposing of time series without giving any economic-theoretical reasons why economic movements should follow some kind of wavelike patterns. The first time he suggested any theoretical explanation of the business cycle phenomenon was at a meeting of Nordic economists in June 1931, where he sketched a large model with 38 variables. It was only a sketch, and he did not work out any cycle model until his famous article from 1933, "Propagation Problems and Impulse Problems in Dynamic Economics." At the meeting he gave a comprehensive presentation of his general research program as applied to the field of business cycle research. Most of the ideas he had presented earlier elsewhere, but as fragmented ideas, not as a comprehensive program.

His first main point was that it was at least as important in business cycle theory to make the theory quantitative as it was in value theory. The paradigm for the development of business cycle research was the empirical work in value theory, like his own studies of consumption behavior: "This development within the field of business cycle theory where the statistician and theoretician is united in the same person mirrors the development of . . . the general theory of value" (Frisch 1931a, p. 128).

A closer integration of mathematical theory construction and empirical studies had been made possible by recent progress in the field of theoretical statistics. Unlike Hayek, Frisch felt convinced that empirical results would be of direct importance for the theoretical explanations given:

> Within many fields of economic theory and especially in the field of business cycle theory the situation is such that the conclusions we are interested in depend in a fundamental way on the numerical

character of the economic relations. . . . I believe we will discover that the problem to a less extent than we have been accustomed to believe consists in demonstrating that this or that factor is present in the mechanism. We will understand that the real problem is the quantitative relations between certain parameters which characterize the economic laws [Frisch 1931a, pp. 129–30].

After mentioning underconsumption theories, monetary theories, and other 'grand' explanations of the cycles, Frisch continued:

If we may ever achieve any explanation of the cycle movement, I believe it will be of another kind. . . . Let us assume that we are studying an exceptionally simple market characterized by the demand elasticities of two commodities. The situation may then be that, let us say, if the demand elasticity of the first commodity is greater than 2.7 times the last one, then we will get a cyclical movement, but if it is less, the movement may be an asymptotic development towards a stationary level [1931a, p. 130].

It may be of interest to compare Frisch's belief in the theoretical importance of empirical work with Hayek's statement:

The means of perception employed in statistics are not the same as employed in economic theory; and it is therefore impossible to fit regularities established by the former into the structure of the latter [Hayek 1933, p. 27].

Frisch was, however, aware of the fact that several important problems of statistical nature might prove very hard to solve despite all the progress in theoretical statistics. Despite his own work, Frisch believed methods for decomposing time series were not completely satisfactory. Another problem he mentioned was the multicollinearity problem. We also know that Frisch at the time was more conscious of the general identification problem of equation systems than most of the other early econometricians.[8]

Frisch not only made a plea for a new way of integrating empirical and theoretical work in his speech at the meeting of Nordic economists; he also put forward some rules of model construction which business cycle theorists should follow.

First, at least one of the relations had to be *dynamic*:

8. Frisch's awareness of these statistical problems may partly explain why he did not follow up his early macrodynamic models with serious empirical investigations as Tinbergen did. Tinbergen thereby took the lead in the field, although he was unable to solve the major statistical problems and made serious mistakes in his interpretations. See Tinbergen 1939.

> In a determinate theory of business cycles at least one of the relations has to be *dynamic*. From this follows that a system of Walrasian equations never can supply a theory of business cycles. A dynamic relation is an equation that embodies the magnitudes a variable may take at two (or more) *different* points of time [1931a, p. 228].

Furthermore the models should be *determinate*. This was a rule which was much sinned against in the business cycle field:

> I venture to say that *none* of the several theories of crises being postulated, have been determined in this sense. Many, if not most theories of crises have held the ambition to explain how the boom generates the depression. However, I do not believe any of them have been aware of the logical consequence that follows, namely that the system of conditions has to be determinate [1931a, p. 139].

The primary reason why business cycle theories were exceptionally weak at this point was the way the turning points were analyzed. When reasoning with a given set of variables, it was very tempting, Frisch suggested, to introduce a new variable to explain why the direction of the movement has to change. Frisch brought this methodological principle home to the profession by a famous discussion with J. M. Clark in the *Journal of Political Economy*, 1931–32.

Frisch initiated the discussion by pointing out that the accelerator principle was not sufficient to explain the turning points of the business cycle as several of Clark's discussions seemed to indicate. According to Frisch, Clark had used the principle to propose that a decrease in the rate of increase of consumption would cause a reduction in the production of capital goods and thereby cause a cyclical downturn. The accelerator mechanism generated only one equation between two variables and was thus unable to determine any determinate movement in the variables over time. As an example, Frisch demonstrated that if the accelerator mechanism was combined with a special reinvestment mechanism, only exponential movements and not cyclical oscillations would be the result. Clark had sinned against the principle of constructing determinate models.

Frisch probably scored his methodological point, or at least so Alvin Hansen and Henry Schultz told Frisch in letters they sent to him. This did not make any great impression on J. M. Clark, who became more interested in the economics of the model Frisch sketched. Frisch, however, was too much occupied by his methodological point to be able to follow up some of Clark's valid criticism and suggestions.

The reason why the discussion with Clark created such widespread interest even outside the group of mathematical economists was that Frisch here demonstrated that some of the exotic problems which were treated by mathematical economics might have great impact on old and much discussed problems such as the mystery of turning points.[9]

VI. *Frisch's Pre-analytical Mechanistic Vision of the Cycle*

Frisch had not formulated any theoretical explanation of the fluctuations before he ventured into decomposing economic time series, but his empirical and methodological research was at least guided by his pre-analytical 'visions' of the cycles. His picture of the cycles was probably pretty clear by the end of the 1920s, but the first time he presented it as a whole was again at the 1931 meeting among the Nordic economists. Like most of the empirically oriented business cycle researchers, Frisch presented a rather mechanistic picture, probably much influenced by the way he was accustomed to analyzing the data statistically. It was, however, more complicated and analytically refined than the common view.

We have already mentioned one of its characteristics: the belief that more than one cycle was present. The observed time series consisted of different cyclical components each with a different frequency. The observed picture was caused by their interference. It later became important for his policy proposals that he firmly believed in a Kondriatiev cycle. He was thus not surprised when the depression in the thirties lasted so long. (Many other business cycle researchers, by concentrating on the 3.5-year cycle, had a tendency to be overoptimistic about when to expect a revival.)

More important was his distinction between *forced* and *free* oscillations. Frisch defined a forced oscillation as

> an oscillation within the system to be explained, when the system in some way or another is tied to a phenomenon outside it, which we have no intention of explaining. If this external phenomenon moves cyclically, it will drag the system behind it in the same cycle [1931a, p. 133].

A free oscillation was different:

> In a free oscillation both the periodical length and the general cyclical properties of the oscillation which we want to explain are caused by the intrinsic properties of the system [1931a, p. 134].

9. Frisch's insistence on the need for determinate models may today look trivial and somewhat pedantic. However, the confusion at that time was serious. Determinate models, for example, were often accused of being logically circular, even among prominent economists like Alvin Hansen (see Hansen 1927, p. 200). It was difficult for economists trained in verbal reasoning methods to avoid using causal or recursive models.

When was the concept of forced oscillation appropriate, and when should the concept of a free oscillation be used? The answer, Frisch believed,

> does not only depend on the character of the phenomenon, but also on our ambitions, how extensive an explanation we are satisfied with [1931a, p. 134].

In the case of business cycle theory, however, Frisch did not believe that one should be satisfied with any explanation which relied on the concept of the cycle as a forced oscillation:

> Here it cannot, so far as I understand, any longer be a question of a forced oscillation. The bundle of phenomena we call business cycle is, I believe, a complex we have to attack as composed of free oscillations if we as economists are ever to be able to understand it. *The explanation of the cyclical character of the oscillations must be sought in the inner structure of the system* [1931a, p. 137].

When one accepted that business cycles should be explained as a system of free oscillations, another pair of concepts became relevant, namely the distinction between the *impulse* and the propagation problem. In order to explain these concepts Frisch used the popular pendulum illustration:

> To remain in the pendulum illustration, the difference between the two types of problems may be explained in the following way. If the pendulum initially is at rest and I walk up to it and give it a kick, then two things happen: (i) the fact that I kick the pendulum, this is the subject of the impulse problem; that may be explained by my mood at the moment and things like that. (ii) The fact that the pendulum when first moving follows its typical trajectory has nothing to do with my state of mind: it has something to do with the inner structure of the pendulum. And that is the subject of the propagation problem [1931a, pp. 134–35].

Frisch believed this distinction to be very important for the construction of any theoretical explanation of the cycles. More concretely, he pictured the cycle as the result of erratic shocks hitting the economy. The shocks maintained the amplitude while the economic structure accounted for the regularity of the movements. By itself the economy was a mechanism which generated friction. Without the outside shocks the economy would only generate damped cycles. This idea Frisch had already expressed in his 1928 role as challenger to

Johan Aakerman's doctoral thesis.[10]

The way Frisch used the distinction between impulse and propagation problems in the later modeling of a business cycle theory in his 1933 article might be regarded as his major theoretical contribution to the field. However, this was not the only way in which the early mechanical vision became instrumental in his later modeling.

VII. *Frisch's Early Model Sketch*

Besides offering an outline of an ambitious research program in the business cycle field, Frisch's paper at the meeting of Nordic economists in 1931 contained a rather loose sketch of a large dynamic model, as we mentioned above. The model suggested 38 variables and 37 equations. Frisch could not decide upon the last equation. This hesitation was due to the model's unwieldiness. He would have liked to introduce the saving-investment equation, but he was not sure if a subset of the other equations defined implicitly a saving-investment relation.

The model was too unfinished to make it possible to tell what kind of economic story Frisch had in mind. It was too large and unspecified. For example, in the listing of equations, when he reached equation 36, the aggregate consumption, he gave no hints whatsoever as to which arguments the aggregate consumption should be a function of. However, some features of the model should perhaps be mentioned.

Like many business cycle theorists, Frisch distinguished between a capital-goods- and a consumer-goods-producing sector, each with a production function showing labor and capital as arguments. In both sectors profits were maximized. The reinvestment and capital stock sector of the model was rather complex, and he distinguished between investment orders, capital goods production, and investment deliveries. The model had to be non-linear, as both construction time and the length of reinvestment lags were to be endogenously determined.

The description of the flows and stocks of consumption goods was another exceptionally complex part.

In the monetary part of the model Frisch distinguished between the credit granted by the banks and the credit used by the public. Only monetary policy instruments were mentioned: the discount rate, the gold stock, and the amount of loans granted to the commercial banks.

At least at the time when Frisch wrote, the model was of course hopelessly ambitious as a starting point for rigorous empirical investigation and too complex to be analytically explored. (It implied a system of 37 to 38 mixed non-linear difference-differential-integral equa-

10. The opposition was later published in Frisch 1931b. According to his own statement Frisch was here inspired by some remarks of Wicksell.

tions.) Even so, Frisch was typically optimistic and believed that the number of variables made "a useful starting point for a theory of crises which should be tolerably extensive and concrete" (Frisch 1931a, p. 144). He even promised that "somewhat more extensive discussion will be published in the near future" (p. 230).

Experience taught him otherwise, in the short run. In the analytical studies which followed, he was satisfied to work out models with only a small number of variables. In the longer run the vision of a large, empirically estimated model was no foolish dream. Frisch's hasty model sketch may be considered to have been a rather direct predecessor of the large macroeconometric cycle models which were developed after World War II, particularly in the United States.

VIII. *The Aftalion Model: Formal Macrodynamics*

The late twenties and early thirties were a time when economic model builders for the first time seriously explored the possibilities of alternative systems of functional equations. The new tool was tried out on several fields. One of the most popular was business cycle theory. The new mathematical techniques, although they forced many restraints upon the researchers, opened up new areas to conquer. Not hampered by old traditions, mathematical economists felt rather free to construct new models. The tool was new; thus some kind of playing with it seemed unavoidable. Moreover, if the model in question could generate complex roots for reasonable parameter values, the temptation to use it as a possible explanation of business cycles was often too great.

The journals received many papers of this kind, and some were even published. At least from today's point of view, the economics of most of these papers may look rather naive—forerunners of the kind of work Frisch himself later branded as "playometrics." Then, however, it was easier to excuse such playing since mathematical economics was still in its adolescence, and the development of new mathematical tools was badly needed. Several articles by Frisch, Tinbergen, da Vinci, and Creedy might seem to be of this kind, at least at first glance.

In the case of Frisch, however, some of his seemingly arbitrary assumptions were in fact made as attempts to model some rather strong prior convictions about how the economic system worked and what kind of economic forces were responsible for cyclical maladies such as unemployment, bankruptcies, and rural poverty.[11]

At least from the autumn of 1931 Frisch became deeply concerned

11. We would probably find that something similar may have been the case for Tinbergen's models as his ideas and activities in this period come to be scrutinized.

about the social and political effects of the depression. He voiced his concern in many places, such as his popular radio lectures in 1932 about business cycles. Based on his empirical studies of the most important time series, he had estimated that a Kondriatiev kind of cyclical depression had occurred which should last until about 1947. He continued:

> This is the future prospect if human beings still accept that they will be pushed along with the movement of the business cycles, without a will of their own [1932c, p. 138].

After stating his belief that it was possible to change this situation by means of policy, he continued:

> When people become aware of this situation, it is not impossible that an uprising will take place which will force through means of regulating the cycles, in one or more countries. This will be a victory for all the constructive forces of the country, because everybody has to agree that it is a disgraceful state when people are living in a world of real economic surplus while at the same time living with an economic system that regularly re-creates destitution and worries for almost all classes of people [1932c, p. 139].

The concern about the effects of depressions on people's living conditions did have an impact on his thinking, making the task of supplying a clear understanding of the causes of depressions more urgent. His political involvement in many economic-policy debates was probably also, to a certain extent, influential in giving his originally rather empty mechanical 'vision' of the business cycles more definite economic shape. These influences reached his scientific macrodynamics only through the filter of academic norms and interests and became in most cases operative only to the extent that they had some bearing on a scientific problem in the field as perceived by Frisch. I will, therefore, still discuss the development of Frisch's macrodynamics in its rather isolated academic setting, and only here and there indicate how his perception of social forces at work may have influenced his choice of assumptions.

Frisch's famous article "Propagation Problems and Impulse Problems in Dynamic Economics" was published in *Economic Essays in Honour of Gustav Cassel*, edited by Karin Koch. This volume became widely read, and Frisch's article was perhaps the first formal mathematical formulation of a dynamic model used for explaining economic crises and fluctuations that won general recognition. Even economists not otherwise interested in mathematical economics had from that time on to make at least passing remarks about the merits or drawbacks of formal dynamic analysis.[12]

In the article, Frisch discussed most of the methodological ideas we have already described. In addition he underlined the need for a simplified, openly macroeconomic approach. In contrast to the microdynamic analysis, "macrodynamic analysis . . . tries to give an account of the fluctuations of the whole economic system taken in its entirety. Obviously in this case it is impossible to carry through the analysis in great detail."[13]

Frisch may have drawn the conclusion from his own experience of trying to handle his 38-variable model. It was not only impossible to construct a business cycle theory from a micro foundation, it would also be an unfruitful approach, which could not answer the proper questions in business cycle theory:

> Of course, it is always possible to give even a macro-dynamic analysis in detail if we confine ourselves to a purely *formal* theory. . . . Such a theory, however, would only have a limited interest. In such a theory it would hardly be possible to study such fundamental problems as the *exact time shape* of the solutions, the question of whether one group of phenomena is lagging behind or leading before another group, the question of whether one part of the system will oscillate with higher amplitudes than another part, and so on. But these latter problems are just the essential problems in business cycle analysis. In order to attack these questions on a macrodynamic basis so as to explain the movement of the system in its entirety, we must deliberately disregard a considerable amount of the details of the picture. We may perhaps start by throwing all kinds of production into one variable, all consumption into another, and so on, imagining that the notions 'production,' 'consumption,' and so on, can be measured by some sort of total indices [1933, pp. 172–73].

12. As I have already indicated, Frisch was not a lonely pioneer. Several economists had already argued for the use of dynamic analysis for a decade (Evans, Roos) and some had already applied it in order to study economic fluctuations, e.g., Tinbergen (1929) and Roos (1930), inter alia; I have nonetheless found none of them to be so elaborate as Frisch's was. Kalecki may be a partial exception. His model, which should prove to have a more lasting value than the others, was published in Polish. In addition, Kalecki was an outsider and his models reflected political tastes too much at odds with the majority values within the profession. Consequently Frisch became the first to make an impact.

13. Frisch 1933, p. 172. Incidentally, according to Schumpeter 1954, p. 278, this was also the introduction of the term 'macro'-analysis into the field of economics.

The ideas expressed here were interesting from several points of view. On the one hand Frisch expressed his interest in the mechanical features of the cycle, a preoccupation he shared with the business cycle researchers from the inductionist school. On the other hand, although the analysis had to be on a highly aggregate level, it was not sufficient to construct one aggregate index, a business 'barometer.' More structure was needed, and several indices had to be constructed. The macrodynamic analysis thus demanded that new aggregates had to be constructed if it was to be supplied with an empirical foundation.[14]

This was of course in a theoretical sense a less ambitious program than Hayek had started on, as it did not demand that the business cycle theory had to be explicitly based on some kind of individual rational behavior. At this point Frisch's program for theory construction was more pragmatic, not demanding reconciliation between basic economic theory and the explanation of business cycles. Many would perhaps say that he left the door wide open for all kinds of shallow ad hoc model constructions. On the other hand the program made it easier for him and others following his approach to avoid much of that obscurity which surrounded most of the discussions initiated by the theoreticians (Keynes' *General Theory* included) who tried to tie the phenomenon of depression to some kind of economic equilibrium, without being able to specify their theories.

However, the core of Frisch's article was not its suggestions of the proper way to explain business cycles, but a specification of a dynamic model which was to exemplify what rigorous model construction could do in the field. The model consisted of three variables: investment orders or "capital starting," capital goods production or "carry-on activity," and aggregate consumption. Frisch had, of course, determined the model and postulated three equations. One was basically a definitional relation between capital production and the preceding flows of investment orders. The average lag between an investment order and its completion played an important role in determining the length of the cycles the model generated. This was a factor Aftalion had emphasized earlier.

The second equation was an accelerator mechanism which related the flow of investment orders to the level and the change of aggregate consumption. The level of consumption influenced investment orders via its influence on the rate of depreciation of the capital stock.

14. Frisch did not attempt to estimate any of his macrodynamical models until after World War II. His empirical interest in macroeconomics was for years concentrated on the development of these indices, the development of national income statistics. That task proved to be far more time-consuming than Frisch initially believed, and he worked on it from the middle thirties and until the end of the war.

The third equation was rather strange. Literally, it stated that the change of consumption was the result of the combined effect of a positive exogenous growth factor and a negative factor coming from the existing levels of consumption and capital goods. How this was to come about was unclear, but the relation was clearly intended to model Frisch's belief that existing monetary institutions might put serious brakes on the real growth in the economy:

> It seems plausible that one effect of the tightening of the cash situation, and perhaps the most important, will be a restriction in consumption. In the boom period when consumption has reached a high level . . . consumption is one of the elastic factors in the situation. It is likely that this factor is one that first will yield to cash pressure. To begin with this will only be expressed by the fact that the rate of increase of consumption is slackened. Later, consumption may perhaps actually decline [Frisch 1933, p. 179].

Although the last equation closed the model in a formal sense, it did this by introducing an exogenous and unexplained factor—the banking system. This fits awkwardly in a model in which only consumers and producers are present. It is a pity that Frisch did not take greater notice of Clark's suggestion of a Keynes-type aggregate consumption function during the Frisch-Clark discussion in the *Journal of Political Economy*, 1931–1932. It would not have created any analytical problem to have introduced a consumption function, and the economics of Frisch's model would have been much more convincing.

The 'monetary brake' mechanism met with criticism from the start. Tinbergen, for example, was rather skeptical in his influential survey of quantitative business cycle theory, and suggested that the monetary brake relations should have been "analyzed economically and statistically before they are made a basis for the theory, especially when the number of competing possibilities is as large as here. It might be that the brake included in the mechanism . . . works in a different way" (Tinbergen 1935, p. 221).

Frisch never answered in public either Tinbergen's or other economists' criticism of his monetary brake mechanism. In spite of the criticism he never seems to have lost his belief in it. As late as 1955, in a lecture at the Institute of Economics in Oslo, he mentioned that he considered the criticism directed against the monetary brake mechanism to have been misplaced.[15]

I believe that Frisch's rather irrational attachment to his monetary

15. The lecture was reported by Per Meinich, *IQ*, 24 May 1955. The report is to be found in Archive Box 34. The lecture was delivered in Norwegian.

brake mechanism may be to a large extent explained by the fact that it was an attempt to model some of Frisch's basic 'visions' of the forces at work during depressions. Frisch was clearly convinced that the monetary system somehow played an important role in generating economic crises and depressions. A consumption function would have left the banking system out of the picture. The monetary brake mechanism left the banking system with a part to play. Frisch's political activities and popular writings concentrated to a large extent on the role of the banking system and the need for a change in monetary policies. Unlike Hayek, he was not so much worried about the banking system's behavior during booms as he was about its behavior during depressions.

The article in the Cassel volume was, however, primarily a contribution to the scientific development of business cycle research, introducing new analytical techniques and a new way of looking at questions of turning points, periodicity, and so on. When we look at the article from this point of view, the conceptual weakness of the monetary brake mechanism was not essential.

The mathematical structure of his model was fairly complicated, a linear–mixed difference–differential equation which was too difficult to solve generally. Frisch had to choose specific values of the parameters and to see how the system behaved when different values were chosen. The choice of the parameter values was not based on any rigorous statistical estimation methods. Frisch used only rough guessing.

Using a specific set of parameter values, Frisch found three significant cyclical components in the solution, one with a length of period around 8.5 years, another around 3.5 years, and finally an ultra-short cycle. Frisch believed the first two results provided evidence in support of the model, since they conformed roughly to empirical evidence. The last cycle he believed could prove to be an interesting hypothesis for empirical studies.

The results were based on Frisch's choice of parameter values—a shaky foundation. The lengths of the periods were determined by an average lag between "production starting" and delivery of three years, probably far too long a lag, as Tinbergen pointed out in his survey of economic dynamics (Tinbergen 1935, p. 271). This estimate of the lag was another considerable weakness of Frisch's model if interpreted as a serious attempt to simulate the empirically observed business cycles. However, it was, of course, of little consequence for the methodological points Frisch was making, which would seem rather startling for an economist trained only in a literary tradition.

First of all, turning points did not need a separate explanation. They followed from the solution of the system which was able to explain the whole business cycle. The same set of forces was at work all the time.

Secondly, the model was able to generate several cycles with different periodicity. The same set of forces was thus able to generate different cycles. If one accepted that empirical evidence indicated the presence of several cycles, one did not have to construct a separate explanation for each of them.

The problem with Frisch's solution was that all the cyclical fluctuations were damped. Empirically speaking, that does not seem to have been the case. By inserting other values of the parameters, Frisch could only get explosive fluctuations, which did not seem more reasonable. In one exceptional and improbable case, however, it would have been possible to make the system generate cycles with unchanged amplitudes. This was the unlikely case Kalecki studied.[16] The mathematical structure of a linear functional equation system was simply not rich enough to generate more than the three possibilities—damped, exactly regular, and explosive fluctuations. None of them were empirically plausible.

The main contribution of Frisch's article was his solution to the problem of how to reconcile a damped solution with the observed non-dampening of the cycles. He thereby also saved the use of linear functional equation systems as a method of theoretical study of business cycles. In order to solve the problem Frisch used his conceptual distinction between the impulse and the propagation problem.

The linear functional system only simulated the propagation phenomenon. The economy if left to itself would generate fairly regular but damped oscillations. The economy was, however, frequently hit by more or less erratic shocks. These shocks would cause the empirical time series to be more irregular; but more important, they would supply energy to the system, thereby making the system behave in an undamped way. Frisch's solution also had some appeal from the theoreticians' point of view. Frisch's economy fluctuated around some stationary state or equilibrium growth path in a damped way. Left to itself the economy would approach some kind of equilibrium state, which made static reasoning methods relevant. The fluctuations were only kept going by external shocks and this agreed with most of the theoreticians' intuition.

16. I believe that Kalecki's choice of this clumsy method with its implausible manipulation of parameter values explains at least in part why Kalecki's early papers did not make any greater impact on the group of mathematical economists who, like Frisch, were preoccupied with the problem of the mechanical characteristics of the cycle. Kalecki later adopted Frisch's method. As a methodological exercise, it would, of course, also be of importance to study the special Kalecki case, but it could not be convincing as an explanation of observed cycles.

In the Cassel-volume article Frisch did not actually expose his Aftalion model to erratic shocks.[17] Instead, he exposed a simpler dynamic system, simulating a pendulum with friction to erratic (auto-uncorrelated) shocks. He demonstrated that in this case the trajectories would be undamped and fairly irregular.

To judge from some mimeographed lecture notes in Norwegian from 1934, it is clear that Frisch had worked more on the problem of how the Aftalion model behaved when it was influenced by erratic factors of various kinds (1934a, pp. 856. 1–4). He reached several interesting results. First, "It is the shocks directed against consumption which proved to be the most important in the maintenance process." From this property of his Aftalion model, Frisch jumped to a conclusion about the real world: "This illuminates in an interesting way the correctness of Clark's proposition that consumption is primary and that capital production hinges upon consumption." A second striking result that Frisch discovered when he exposed the model to shocks was that it now generated a new kind of cycles which could not be found in the theoretical solution. For example, a Kondriatiev type of cycle could be discovered. Frisch commented:

> The form of the curve is noteworthy. First we recognize the components of 8½ and 3½ years. Especially the 8½-year cycle is prominent. Now, no tendency of dampening is to be found. . . . The result in fig. (3) shows an additional peculiarity. We have got a completely new cycle, namely a 50-year cycle. It appears as an underlying movement. . . . This does not . . . immediately appear from the theoretical solution. It is a cycle primarily generated as a result of the cumulation process of the erratic shocks.

This was a striking result indeed. It confirmed Frisch's belief in the Kondriatiev cycle, and thereby reinforced his belief in the Aftalion model. At the same time it seemed to give a precise statement of the common belief that if a Kondriatiev cycle was to be found, it had to be more influenced by stochastic exogenous events.[18]

The most important result, however, was that Frisch could confirm his intuitive conviction about the non-dampness of the cyclical trajectories in the case of his specification of the Aftalion model. Despite the work involved in reaching these results and their importance at the time, Frisch, for some strange reason, never published them in an ac-

17. When Frisch on other occasions did this, he picked his random numbers from the winners of the Norwegian state lottery.

18. See, for example, Alvin Hansen 1964, p. 308, or Paul A. Samuelson 1947, p. 341.

cessible form. However, this was rather typical for him. When he had solved a problem, he was always rushing on to new problems without bothering much about publishing his results.

IX. *Various Other Macrodynamic Models*

In addition to his Aftalion model Frisch constructed several other macrodynamic models in which he tried to model some of his ideas about the processes at work creating cycles or depressions. The most important was the depression model he published in *Econometrica*, 1934, "Circulation Planning." There he developed a shoemaker-farmer model, in which the depression was primarily created by the different groups fearing to buy from each other. Each group's sales was determined by its sales to the other group in the preceding period. If both groups became pessimistic and dared not buy for the whole amount of the last period's sales, the economy would plunge down into a bottomless depression.

Frisch tried to make a cycle model out of the shoemaker-farmer model. By making one group consistently pessimistic and the other consistently more optimistic, and introducing the stock of their mutual claims and debts as a motivating factor for the exchange activities, Frisch was able to make the model generate cycles. He called them "pure exchange cycles." In my opinion, the model was totally unconvincing as a cycle model. It was almost a contradiction in terms of his own analysis to assume that the purchasers kept the same attitude to buying over the cycle. In a second model Frisch focused on the role of profits. This profit accumulation model was published only in Norwegian in his mimeographed lecture notes in macrodynamics (Frisch 1934a, subsection 856).

The model portrayed a corn economy in which the capitalists saved all their corn profits and put them into their stocks while the workers ate up all their wages. The stock of corn depreciated at a given rate and pressed down the level of profits. Frisch made two different cyclical stories out of this Ricardian type of economy. In the first, he made the capitalists change production at a rate varying (negatively) with the accumulated difference between the 'normal' and the actual flow of production. In the second, he made the wage rate vary with the workers' and capitalists' accumulated experience of the size of the industrial reserve army during the preceding periods. Considered as a way to graft cyclical fluctuations on the stem of a Ricardo model, the models were rather interesting. However, he made the capital stock only drain the profits and did not allow it to have any positive influence on production. It is then difficult to see how it was possible for Frisch to believe that the model was relevant for an analysis of the cyclical fluctuations in an industrial capitalistic economy.

In addition to these models, Frisch suggested a couple of others of less interest. One treated the possibility of producers overreacting to a 'wrong' mix of production factors. Another explored the possibility of an interaction between reinvestment and 'new' investment which could generate cyclical fluctuations. The last problem received considerable attention among Norwegian economists during the interwar years.[19]

X. *Conclusions*

The econometric approach to empirical macroeconomic research has been dominant for decades and is in a way considered so obvious that it is seldom a subject for reflection except by the few who do not believe in regularities at all. Thus, everybody believes one should first specify a quantitative model and then estimate or test it empirically. Theory must explicitly play an active role in this way of doing empirical research.

The situation was different in the twenties. The statistical techniques then used did not need much theoretical information, or the researchers were at that time not aware of such a need. On the other hand, the theoretical economists did not even try to make their theories operational. Frisch and other economists and statisticians like Tinbergen, Hotelling, and Roos tried to bridge that gap.

If the attempt was to be more than empty talk, new analytical techniques in theory construction, new statistical techniques, and new ways of collecting data were all necessary. Achieving them proved to be a rather long process.

In many ways Frisch was more influenced by the inductionist than the theoretical program. He always had a lively interest in numerical and computational problems. He used and refined the empirically oriented school's stock of methods. His daily research life was more like theirs. Furthermore, he basically shared their mechanical vision of one cycle or several cycles which could be discovered by statistical methods without the help of any specified economic theory. On the other hand he insisted on the importance of economic model construction; but when he finally constructed a theory, he did not make any attempt to relate it to basic economic theory about individual rational behavior. His attitude toward economic theory was more pragmatic than the theoreticians'. In this he was also more in tune with the empirical school. It was perhaps also significant that Frisch's technique for estimating

19. See for example Einarsen 1938 and Schoenheyder 1927.

parameters in equation systems, the confluence analysis, made empirical observations play a more active role than the later standard approach by assisting in the specification of the variables to be included.

It was, then, perhaps somewhat paradoxical that Frisch's main contribution to the development of the new empirical research program in microeconomics was this development of the new analytical theoretical technique in the Cassel-volume model. His laborious work in time series analysis was soon forgotten, as it was tied to the older business cycle research tradition.

Frisch's main contribution proved to be his use of the distinction between impulse problems and propagation problems. At one stroke he both saved the linear dynamical approach and suggested how stochastical elements could be introduced into the model, thereby also opening it up for some kind of empirical scrutiny.

His defense of linear models was, however, a mixed blessing, at least for the theoretical study of cycles, as Samuelson later confessed (Samuelson 1974). For a while, it hampered the development of the richer non-linear models, which in many respects could be made more realistic. From a priori considerations it seems inherently implausible to assume that people behave in the same way during booms as in depressions.

Frisch himself was aware of the possibility of constructing non-linear models, but he could only with great difficulty move away from his basically linear vision cycles. This was particularly evident in his criticism of literary economists. In many cases they were discussing non-linearities when Frisch blamed them for creating non-determinate models.

Despite his strong motivation for empirical studies, Frisch did not scrutinize his macrodynamic models empirically during the period when the new macroeconometric program was developed, i.e., approximately the period between the beginning 1930s and the late 1940s. This paradox may be partly explained by Frisch's tendency to move quickly from one field of research problems to another and to branch out in too many directions. He may also have been troubled by the Faustian problem of knowing too much. Frisch was probably more aware of the statistical problems which had to be solved before the model could be rigorously explored empirically than, for example, Tinbergen was.

Whatever the reasons, Tinbergen was to take the lead in empirical macrodynamical research. His results were gathered in his monumental *Statistical Testing of Business-Cycle Theories*. This work was published in 1939, but it had been discussed for a long time. As Frisch pointed out in his influential but unpublished paper from 1938, "Statistical Versus Theoretical Relations in Economic Macrodynamics," Tinbergen had not understood the identification problems well enough and thereby made some serious mistakes in the interpretations of his results. Both the mistakes and the achievements proved to be important. When Tinbergen's work was attacked from the theoretical schools under Keynes' leadership, the new school of empirical researchers, the econometricians, closed ranks and defended Tinbergen against Keynes.

The new school of macroeconometric research was able to supersede the old empirical business cycle research program. As just indicated, this was a long-drawn-out process demanding new theoretical and statistical tools as well as new ways of collecting data. Frisch was very influential in shaping this change, especially in its early stages. Roughly the change in empirical business cycle research coincided in time with the so-called Keynesian Revolution. Although the econometric school was at times actively opposed by Keynes himself, the Keynesian ideas and econometric methodology mixed, and together they became the basis of most empirical macroeconomic research for at least two decades after World War II.

Frisch was, of course, not the only econometrician to bring about this new way of blending theoretical and empirical research in the field, but he was influential. In addition, to view the change from his point of departure gives us a chance to increase our understanding of this development from *one* historical perspective.

The econometric school was never able to bring about the decline of the pure theoretical schools. It proved to be more difficult to base theoretical macroeconomics on an empirical foundation than Frisch with his inductionist leanings once believed. For good or bad reasons, 'idle' speculation flourishes more than ever.

The research connected with this study has been financed by the Norwegian Research Council for Science and Humanities, and the Bank of Norway's Foundation for Economic Research.

References

A basis for documentation is to be found in unpublished letters and papers from the collection of Ragnar Frisch's papers in the Manuscript Department of Oslo University Library and from the collection of his papers at the Institute of Economics, University of Oslo. More thorough documentation is given in an unpublished manuscript by Jens Christopher Andvig, "Draft of Chapters 1–4 of Ragnar Frisch in the Thirties," Los Angeles, 1.12.1978. Available from the author.

Aakerman, Johan. *Om det ekonomiska livets nytmik*. Stockholm, 1928.

Aftalion, Albert. "The Theory of Economic Cycles Based on the Capitalistic, Technique of Production." *Review of Economic Statistics*, Oct. 1927.
Andvig, Jens Chr. "Den historiske bakgrunnen til Frisch's analyse av forholdet sak og vurdering." Memorandum fra Sosialoekonomisk Institutt Universitetet i Oslo. 21 April 1977.
——— "Wicksell's Influence on Frisch's Macroeconomics in the Thirties." *Scandinavian Journal of Economics*, 1978, no. 2.
Arrow, K. "Ragnar Frisch, Econometrician." *Econometrica*, 1960.
Clark, J. M. "Capital Production and Consumer-Taking: A Reply." *Journal of Political Economy*. 1931.
———. "Capital Production and Consumer-Taking: A Further Word." *Journal of Political Economy*, 1932.
———. *Strategic Factors in Business Cycles*. New York, 1935; reprint, 1949.
Davis, Harold T. *The Analysis of Economic Time Series*. Bloomington, Ind., 1941.
Edvardsen, Kaare. "A Survey of Ragnar Frisch's Contribution to the Science of Economics." *De Economist*, 1970.
Einarsen, Johan. *Reinvestment Cycles and Their Manifestation in the Norwegian Shipping Industry*. Oslo, 1938.
Feiwel, George R. *The Intellectual Capital of Michael Kalecki: A Study in Theory and Policy*. Second printing, Knoxville, Tenn., 1975.
Fisher, Irving. "The Business Cycle Largely a 'Dance of the Dollar.' " *Journal of the American Statistical Association*, 1923, pp. 1024–28.
———. "Our Unstable Dollar and the So-Called Business Cycle." *Journal of the American Statistical Association*, June, 1925.
Frisch, Ragnar, "Sur un problème d'économie pure." *Norsk Matematisk Forenings Skrifter*, ser. 1, no. 16, 1926a.
———. "Kvantitativ formulering av den teoretiske oekonomikks lover." *Stasoekonomisk Tidsskrift*, 1926b.
———. "Changing Harmonics and Other General Types of Components in Empirical Series." *Skandinavisk Aktuarietidskrift*, 1928.
———. "Statikk og dynamikk i den oekonomiske teori." *Nationaloekonomisk Tidsskrift*, 1929.
———. "Konjunkturbevegelsen som statistisk og oekonomisk fenomen." In *Forhandlingar ved Nordiska Nationalekonomiska moetet i Stockholm, 15–17 juni 1931*. 1931a.
———. "Johan Aakerman: Om det ekonomiska livets rytmik." *Statsvetenskaplig Tidskrift*, 1931b.
———. "A Method of Decomposing an Empirical Series into Its Cyclical and Progressive Components." *Journal of the American Statistical Association*, 1931c.
———. "The Interrelation between Capital Production and Consumer Taking." *Journal of Political Economy*, 1931d.
———. "Rejoinder," and "A Final Word" (the discussion with J. M. Clark). *Journal of Political Economy*, 1932a.
———. "New Orientation of Economic Theory: Economics as an Experimental Science," Public lecture delivered at the University of Norway, 8 Feb. 1932. *Nordic Statistical Journal*, 1932b.
———. "Konjunkturene." *Verdensoekonomien i efterkrigstiden*. Universitets radiofordrag, serie B, 1932c.

———. "Propagation Problems and Impulse Problems in Dynamic Economics." In *Economic Essays in Honour of Gustav Cassel* (London, 1933).

———. *Forelesninger holdt 1933 II og 1934—over Makrodynamikk*. Oslo, 1934a.

———. "Circulation Planning." *Econometrica*, 1934b.

———. *Statistical Confluence Analysis by Means of Complete Regression Systems*. Publication No. 5 from the University Institute. Oslo, 1934c.

———, and Harald Holme. "The Characteristic Solution of a Mixed Difference and Differential Equation Occurring in Economic Dynamics." *Econometrica*, 1935a.

———. *Et generelt monetaert begrep- og symbolsystem*. Oslo, 1935b.

———. "On the Notion of Equilibrium and Disequilibrium." *Review of Economic Studies*, Feb. 1936.

———. "Statistical versus Theoretical Relations in Economic Macrodynamics." A memorandum prepared by Professor Frisch for the Business Cycle Conference at Cambridge, England, 18–20, July 1938, to discuss Professor J. Tinbergen's publications of 1938, for the League of Nations, 1938.

———. *Noen trekk av konjunkturlaeren*. Oslo, 1947.

———. "From Utopian Theory to Practical Applications: The Case of Econometrics." In *Les Prix Nobel en 1969* (Stockholm, 1970).

Gordon, Robert Aaron. *Business Fluctuations*. New York, 1952.

Haavelmo, Trygve. "The Inadequacy of Testing Dynamic Theory by Comparing Theoretical Solutions and Observed Cycles." *Econometrica*, 1940.

Haberler, G. *Prosperity and Depression: A Theoretical Analysis of Cyclical Movement*. Fifth edition, second impression. London, 1968.

Hagstrom, Warren O. *The Scientific Community*. New York, 1965.

Hansen, A. H. *Business-Cycle Theory*. Boston, 1927.

———. *Business Cycles and National Income*. Expanded edition. New York, 1964.

———, and Richard V. Clemence. *Readings in Business Cycles and National Income*. New York, 1953.

Hardy, Charles O. *Forecasting Business Conditions*. New York, 1927.

Hayek, F. A. *Monetary Theory and the Trade Cycle*. London, 1933; reprint 1975.

Hicks, J. R. *Value and Capital: An Inquiry into Some Fundamental Principles of Economic Theory*. Second edition. Reprint, London, 1968.

Hotelling, H. "Differential Equations Subject to Error and Population Estimates." *Journal of the American Statistical Association*, 1927.

Johansen, Leif. "Ragnar Frisch's Contributions to Economics." *Swedish Journal of Economics*, 1969.

Kalecki, M. *Studies in the Theory of Business Cycles, 1933–1939*. Oxford, 1969.

———. *Essays in the Theory of Economic Fluctuations*. New York, 1939.

Klein, L. *The Keynesian Revolution*. Second edition. London, 1966, 1970.

Lakatos, I., and A. Musgrave, eds. *Criticism and the Growth of Knowledge*. Cambridge, 1970.

Landgren, Karl-Gustav. *Den nya ekonomien i Sverige*. Uppsala, 1960.

Laudan, Larry. *Progress and Its Problems: Toward a Theory of Scientific Growth*. London, 1977.

Metzler, L. A. "Keynes and the Theory of Business Cycles." In Seymour E. Harris, ed., *The New Economics: Keynes' Influence on Theory and Public Policy* (London, 1947; 3d impression, 1952).

Moore, H. L. *Economic Cycles: Their Law and Cause*. New York, 1914.

———. *Generating Economic Cycles*. New York, 1923.

Mitchell, W. C. *Business Cycles, the Problem and Its Setting*. New York, 1927, 1963.

Myrdal, Gunnar. *I staellet foer memoarer*. Vaenessborg, 1973.

Neyman, Jerzy. "The Emergence of Mathematical Statistics." In D. B. Owen, ed., *On the History of Statistics and Probability* (New York, 1976).

Ohlin, Bertil. *Den vaerldsekonomiska Depressionen*. Stockholm, 1931.

Patinkin, Don. "Keynes and Econometrics: On the Interaction between the Macroeconomic Revolutions of the Interwar Period." *Econometrica*, 1976.

Persons, W. M. *Forecasting Business Cycles*. New York, 1931.

Pigou, A. C. *Industrial Fluctuations*. Second edition. London, 1929.

Samuelson, Paul A. *Foundations of Economic Analysis*. New York, 1965.

———. "Remembrances of Frisch." *European Economic Review*, 1974.

Schoenheyder, K. "Produktionscyklerne og krisene." *Statsoekonomisk Tidskrift*, 1927.

Schumpeter, J. A. *Business Cycles*. Vol. 1. New York, 1939.

———*History of Economic Analysis*. London, 1954, 1972.

Steiger, Otto. *Studien zur Entstehung der Neuen Wirtschaftslehre in Schweden. Eine Antikritik*. Berlin, 1971.

Tinbergen, Jan. "Konjunkturforschung und Variationsrechnung." *Archiv für Sozialwissenschaft und Sozialpolitik*, Juni 1929.

———. "Der Einfluss der Kaufkraftregulierung auf den Konjunkturverlauf." *Zeitschrift für Nationalökonomie*, 1934.

———. "Annual Survey: Suggestions on Quantitative Business Cycle Theory." *Econometrica*, 1935.

———. *Statistical Testing of Business-Cycle Theories*. Vols. 1–2. Geneva, 1939.

———, and J. J. Polak. *The Dynamics of Business Cycles*. Chicago, 1950, 1974.

Wagemann, Ernst. *Economic Rhythm: A Theory of Business Cycles*. New York, 1930.

[5]

History of Political Economy 14:1

Discovery of the money-income relationship in the United States, 1921–1944

Paul B. Trescott

I

The influence of changes in the stock of money (M) on the flow of national money income and expenditure (Y) has been a central topic of modern macroeconomics. In his *General Theory* (1936), J. M. Keynes argued that monetary policy would not produce roughly proportional changes in Y and that major income changes would originate from disturbances involving investment or fiscal policy.[1] In contrast, as Thomas Mayer recently stated, monetarism "is the view that changes in the money stock are the predominant factor explaining changes in money income."[2] The plausibility of viewing M as a major influence on Y is supported by the very high empirical correlation between them in time-series data. Long-period regressions indicate approximately unitary elasticity for the relationship.[3]

The close correlation was first observed by James W. Angell, who was the first to present time-series correspondence graphically (1936), and the first to calculate regression equations explaining income by money (1941). His work is examined at length in Section V below,

Correspondence for the author may be sent to Professor Paul B. Trescott, Dept. of Economics, Southern Illinois University at Carbondale, Carbondale, IL 62901 USA.

1. John Maynard Keynes, *The General Theory of Employment, Interest, and Money*, 1936, pp. 298–99.

2. Thomas Mayer, *The Structure of Monetarism*, 1978, p. 1. This view traces most directly to Milton Friedman's "Restatement" of 1956. Friedman expressed Y as a function of M and derived that function from a demand schedule for M on the assumption that M was exogenously determined. Friedman showed that Y would have unitary elasticity with respect to M if the other variables in the demand schedule were held constant. "The Quantity Theory of Money: A Restatement," in Friedman, ed., *Studies in the Quantity Theory of Money*, 1956, reprinted in Richard Thorn, ed., *Monetary Theory and Policy*, 1966, pp. 74–80.

3. Logarithmic regressions explaining nominal GNP by either $M1$ or $M2$ (current and one-year-lagged) for 1897–1970 have essentially unitary elasticity (i) when estimated without other variables and (ii) when estimated using also measures of long- and short-term interest rates. Without interest rates the R^2 values are .977 and .988; with interest rates, they are .9946 and .9956. Details are in the author's unpublished paper, "The Velocity of High Powered Money."

where it is compared with that of Lauchlin Currie, who presented income-velocity estimates very nearly simultaneous with those of Angell.

However, correlation does not prove causation. Many economists have argued that *M* adjusts in a relatively elastic manner to variations in the demand for money or bank credit. To establish a persuasive view of monetary causation required evidence that significant variations in the stock of money are exogenous.

The present article traces the evolution of two related ideas: first, recognition of the close empirical correspondence between money and national income, and second, an analytical view assigning to *M* an important role in the determination of *Y*.[4]

Economists' perceptions of the money-income relationship evolved in the perspective of a growing understanding of the theory and measurement of both money and national income. Undoubtedly monetary economists from the time of Cantillon and Hume viewed monetary adjustments in an implicit national-income framework; linkage relating money to spending, output, and prices was clearly spelled out by Henry Thornton and Thomas Attwood in the nineteenth century. But the conscious attention directed to transactions on 'income and product' account, as distinct from money payments of all kinds, became evident only toward the end of the nineteenth century. The first time-series estimates of national money income for the United States were published in 1921, covering the period 1909–1919. Data for other countries were not available until much later. Discussions of the money-income relationship prior to 1921 were thus of necessity lacking in empirical support. In Section II below, we review a number of important early contributions to the theory of the relationship, as presented by Newcomb, Fisher, Wicksell, Hawtrey, and Schumpeter.

In Section III we examine the data on national income and the stock of money which were readily available to scholars from 1921 on. With regard to both money and national income, theory and measurement evolved in close interaction. Double-entry systems of definitions and measurement conventions were ultimately developed which helped to eliminate many sources of fallacious argument and to clarify causal

4. The present article does not attempt to deal with the evolution of the quantity theory of money as such. Important earlier secondary surveys are Arthur Marget, *The Theory of Prices*, vol. 1, 1938, and Hugo Hegeland, *The Quantity Theory of Money*, 1951. Useful recent items include Thomas Humphrey, "Empirical Tests of The Quantity Theory of Money in the United States, 1900–1930," *History of Political Economy* 5 (Fall 1973); Humphrey, "Role of Non-Chicago Economists in the Evolution of the Quantity Theory in America, 1930–1950," *Southern Economic Journal*, July 1971; Don Patinkin, "On the Monetary Economics of Chicagoans and Non-Chicagoans: Comment," *SEJ*, Jan. 1973, and the reply by Humphrey, ibid.

linkages, but these were evolved slowly. It was not until the 1930s, for instance, that national income came to be generally recognized as a measure of aggregate expenditure and demand, with appropriate empirical categories and measures—even though both Hawtrey (1913) and Schumpeter (1917) clearly perceived national income in terms of aggregate demand. And while measures of such monetary aggregates as currency and deposits had long been available, the double-entry underpinnings necessary to show the determinants of the stock of money did not come into place until the 1940s.

In Section IV we look at some research by Irving Fisher and Willford King which came close to expressing the money-income relationship in the 1920s. We also examine some reasons why it took so long for that relationship to be identified.

After Angell, the economist who did most to stress the closeness of the money-income relationship was Clark Warburton. His contributions are noted briefly in Section VI. With those, much of the evolution of modern monetarism from Fisher to Friedman is filled in.

II

Irving Fisher's version of the equation of exchange focused attention on the total flow of money payments, rather than isolating purchases of current production. There is no evidence that Fisher ever adopted an income version of the equation. However, a national-income interpretation is much more plausible for the work of Simon Newcomb (1886), from whom Fisher adapted the equation.[5] Newcomb wrote his "equation of societary circulation" as follows:

$$V \times R = K \times P.$$

He used R to stand for the "rapidity" of circulation, thus retaining the traditional term apparently coined by Henry Thornton and used by John Stuart Mill. P represented the "scale" of prices. V represented the total volume of "currency," by which Newcomb meant the sum of coins, paper money, and bank deposits. Finally, and perhaps most important for this article, Newcomb's identification of K sounds very much like a measure of national output or income. The nature of, determinants of, and consequences of production form the central theme of his book. His references to K generally involve production of goods and services.[6] Newcomb explicitly excluded borrowing and lending from his measure of transactions, as well as speculative transactions

5. Simon Newcomb, *Principles of Political Economy*, 1886.

6. Ibid., pp. 326–29. A good illustration of his national-income orientation appears at p. 381, where he argues that if there were a 1 percent decrease in the expenditure flow, "one per centum of the industrial population would be thrown out of employment so long as the scale of prices remained the same as before."

settled by offsets (pp. 327, 332–34). His account of the structure of the payments flow captures the modern idea that value added by each production sector is represented by the factor payments from that sector (pp. 328–29).

Fisher first published his version of the equation of exchange in 1899.[7] It altered Newcomb's approach in several ways. First, Fisher substituted the term 'velocity' for 'rapidity.' The new term caught on and may have conveyed an impression of natural stability not implied by 'rapidity.' Second, Fisher divided 'currency' into two components, one (M) composed of paper money and coins, and the other (M') of bank deposits, each with its own velocity. The justification for this division became clearer in his full development of the analysis in *The Purchasing Power of Money* (1911), where empirical estimates of the two velocities were presented. Fisher's presentation thus worked against the idea of combining the different money forms into a single magnitude with a single velocity. Neither his exposition nor his data implied that velocity was constant, merely that it was invariant with respect to changes in M. In fact, velocity underwent considerable change in the period 1896–1909 for which he presented data.[8]

Third, Fisher's measure of transactions (T) was implicitly broader than Newcomb's. This difference was not stressed in 1899, but was evident in 1911 with presentation of the empirical estimates. Fisher was attracted by the prospect of using bank clearings as a measure of $M'V'$, but this measure included a large volume of transactions in financial assets. To be sure, most of his discussion of changes in T refers to changes in output and employment (pp. 62, 155). But in general an income interpretation of Fisher's work is not easy to support. It is relevant that Keynes's review of *Purchasing Power* (1911) faulted Fisher for failing to give sufficient attention to the expenditure flow as the channel through which changes in M would alter prices.[9]

At the same time that Fisher's ideas were being put forward and disseminated, the view now known as 'reverse causation' was being articulated by major figures in several countries: Wesley Mitchell, Knut Wicksell, A. C. Pigou, and Joseph Schumpeter. To be sure, the idea had a long history. Elements of it stemmed from Adam Smith's espousal of the 'real-bills doctrine,' and it received strong support from Thomas Tooke and the 'banking school' in nineteenth-century British monetary controversy.[10]

7. Irving Fisher, "The Role of Capital in Economic Theory," *Economic Journal*, Dec. 1899, pp. 515–21.

8. *The Purchasing Power of Money*, 1911, pp. 284–90.

9. *Economic Journal*, Sept. 1911, p. 395.

10. See Lloyd W. Mints, *A History of Banking Theory*, 1945, esp. ch. 6.

As ordinarily understood, 'reverse causation' refers to the notion that changes in the money supply are the consequence, rather than the cause, of changes in national money income. However, the authors in question believed that the changes in income originated from disturbances in the spending impulses of the various sectors of the economy, principally from variations in the profit outlook for business investment. Variations in investment would in turn lead to variations in demand for bank credit, calling forth variations in the volume of loans and deposits.

Wicksell, Pigou, and Schumpeter all acknowledged the formal validity of the quantity theory of money. And both Wicksell and Schumpeter cast their analysis heavily in a national-income frame of reference.[11] Considering the prominence of Mitchell, Wicksell, Pigou, and Schumpeter in the evolving literature on business cycles, it is highly significant that they tended to view money as a relatively passive and permissive element in economic fluctuations.

In the second volume of his *Lectures*, originally published in 1906, Wicksell outlined a path-breaking analysis of the economy's response to such genuinely exogenous monetary disturbances as a gold discovery or government issue of fiat currency. Such disturbances would raise the flow of aggregate demand for goods and services and through that channel would act on prices and, quite possibly, on output and employment as well.[12]

However, such exogenous monetary disturbances were not stressed. Under ordinary circumstances, disturbance in the macroeconomy was believed to originate in variations in the profit outlook of business, as embodied in the 'natural rate' of interest. Wicksell expected that money and bank credit would be highly elastic with respect to variations in the demand for credit. The spread of bullish expectations would thus generate a monetary expansion and a rise in aggregate de-

11. Mitchell's ideas and those of his teacher Laughlin are abundantly documented by Abraham Hirsch in "Wesley Clair Mitchell, J. Laurence Laughlin and the Quantity Theory of Money," *JPE* 75 (1967): 6.

On Wicksell's support of the quantity theory, see *Interest and Prices*, 1898, pp. 35–43; *Lectures on Political Economy*, vol. 2, 1906, esp. pp. 159–68; Don Patinkin, *Money, Interest, and Prices*, 2d ed., 1965, pp. 587–88. The national-income orientation of Wicksell's anslysis is stressed in Carl G. Uhr, *The Economic Doctrines of Knut Wicksell*, 1962, p. 224. Wicksell explicitly designated national income as the appropriate scale variable for velocity analysis in his *Lectures*, 2:71. This viewpoint is foreshadowed in *Interest and Prices* by examples relating the quantity and turnover of cash and deposits to "the value of the annual produce" (pp. 56, 72–73). I am indebted to Professor Uhr for verifying that these passages appeared in the original Swedish editions and for calling my attention to the passages in *Interest and Prices*. On Pigou and Schumpeter, see below.

12. *Lectures*, 2:161–70.

mand. Money would be an accommodating element, not the exogenous cause of the upswing.[13]

A crucial assumption required for this view of passive monetary adjustment is that either the quantity of bank reserves or the banks' desired reserve ratios readily respond to variations in demand for credit. None of the four authors discussed this issue directly at length. Wicksell made numerous references to bank reserve positions, but his treatment was ambiguous, for several reasons. He defined money as currency alone, excluding bank deposits. In his view, deposits were an influence on 'virtual velocity' of currency.[14] His discussion of bank reserves sometimes treated them as a binding constraint, but often dwelt on the banks' ability to expand at will, if acting concurrently.[15]

In contrast, Ralph Hawtrey's *Good and Bad Trade*, which appeared in 1913, presented one of the clearest and most forceful statements of the money-income relationship. Hawtrey's emphasis throughout was on the determination of national money income, viewed as a measure of the aggregate demand for current output. In the short run, variations in national income affect chiefly output and employment, while in the long run the effects are on nominal wages and prices. While avoiding any reference to velocity, Hawtrey stressed that the public has a desired ratio between money holdings and income, and he described processes by which money and income adjust to each other. Following Fisher, he developed a model of the money-supply process stressing relatively fixed desired ratios of currency to deposits and of bank reserves to deposits. He felt that fluctuations originated in disturbances either to the stock of specie or to the banks' reserve ratio and that the response of the economy reflected lags in wages and in the adjustment of currency holdings. Hawtrey made no effort to support his analysis empirically in this volume.

Although Hawtrey did not refer explicitly to Wicksell, he presented a theory of bank behavior which incorporated Wicksellian views. When bank reserves exceeded their desired ratio, banks would lower their interest charges below the "natural" rate (Hawtrey retained Wicksell's term), and that discrepancy would generate the adjustment

13. *Lectures*, 2:205–9.

14. *Lectures*, 2:67, 168–69; *Interest and Prices*, pp. 41–42.

15. *Interest and Prices*, pp. xxvii, 110–14; *Lectures*, 2:24, 85, 205–9. In the abbreviated version of his theory presented to the Royal Economic Society, Wicksell stressed bank credit elasticity with little qualification—"in our days demand and supply of money have become about the same thing, the demand to a large extent creating its own supply" ("The Influence of the Rate of Interest on Prices," *Economic Journal*, June 1907, p. 215). That Wicksell downplayed monetary disturbance and stressed variations in profit expectations (the 'natural rate of interest') is documented by Uhr, pp. 24–26, 222–24.

process involving expanding bank credit and money and rising investment spending. However, by insisting on relatively rigid demand functions for currency and deposits (by the public) and for reserves (by the banks), Hawtrey ruled out the sort of reverse causation stressed by Wicksell.[16]

Reviewing *Good and Bad Trade* in the *Economic Journal*, Pigou took the opportunity to defend the reverse-causation view. According to Pigou,

> the whole drift of [Hawtrey's] discussion implies that the causes of fluctuations are exclusively monetary and banking causes. Such a point of view is exceedingly superficial. . . . It is undoubtedly the case that the fundamental causes of industrial fluctuations often make use, as it were, of monetary and banking systems as the medium through which they act. But there is no reason to suppose —indeed, there is abundant reason to deny—that they are themselves in any sense resident in those systems. Variations, for example, in the general bounty of nature, or waves of confidence or depression in the outlook of the business community, exercise much of their influence upon industry through the banking system, but they themselves lie wholly outside it. Mr. Hawtrey has failed to grasp this important point.[17]

Schumpeter in 1917 went beyond Wicksell in urging that national income was the most desirable variable to use in defining the equation of exchange. He argued: "The sum of incomes is the monetary expression of 'total demand' " (p. 182). However, he believed *M* should include only money in active circulation, explicitly excluding "hoards" and "unemployed sums waiting to be used" (p. 176). This interpretation would have made it impossible to estimate Schumpeter's version of the equation of exchange directly, and in fact his article contained no efforts at empirical application.[18] While acknowledging that gold discoveries and government fiat-money issues would affect national income, Schumpeter consistently stressed the view that the origins of

16. Hawtrey followed Fisher in assuming that the public's desired ratios of money to income and currency to deposits, and the banks' desired ratio of reserves to deposits, were relatively invariant. See Fisher, *Purchasing Power*, pp. 50–52; Hawtrey, *Good and Bad Trade*, pp. 59, 71–72, 189–90. If bank reserve ratios are invariant, the banks are always 'loaned up' and loans and deposits have no scope to vary with the state of business, unless the monetary base itself is elastic.

17. *Economic Journal*, Dec. 1913, p. 582.

18. Joseph Schumpeter, "Das Sozialprodukt und die Rechenpfennige," *Archiv für Sozialwissenschaften*, 1917–18; a translation entitled "Money and the Social Product," prepared by Arthur Marget, was published in *International Economic Papers*, 1956. Page references are to the translation.

peacetime fluctuations lay with variations in business investment, to which bank credit and money would respond.[19]

Sporadic references to circuit velocity or income velocity of money appeared in the literature in the 1920s. In 1922 William T. Foster approximated the order of magnitude of 'circuit velocity' by comparing the NBER (National Bureau of Economic Research) estimate for 1909 national income with Fisher's estimate of the money stock, but did not attempt to form a time series.[20] Pigou explicitly referred to income velocity in a theoretical context in 1927, and Lionel Edie used the same term in the United States in 1928.[21] But no time-series calculation of income velocity behavior was made prior to 1932.

III

The lack of attention directed to the empirical money-income relationship in the 1920s cannot be attributed to lack of national-income data. When the National Bureau of Economic Research was formed in 1920, the first task to which its associates directed their attention was national-income estimation. In 1921 they produced *Income in the United States, 1909–1919*, which contained annual estimates for the eleven years indicated in the title. The work was the joint product of Wesley Mitchell, Willford King, Frederick Macaulay, and Oswald Knauth. Of these, both Mitchell and King had done considerable work with monetary data. Mitchell had devoted a lengthy section of his 1913 *Business Cycles* to estimates of currency and checking deposits. And King had published in 1920 a long set of time-series estimates of monetary data. It is noteworthy that neither King nor Mitchell attempted to bring money-stock and national-income estimates into a confrontation. Considering Mitchell's beliefs about reverse causation, this is not surprising.

Work on national-income estimates continued through the 1920s

19. Ibid., pp. 200–209. This view had already been spelled out in his earlier *Theory of Economic Development* (1911).

20. William T. Foster, "The Circuit Flow of Money," *AER*, Sept. 1922, p. 468. "For some purposes, the general equation $MV = pQ$ is not as useful as the equation $MC = \Sigma pq$, in which C is the circuit velocity of money and q is the volume of new consumers' goods sold to consumers" (p. 461). See also Foster and Waddill Catchings, *Money*, 1923, pp. 311–12. Their circuit velocity is thus not quite income velocity. Their underconsumptionist view did not stress monetary causation.

21. A. C. Pigou, *Industrial Fluctuations*, 1927, pp. 168–72; Lionel Edie, *Money, Bank Credit and Prices*, 1928, pp. 395–98. To be sure, both Pigou and, earlier, Alfred Marshall had cited income as an appropriate scale variable in the demand schedule for money. But they did not transform this into an explicit statement about determination of money income. See Marshall, *Money, Credit, and Commerce*, 1923, pp. 44–45; Pigou, "The Value of Money," *QJE*, 1917–18, reprinted in Friedrich Lutz and Lloyd Mints, eds., *Readings in Monetary Theory*, p. 166.

chiefly under King's direction. In 1925 Maurice Leven's *Income in the Various States* presented King's estimates for 1920 and 1921, as well as revising that for 1919. Mitchell's 1927 *Business Cycles* contained estimates for 1922–26. King finally published consistent annual estimates for 1909–28 in his 1930 volume, *The National Income and Its Purchasing Power*; some of these data appeared the previous year in an article by Morris Copeland. Simon Kuznets joined the National Bureau in 1929 and soon took over the national-income work there. In 1933 he moved 'on loan' to the Department of Commerce and in 1934 produced the first official income estimates.[22]

One might suppose, then, that there was a problem in obtaining data for the stock of money. Friedman and Schwartz have demonstrated the many pitfalls involved in using the aggregate monetary data available for the early twentieth century.[23]

But in truth, a researcher interested in getting a general idea of the money-income relationship, and willing to use annual time series estimates for currency and commercial-bank deposits, would have been able to obtain such data quite easily. The *Annual Report of the Comptroller of the Currency* for 1920 contained June 30 estimates for "individual deposits" of all banks going back beyond 1909 (pp. 260–61). If he wished, the researcher could deduct "cash items" in process of collection shown in the same table. To convert the data to commercial-bank deposits only, he would have had to deduct mutual-savings deposits for which separate data were given in another table (p. 236). Then he would have been ready to add in currency outside banks and the Treasury, shown in still another long time-series table (p. 22). The Comptroller's reports continued to carry data in this form through 1928. Thus at each point when a new set of national income data came forth, it would have been possible to confront them with plausible time-series estimates of what was long called *M*2.

Our hypothetical researcher would have had a much more difficult time in obtaining estimates of commercial-bank demand deposits. In fact, economists of the 1920s were strongly inclined to prefer a narrow to a broad measure of money. Isolating deposits subject to check had been a major task of Mitchell's 1913 study. In his 1927 *Business Cycles*, he cited new estimates of checkable deposits prepared for 1919–26 by

22. Wesley C. Mitchell, *Business Cycles: The Problem and Its Setting*, 1927, pp. 140–41; Morris Copeland, "National Income and Its Distribution," *Recent Economic Changes*, NBER, 1929, vol. 2; *National Income, 1929–1932*, U.S. Senate Document 124, 73d Congress, 2d Session, 1934. On the evolution of the national-income accounts, see Carol S. Carson, "The History of the United States National Income and Product Accounts," *Review of Income and Wealth*, July 1975, esp. pp. 154–59.

23. Milton Friedman and Anna J. Schwartz, *Monetary Statistics of the United States*, NBER, 1970, pp. 260–62, 267–72.

Carl Snyder. Mitchell also helped direct the research of Y. S. Leong, who in 1929–30 published time-series estimates of checking deposits and currency.[24]

Had our researcher consulted the *Statistical Abstract of the United States*, however, he would not have had to wait for Leong's estimates of what we would call *M*1. In 1926 the *Statistical Abstract* began to carry annual time-series data beginning with 1910 on time and savings deposits in all banks, data prepared by the American Bankers Association (p. 26). By deducting these from total "individual deposits," the researcher could make a fair approximation to demand deposits.[25]

Whatever their faults, the money-stock data available in the 1920s would have been sufficient to demonstrate the extremely close correlation between national income and money. In Table 1 we present regression results obtained from various combinations of these. For example, confronting the 1909–19 income data with crude early *M*2 estimates would have yielded a regression with R^2 of .983, and 1909–21 income data regressed against the estimates of *M*1 yielded $R^2 = .991$. Admittedly, regression analysis as we know it was not practiced in the 1920s. But it was not uncommon in statistical work to calculate the coefficient of correlation; and to find a relationship with *R* on the order of .99 should have whetted interest in further investigation.

Regressions run on the data through 1928 generally yielded regression coefficients of about 2 for broad money (Equations 1, 2, 3, 4) and 3 for narrow money (Equations 8–12), with R^2 values of .968 and upwards. Comparison with estimates extending into the 1930s, especially using Angell's 1936 data, demonstrates that the statistical relationship deteriorated badly after 1929. The general results of Equations 5, 6, 7, 13, and 14 are discussed elsewhere in the article.

IV

Before assessing reasons for the long neglect of the empirical money-income relationship, it is useful to make brief note of two in-

24. Wesley C. Mitchell, *Business Cycles*, 1913, pp. 294–322; *Business Cycles: The Problem and Its Setting*, 1927, pp. 126–27; Y. S. Leong, "An Estimate of the Volume of Deposit Currency in the United States," *JPE*, Oct. 1929; "An Estimate of the Amount of Money Held by the Banks and the Amount of Money in General Circulation in the United States," *JPE*, 1930.

25. It was not until much later that the Federal Reserve began to publish adequate money-stock data. Their *Banking Studies* (1941) contained crude estimates of currency plus all bank deposits for 1890–1940 (p. 447). *Banking and Monetary Statistics*, the 1,000-page showpiece volume published in 1943, devoted a single two-page spread to "adjusted deposits of all banks and currency outside banks" (pp. 34–35). For 1892–1922, estimates were given for one date each year (June 30) and for the remaining years for June 30 and December 31. *The Federal Reserve Bulletin* began to carry a comparable tabulation on a current monthly basis in February 1944.

quiries that may be regarded as near misses in the work of Irving Fisher and Willford King. Fisher never made any effort to incorporate national income data into the equation of exchange. As late as 1932 (*Booms and Depressions*) he was still presenting the equation in its transactions form.

In the 1920s, however, Fisher became engaged in a highly original inquiry into the influence of the rate of change of prices on output and employment. His analysis was probably the first use of distributed lag analysis in economics. It pioneered in stressing the rate of change of prices, as well as their level. And Fisher boldly argued that the supposed inherent cyclical tendencies of the economy, so much stressed in both the U.S. and British literature, were in reality simple reflections of monetary instability.[26]

But while the innovative quality of this work is apparent to the modern reader, it did not attract much attention at the time. Fisher published his results in relatively obscure journals. And although, as Humphrey suggests, he undoubtedly meant to stress prices as a link between monetary disturbance and changes in output and employment, references to money were brief and elliptical.[27]

Fisher's analysis was structured around the implicit assumption that monetary disturbance would affect prices first, with output and employment then responding to price changes. Had he cast his presen-

26. Irving Fisher, "Our Unstable Dollar and the So-Called Business Cycle," *Journal of the American Statistical Association*, June 1925.

27. In the major article, which occupies 23 pages, there are only about six sentences which suggest that price change should be seen as a response to monetary change, "Our Unstable Dollar and the So-Called Business Cycle" (pp. 194, 199). The strongest comment is this: "Monetary theory ought . . . to be able to help us analyze and predict the price level. Professor Alvin Hansen and Professor Holbrook Working have already pointed out that, conformably to the quantity theory, the price level follows bank deposits with a few months lag. The lag, Professor Working tells me, that gives the highest correlation is six months" (p. 199). See Humphrey. "Empirical Tests," pp. 297–304.

Fisher duplicated much of this material in "Banking Policy and Unemployment" (*American Labor Legislation Review*, 1926, pp. 24–29), but the text of the article contains no reference at all to banking policy. In "A Statistical Relation Between Unemployment and Price Changes" (*International Labor Review*, June 1926), the only reference to money is a single sentence at the end, where Fisher concluded: "The ups and downs of employment are the effects, in large measure, of the rises and falls of prices, due in turn to the inflation and deflation of money and credit" (p. 792).

Wesley Mitchell commented scornfully on the 1925 article in his 1927 *Business Cycles*, stressing the apparent exogenous status of price changes: "Thus, most of the time, P and T are the 'active' factors in the equation of exchange; they bring about changes in M', V, and V'; to a less extent they affect even M" (p. 137).

Fisher updated his work in 1932; but his reluctance to stress the monetary influence was repeated. The only reference is this: "A contraction in the currency and credit causes a fall of prices which in turn reduces employment." "The Relation of Employment to the Price Level," in *Stabilization of Employment*, ed. Charles F. Roos, 1933, p. 159.

Table 1. Regression results: national income and money stock, using data available in the 1920s and 1930s

Regression Number	Years included	Nat. income variable	Money-stock variable	Reg. coefficient	*t*-ratio	const. (billions)	R^2	DW
			I. Broad Money (M2)					
1.	1909–19	Y21	M20	2.17	23.87	$ 1.6	.984	1.61
2.	1909–21	Y25	M26	1.97	18.21	4.9	.968	0.93
3.	1909–28	Y30a	M28	1.79	43.84	8.4	.991	1.27
			Angell's data of 1932					
4.	1909–28	Y30a	MA32	1.42	40.69	6.0	.989	0.94
			Currie's data of 1933					
5.	1921–30	Y32	MC33	1.86	11.29	5.9	.941	1.68
			Angell's data of 1936					
6.	1909–32	Y34	MA36	1.20	9.75	11.4	.812	0.27
			Warburton's data of 1945					
7.	1919–43	Y45	MW45	1.16	8.76	23.4	.770	0.34
			II. Narrow Money (M1)					
8.	1910–21	Y25	M126	2.76	34.29	5.1	.992	1.16
9.	1910–28	Y30a	M129	3.11	26.35	1.0	.976	0.37
10.	1910–28	Y30b	M129	2.91	24.40	0.9	.972	0.36
			Leong's data of 1929–30					
11.	1909–26	Y30a	M1L	3.40	28.53	−0.7	.981	1.05
12.	1909–26	Y30b	M1L	3.17	26.13	−0.5	.977	0.99
			Currie's data of 1933					
13.	1921–30	Y32	M1C33	5.10	11.97	−45.6	.947	1.37
			Angell's data of 1936					
14.	1909–32	Y34	M1A36	2.83	12.24	2.5	.872	0.37

Continued overleaf

Table 1 (continued)

Note: Numbers in income and money data refer to the year in which those data (or their most recent components) became available.

Sources:

Y21: Wesley C. Mitchell, Willford I. King, Frederick R. Macaulay, and Oswald W. Knauth, *Income in the United States, 1909–19*, NBER, 1921, p. 72.

Y25: Maurice Leven and Willford I. King, *Income in the Various States*, NBER, 1925, p. 32, which provides observations for 1919, 1920, and 1921, added to Y21.

Y30a: Willford I. King, *The National Income and Its Purchasing Power*, NBER, 1930, p. 74.

Y30b: Same source as Y30a, but excludes imputed income items.

Y32: Lauchlin Currie, "Money, Gold, and Income in the United States, 1921–32," *QJE*, Nov. 1933, p. 92; originally published by Morris Copeland, "How Large is Our National Income?" *JPE*, Dec. 1932, p. 773.

Y34: James W. Angell, *The Behavior of Money*, 1936, p. 190; using King's data (Y30b) plus Kuznets's data for 1929–32, "National Income, 1929–1932."

Y45: Clark Warburton, "The Volume of Money and the Price Level Between the World Wars," *JPE*, June 1945; reprinted in *Depression, Inflation and Monetary Policy*, p. 130; compiled from a variety of primary sources.

M20: *Annual Report of the Comptroller of the Currency* for 1920, vol. 1; individual deposits for all banks minus cash items in process of collection (pp. 260–61) minus deposits of mutual savings banks (p. 236) plus currency in circulation (p. 22).

M26: M20 for 1909–16. For 1917-21, *Comptroller's Report*, 1921, pp. 171, 761. For 1922–26, *Comptroller's Report*, 1926, pp. 102, 104, 603.

M1 26: Same as M26 adjusted with data from *Statistical Abstract*, 1926, p. 263.

M28: Same as M26, extended with data in *Comptroller's Report*, 1928, pp. 103, 104, 717.

M1 29: Same as M28 adjusted with data from *Statistical Abstract*, 1929, p. 275.

M1 L: Y. S. Leong, "An Estimate of the Volume of Deposit Currency in the United States," *JPE*, Oct. 1929, p. 596, and "An Estimate of the Amount of Money Held by the Banks and the Amount of Money in General Circulation in the United States," *JPE*, April 1930, p. 171.

MA32: Angell, "Money, Prices, and Production: Some Fundamental Concepts," *QJE*, Nov. 1933, p. 75. The money-stock data are not actually shown, but can be derived from the velocity figures shown and from the income figures (Y30a) which he used.

MC33, M1 C33: Currie, *QJE*, Nov. 1933, pp. 90, 92.

MA36, M1 A36: Angell, *The Behavior of Money*, p. 190.

MW45: Warburton, p. 130, using Federal Reserve data.

tation in national-income terms, it would have been more persuasive to show that output and prices would tend to respond in the same direction to monetary disturbance. His analysis implied a strong influence from money to national income, but he did not make the connection explicit.

We have already noted that Willford King, who pioneered in generating national-income estimates, had also worked extensively with money-stock estimates. King's 1930 national-income volume contains a rather surprising section in which he compares national income with various monetary and banking measures. Instead of a money stock total, however, King added together bank loans and individual deposits and compared that incongruous total with national income. He presented the annual values of the ratio of the two, which ranged from .833 to 1.036 for 1909–28. Regressing national income on this improbable monetary aggregate would have yielded a regression coefficient of .945 and R^2 of .984. King's brief commentary indicated he did not perceive any functional relation between the two series (p. 355).

While most economists ignored the empirical money-income relationship, J. M. Keynes denied it. In his *Treatise on Money* (1930), Keynes wrote "it is misleading to represent the total cash deposits [chief elements in the stock of money] . . . as bearing any stable or normal relationship to the national money income" (1:43). Keynes could have tested this assertion against the data on U.S. checking deposits and U.S. money income published in 1929 by Leong and Copeland, respectively. Taking the period 1913–26 covered by both series, a regression of deposits on income would have yielded $R^2 = .964$.

Why were economists so slow to bring the money-stock and national-income data into confrontation? Several main reasons can be cited. First, national-income data were not seen as measures of aggregate demand and expenditures. The early estimates were presented on two bases, by income shares and by industrial origin. The division into categories of expenditure did not come until the 1930s.

Second, as Friedman and Schwartz have stressed, most researchers prior to the 1930s did not think in terms of a single monetary aggregate combining currency and deposits.[28] The separation of currency and deposits tended to become stronger in the 1920s when the Federal Reserve's data on bank debits provided such an attractive measure of the total volume of check transactions. The preoccupation with debits tended to keep the equation of exchange focused on total transac-

28. Note that Keynes did not combine currency and deposits into a single entity. As late as the *General Theory* he was still willing to "assume that money is co-extensive with bank deposits" (p. 167 n.). This usage seems inconsistent with his observations about inelastic production of money at p. 230.

tions.[29] Angell and Currie were the first to add currency and deposits empirically and assign a single velocity to the sum.

Third, researchers were, perhaps justifiably, preoccupied with finding measures of checking deposits and did not make use of the more readily available data on total deposits.

Fourth, it is worth recalling that, as Humphrey has pointed out, the period of the 1920s abounded in statistical *ad-hoc*ery, of the sort exemplified by the work of the Harvard Economic Service and by some of the National Bureau's publications. For a researcher to have identified a purely statistical correspondence, without an analytical system into which to fit it, would probably have made little impression. King's discussion illustrates this. Still, one wonders what difference it might have made had Keynes had more familiarity with these data.

Fifth, U.S. economists did not use the analytical construct of a demand schedule for money, although it was a common topic in the British literature. The close correlation between money and income could be seen as evidence of the existence of a strong and stable income-demand for money, even if one did not stress the causal influence of money on income.

Finally, as Alan Sweezy has noted, "the concept of the business cycle dominated the thinking of economists and businessmen alike."[30] With it came the presumption that the roots of cyclical behavior lay outside the monetary system. Such formidable business-cycle experts as Pigou, Schumpeter, and Mitchell adhered to the view that the quantity of money adjusted to exogenous variations in business confidence and investment spending. Hawtrey's defense of monetary causation received little support. No one attempted the systematic analysis of the behavior of bank reserves and bank credit required to determine which way the predominant causal influence was operating.

V

The first time-series estimates of U.S. income velocity were published in 1933 by James W. Angell and Lauchlin Currie. Angell's esti-

29. The present article does not attempt to review the extensive literature of empirical studies based on the transactions version of the equation of exchange by such economists as Holbrook Working, Morris Copeland, Carl Snyder, and many others. See Humphrey, "Empirical Tests"; George Garvy, "Carl Snyder, Pioneer Economic Statistician and Monetarist," *History of Political Economy* 10 (Fall 1978). Copeland, like Mitchell and King, worked extensively with both money and national-income data but did not integrate them until much later. His analysis of money flows can be viewed as an attempt to integrate the income and transactions approaches. See his *A Study of Moneyflows in the United States*, NBER, 1952. This was the forerunner of the Federal Reserve flow-of-funds accounts.

30. Alan Sweezy, "The Keynesians and Government Policy, 1933–1939," *AER*, May 1972, p. 116.

mates were initially presented at the 1932 meeting of the American Association for the Advancement of Science.

Currie's article in the November 1933 *Quarterly Journal of Economics (QJE)* was devoted primarily to presenting his carefully derived estimates of demand deposits, time deposits, and currency for 1921–32.[31] Currie compared his money-stock estimates with national income estimates for 1921–30 published by Copeland in 1932. Had he regressed income on his two money-stock series, he would have obtained regression coefficients of 1.86 for broadly defined money and 5.10 for narrowly defined money, with R^2 values of .941 and .947 respectively (Equations 5 and 13 from Table 1).

Neither in the *QJE* article nor in his other writings of the period did Currie devote much attention to the behavior of velocity or to the measurement of the impact of money-stock change on income change. His important book *The Supply and Control of Money in the United States* was published in 1934. Although his study was evidently motivated by the belief that money was an important influence on income and expenditures, his assumptions about the impact of money on income are nowhere made very clear. He recently wrote, "After the upturn in business in early 1930 proved abortive, I despaired of the efficacy of monetary measures in the conditions of the times."[32]

Whatever his reservations on that score, however, Currie did present a careful empirical critique of the reverse-causation view, based on detailed examination of the behavior of the determinants of the money stock. He found that banks' excess reserves showed little variations over the normal business cycle. "Our general conclusion is that the demand for loans does not impose a very serious limitation upon

31. Lauchlin Currie, "Money, Gold and Income in the United States" *QJE*, Nov. 1933, esp. pp. 91–93.

32. Lauchlin Currie, "Comments and Observations," *History of Political Economy* 10 (1978): 541. The introductory chapter of *Supply and Control* criticized Keynes's *Treatise* for unduly downplaying the influence of money, but did not provide a systematic alternative. The income velocity data for 1921–29, slightly revised, appeared in a footnote with the comment that "From 1923 to 1929 the income velocity increased by 1.3 per cent per annum. The national money income increased by 4 per cent per annum. Hence the major part of the increase in money incomes was attributable to the expansion of money" (p. 6). He also devoted a paragraph to explaining that "various episodes in monetary history since the war appear to point to the importance of the supply of money as a factor affecting business conditions," noting that "different countries had individual cycles corresponding closely to what one would expect from their various monetary policies" (p. 8).

Currie's work in Washington after 1934 did not indicate a conviction that national income was primarily determined by the quantity of money. See Sweezy, "The Keynesians"; Byrd L. Jones, "The Role of Keynesians in Wartime Policy and Postwar Planning, 1940–46," *AER*, May 1972, pp. 116–18, 125–27, and comments by Currie, pp. 139–41.

the volume of deposits. Unless the depression is abnormally severe, banks can offset the decline in their commercial loans by increasing their investment portfolios. . . . It has not been thought necessary to consider at any length the view that deposits expand in the upswing *because* the demand for loans increases. . . . The absence of any growth in the money supply at a period of the most intense demand for loans in the last decade, 1928–29, and the growth of the money supply in the years of recession 1924 and 1927, would seem to indicate that the main explanation of the variations in the money supply cannot be found in the variations in the demand for loans."[33]

Angell's velocity estimates also appeared in the *QJE* for November 1933.[34] His article was largely a theoretical analysis of the structure of the payments system. The velocity data were presented in a footnote merely to illustrate an order of magnitude. Angell used a very broad definition of money, including commercial and savings bank deposits (including government) plus currency. Thus his estimates for velocity were lower than Currie's. By using more readily available data, Angell was able to cover a much longer time span, over which the stability of the money-income relation was more impressive. For his twenty-year span 1909–28 (using the King national-income estimates of 1930), velocity ranged between 1.50 and 1.80. Had he regressed income on money, he would have obtained a regression coefficient of 1.42 and an R^2 of .989 (Equation 4).

Far more interesting is the paper Angell presented in 1932 to the American Association for the Advancement of Science.[35] Here he made a strong statement about the importance of money as an influence on national income, output, and employment. From his income-velocity data Angell concluded that "the circular velocity of money, also changes only rather gradually. . . . When there is no new voluntary saving and investment, the principal source of fluctuations in the national money income . . . is, at least in fairly short periods, changes in the size of the money stock" (pp. 211–12). Comparing the seriousness of monetary disturbance with disturbance originating with saving and investment, he argued that "the first is far more important, since the most serious consequences of excessive saving and investment appear only when the excessive investment is initially financed in significant

33. *Supply and Control*, p. 124–25.

34. James W. Angell, "Money, Prices, and Production, Some Fundamental Concepts," *QJE*, Nov. 1933, p. 75.

35. "Monetary Prerequisites for Employment Stabilization," in Roos, ed., *Stabilization of Employment*, 1933. Virtually the identical article appeared under the title "Monetary Control and General Business Stabilization," in *Economic Essays in Honor of Gustav Cassel*, 1933.

degree through the creation of additional money" (p. 225). He concluded that "proper manipulation of the monetary and financial mechanism can be made to produce substantial stability of general employment; and indeed that, with our present general philosophy, enduring stability can be secured only through this manipulation" (p. 226).

In his book *The Behavior of Money* (1936) Angell further examined the money-income relationship. His discussion of money and national income came late in the book and in condensed form. Its most striking novelty was a time-series chart comparing money and national income, 1909–32 (p. 145). His diagram, drawn to stress proportional changes in M and Y, showed that their movements were closely parallel from 1909 through 1930, but made clear that income had fallen more, proportionately, than M in 1929–32. He was sufficiently impressed by the close long-run correspondence to entitle his chapter subsection "National Income 1909–1932: Varied Chiefly with the Stock of Money, Not with Circular Velocity" (p. 144). But he pulled back from assuming strict monetary causation: "It is evidently not possible to deduce from these facts either that the national income 'determines' the size of the money stock or that the size of the money stock determines the size and fluctuations of the national income" (p. 147).

The agnostic tone of this passage reflects Angell's lack of a well-articulated analysis of the determination of the money stock which would have enabled him to clarify the direction of causality.[36] Angell's reluctance to assign causal importance to money also resulted from the analysis in his earlier chapters. There he compared the behavior of currency and checking deposits (taken separately) with a variety of business-cycle indicators such as industrial production, freight-car loadings, factory payrolls, and construction contracts awarded. Comparison involved monthly data for 1919–34. From these, Angell was unable to draw any consistent view of causal interactions. Angell's lack of a theory of money *supply* is evident in the following passage:

36. It may seem incorrect to claim that Angell lacked a theory of determination of the money stock, in view of his lengthy article (with Karel Ficek) "The Expansion of Bank Credit," *JPE*, Feb. and April 1933. However, the presentation lacks important elements of a *theory* of money supply. It was not grounded on profit-maximizing behavior by the banks and thus did not present any hypothesis about the probable behavior of their desired holdings of excess reserves and vault cash. It treated the stock of initial reserves as predetermined and thus did not integrate bank reserves into a sources-and-uses framework which would relate them to the monetary base. Currie's *Supply and Control* dealt more directly with these matters; see Karl Brunner's introduction to the reprint edition (1966). Other path-breaking contributions to the theory of money supply include Winfield W. Riefler, *Money Rates and M ney Markets in the United States*, 1930, pp. 124–44; and James Harvey Rogers, "Monetary Initiative in a Traditional World," in Arthur Gayer, ed., *The Lessons of Monetary Experience*, 1937, esp. pp. 110–14. Rogers introduced the term 'monetary base' in essentially its modern usage in this article.

"The data thus provide no prima facie support at all for the view that increasing the quantity of money will start the process of economic recovery. On the contrary, increases in the quantity of money seem to have been the *result* rather than the cause of the onset of business revival" (p. 61). He was very pessimistic about the influence of monetary policy: "A 'moderate' enforced expansion of the money supply therefore seems likely to have little effect on current business activity, and may be absorbed chiefly in . . . 'idle' balances" (p. 160).

In reviewing *The Behavior of Money*, D. H. Robertson confronted Angell's apparent inconsistency: "*Prima facie* it would seem that his methods must be either overestimating the influence of quantity of money on national income, or underestimating its influence on the components of national income, namely output and prices; to suppose that the former is overwhelming and the latter negligible seems to be to suppose inconsistent things."[37]

A much more forthright statement of monetary causation was contained in Angell's contribution to the 1937 festschrift for Irving Fisher.[38] Angell now made use of the national-income estimates for 1899–1908 published by the National Industrial Conference Board to show that relatively stable income velocity had prevailed from 1899 to 1930. Further, he observed from current national-income data that national income was expanding in proportion with money after 1932, although the average velocity was lower than it had been before 1930 (p. 55). Thus, he could stress that the velocity decline of 1930–32 was unique in twentieth-century U.S. experience. Angell cited the results of a League of Nations study giving estimates of money and exchange velocity for nineteen major countries for 1929–35; in most of these the downswing was dominated by decrease in M rather than V (p. 57).

Angell argued:

> It is perhaps not even too rash to suggest that much of the decline in world economic activity between 1928 and 1933 . . . could have been avoided by stabilizing the quantity of circulating money at around the 1928–1929 peaks, or (still better) by causing it to increase gradually from those peaks, say with population. . . . Nor is it wholly improbable that preventing the wide declines which actually occurred in the quantity of money, with their accompaniments of self-feeding waves of liquidation and fear, would have checked the struggle for increased cash liquidity itself, would thus have prevented at least a part of the actual fall in velocity, and in

37. *Economic Journal*, June 1937, p. 332.

38. "The General Objectives of Monetary Policy," in Arthur Gayer, ed., *The Lessons of Monetary Experience*, 1937.

> this indirect way, too, would have checked the decline in general activity [pp. 56–58].

> It seems to me almost certain that if the quantity of money were kept reasonably stable, [the] remaining and perhaps irreducible quasi cycles would become relatively small in size, and would hence be of secondary importance [p. 83].

After the forthright statements in the 1937 article, it is difficult to believe that *Investment and Business Cycles*, published in 1941, was written by the same author. While presenting additional important material about the money-income relationship, the book was primarily devoted to a loosely sketched verbal model of business-cycle theory in which the monetary system played no significant role. The infrequent references to money depicted passive adaptation to variations in business conditions: reverse causation.

In this study, Angell related his estimates of the velocity of active money to the Keynesian multiplier, using the velocity estimates to try to estimate the speed of adjustment of the multiplier process. Yet his material reinforced the earlier stress on the close relationship between money stock and national income. A time-series chart compared annual estimates of M and Y for the entire period 1899–1939, showing their extraordinary parallel (p. 143). Further, Angell calculated the regression relationship between Y and M for the periods 1899–1929, 1929–33, and 1933–39—apparently the first author to make such calculations:

> The data for the first period, 1899–1929, reveal an extraordinarily stable relation between changes in income and changes in money stock. . . . It may be doubted if any other important and directly measurable economic magnitude, except the average circular velocity of money itself, has shown equal stability over as long a period as 30 years, at least in modern times [p. 148].

For 1899–1929, Angell's regression result was as follows (p. 150):

$$\begin{aligned} Y &= -\$0.17 \text{ bil} + 3.03M \\ R &= 0.96 \\ \text{s.e.} &= \$2.52 \text{ bil} \end{aligned} \qquad (15)$$

(In a footnote, he also presented the regression with M as dependent variable, but nowhere interpreted this as a demand schedule for M.)

For 1929–33, his regression was as follows:

$$\begin{aligned} Y &= -\$56.16 \text{ bil} + 4.99M \\ R &= 0.99 \\ \text{s.e.} &= \$1.23 \text{ bil} \end{aligned} \qquad (16)$$

and for 1933–39 as follows:

$$Y = \$12.12 \text{ bil} + 1.75M$$
$$R = 0.96$$
$$\text{s.e.} = \$2.32 \text{ bil} \qquad (17)$$

His 1929–33 regression implied a strong deflationary result from the monetary contraction, and the 1933–39 regression implied that monetary expansion after 1933 was not ineffective.

Angell's monetary regressions were virtually the only empirical material in the book. Yet his discussion proceeded as if money were a relatively passive element in the business cycle (see especially p. 159). In place of the strong defense of monetary policy in his earlier writings, Angell devoted only a few sentences to monetary policy, sufficient to show that he now thought it of little account, relative to fiscal policy (pp. 221, 255).

If one reads Angell selectively, his work is without parallel in discovering the closeness of the money-income relationship. He was the first to make systematic calculation of income-velocity time series, the first to chart money and income together to show their close parallel, and the first to regress income on the money stock. Yet he was never able to decide how much monetary causation they implied.

VI

Just as Angell was giving up his long monitoring of the money-income relationship, it was being discovered by Clark Warburton.[39] Warburton, who was two years older than Angell, had participated actively in the development of national-income accounts in the 1930s, but his work of that period gives no hint of a conviction of strong monetary causation.[40]

Warburton's discovery of the money-income relationship is apparent in three items beginning in 1943. In a note appearing in the June *American Economic Review (AER)* he commented on a variety of measures of the inflationary gap, including some which reflected the in-

39. Warburton's work has been the subject of several recent studies. See Thomas Cargill, "Clark Warburton and the Development of Monetarism Since the Great Depression," *History of Political Economy* 11, no. 3 (1979); Michael D. Bordo and Anna J. Schwartz, "Clark Warburton: Pioneer Monetarist," *Journal of Monetary Economics*, 1979.

40. This can be seen particularly in his contribution to the Mitchell memorial volume, a business-cycle commentary stressing the active role of innovations and referring only incidentally to credit as a permissive element. "Plateaus of Prosperity and Plains of Depression," *Economic Essays in Honor of Wesley Clair Mitchell*, 1935. Warburton commented on his change of views in "The Theory of Turning Points in Business Fluctuations," *QJE*, Nov. 1950, reprinted in *Depression, Inflation, and Monetary Policy*, 1966, p. 51 n.

crease in the quantity of money.[41] In September he published another note entitled "Who Makes the Inflationary Gap?"[42] In a mere five pages, this note sketched a clearly modern monetarist position. By the end of 1943 he had completed a paper titled "The Volume of Money and the Price Level Between the World Wars," which eventually appeared in the *Journal of Political Economy (JPE)* in 1945. He drew on its findings in a reply, published in the June 1944 *AER*, to criticisms of his previous notes. In this, he addressed quantitatively the question later confronted by Friedman and Meiselman: Could one explain consumption spending better by income or by money holdings? He found income superior during the great contraction, 1930–33, but otherwise the two seemed to perform about equally well between the wars. However, he found that the money-consumption relation was holding much more stable in 1941–43 than the income-consumption relation. Moreover, Warburton argued that income was not nearly so exogenous nor predictable as was money.[43] Thus, he advocated looking at monetary data as the best indicator of potential inflationary pressure.

These articles set off a tremendous burst of publication by Warburton. Besides the four items just noted, the *Index of Economic Journals* lists thirteen other articles or notes in 1945–49 (p. 453). The noteworthy elements in his monetary analysis included the following points:

1. He concentrated attention on a broad measure of the money supply, including time deposits.
2. He did not use regression analysis, but stressed deviations of M and V from their time-trend values. He looked for causality in leads and lags related to turning points.
3. He forcefully defended the view that money-stock changes originated with the volume of bank reserves in relation to reserve requirements, and rejected the reverse causation position that M was passively responding to business conditions.
4. He argued that changes in income and expenditure were the main channel through which the economy adjusted to monetary disequilibrium. He was probably the first economist to write the velocity relationship as a function linking income and money: $Y = v(M)$.
5. He relied on an intuitive but shrewd analysis of the demand for

41. Clark Warburton, "Measuring the Inflationary Gap," *AER*, June 1943, esp. pp. 367–69.

42. "Who Makes the Inflationary Gap?" *AER*, Sept. 1943.

43. "Monetary Expansion and the Inflationary Gap," *AER*, June 1944. It is interesting to compare Warburton's three articles with one by Milton Friedman on the same topic: "Discussion of the Inflationary Gap," *AER*, June 1942. Friedman's note makes no reference to the money supply at all.

money. He accepted but did not stress the Keynesian conviction that interest rates would affect desired money holdings.

6. He spelled out an adjustment sequence whereby monetary expansion could initially tend to lower interest rates but in which interest rates would ultimately rise.

Points 3, 4 and 5 represent areas in which Warburton's analysis improved significantly over Angell's. While he used variants of the velocity concept, Warburton was always analytically secure in a supply-and-demand framework. Thus, he escaped the preoccupation with the structure of payments which stultified Angell's work.

Despite the fact that Warburton's views were widely disseminated, they had little apparent influence on economic thinking in the 1940s. The Keynesian ideas, which had been slow to catch on in the 1930s, were gaining support during and after the war. But on virtually every major point listed, Warburton's views correspond with those later articulated by Milton Friedman. Exactly how that correspondence came about would make for an interesting study, but is beyond the scope of this essay.

VII

In sum, noteworthy features in the evolving view of the money-income relationship include the following:

1. Prominent advocates of a monetary point of view, notably Fisher and Hawtrey, failed to follow through with an effective campaign of evidence, analysis, and persuasion. Fisher never cast his analysis into a national-income frame of reference and failed to make sufficiently explicit the role of monetary disturbance in his path-breaking studies of unemployment and prices in the 1920s. Hawtrey did not develop a strong empirical presentation to support the elegant theoretical system laid out in *Good and Bad Trade*.

2. Just as the close statistical relation between money and national income was being discovered by Angell and Currie, that relationship was undergoing its first serious instability of the twentieth century. Although Angell's argument that the velocity decline after 1929 could have been induced by the monetary contraction was probably sound, most economists were not persuaded.

3. The reverse causation argument was strongly defended early in the twentieth century by a variety of prominent economists and has remained to this day the chief anti-monetarist argument. Significantly, this view was held by Wicksell, Mitchell, Schumpeter, and Pigou, all of whom contributed in significant degree to the increasing emphasis, in both theory and measurement, on national income. Currie's denial of

reverse causation could not overcome the apparent evidence that it was operating in the 1930s. That same evidence was also used against Warburton's subsequent argument that profit maximization by banks would not lead to a highly elastic supply of bank credit. The extent of monetary causation remains a highly controversial issue.

An earlier version of this paper was presented to the History of Economics Society at Champaign-Urbana, May 1979. I am grateful for comments on earlier drafts from James W. Angell, Lester Chandler, Don Patinkin, Thomas Humphrey, Clark Warburton, Anna J. Schwartz, John Henderson, William Waters, Carl Uhr, and the referees.

[6]

History of Political Economy 15:1

Allyn A. Young: a curious case of professional neglect

Charles P. Blitch

I. *The Foundational Years: 1876–1917*

One of the most neglected persons in the annals of modern economic thought is Allyn Abbott Young. It was by an ironic twist of fate that from a position as one of the most eminent American economists in the interwar period he became by the fifth decade of the century a shadowy but fascinating figure in the footnotes and acknowledgments of many of the leading economists of the day. Joseph A. Schumpeter, writing of Young shortly after the latter's death said, "Rarely if ever has fame such as his been acquired on the basis of so little published work" (Schumpeter 1937, 514). Scarcely a decade had passed when Schumpeter, again referring to Young, wrote: "I take this opportunity of saying a few words on Allyn Young. . . . This great economist and brilliant theorist is in danger of being forgotten" (1959, 875 n. 23). The reason for this paradoxical development might appear to be Schumpeter's observation of great fame "on the basis of so little published work." As a matter of fact Schumpeter was wrong, for Young's publications constitute an impressive bibliography. Unfortunately many items are not easily accessible to the student of the history of economics, since they are printed in the newspapers and magazines of the era or in the pages of out-of-print textbooks and encyclopedias rather than in the professional journals.

Young's main focus in university work was graduate teaching. He was on the faculty of the leading American graduate school of the day, Harvard University. He acted as thesis director or adviser to a large number of students who were to gain fame or noteworthiness in economics in later years. His professional and public service was wide in scope and variety and acknowledged by honors and reputation. Yet, despite this very distinguished résumé, it is an anomaly in the history of economics that outside a short but concise summary of Young's life and accomplishments in Dorfman's *The economic mind in American civilization* (1969, 4: 222–23) and a very brief sketch of his work at the London School of Economics in Lord Robbins' *Autobiography* (1971, 119–22), there is not a professional

Correspondence for the author may be sent to Professor Charles P. Blitch, Dept. of Economics, Old Dominion University, Box 6173, Norfolk VA 23508

reference for the life and thought of a leading member of the economics community of the interwar period.

Allyn Abbott Young was born in Kenton, Ohio, on September 18, 1876, the first of three children of Sutton E. Young by his marriage to Emma Matilda Stickney.[1] His given name was a combination of the maiden names of his paternal (Allyn) and maternal (Abbott) grandmothers. The family was of sturdy English stock, as forebears on both sides had emigrated from England to the Colony of Massachusetts in the 1630s. The Young family settled in Connecticut, but in 1810 Allyn's great grandfather migrated to Ohio to clear and farm a tract of land which he had purchased in Hiram township. Allyn's grandfather, a successful carpenter and cabinetmaker, was a devout member of the Church of the Disciples of Christ and was instrumental in the establishment of Hiram College by that faith in 1850. Allyn's father graduated from there in 1871. At first he was a schoolteacher, but later as a result of reading law on his own he was admitted to the Ohio bar. Allyn's mother was a graduate of Oberlin College and was a teacher in the public schools of Kenton at the time of her marriage.

When Allyn was five years old the family moved to Sioux Falls in the Dakota territory, where his father became superintendent of the public schools. There Allyn received his early education. Evidently he was a precocious student, for when the family moved to Hiram in 1890 to enter him in Hiram College, he was only fourteen years old. When he graduated with honors on the evening of June 19, 1894, he was just seventeen and the youngest graduate on record. His course of study was heavily weighted in mathematics and the physical sciences, but he also took Latin, French, and German. His transcript shows that he took one course in political economy in the spring of 1893 and received a grade of 96%. It is interesting to note that the textbook used was the first edition of Richard T. Ely's *Outlines of economics*, a book that Young was to co-author in its second edition some fifteen years later. While in college Allyn helped pay his expenses by doing job printing on a hand press that he owned. He was granted the Bachelor of Philosophy degree (Ph.B.) at a time of economic depression. In order to earn money to continue his education he worked as a printer for firms in Cleveland, Ohio, and Winona, Minnesota, from 1895 until August 1898.

In September 1898 Young entered the University of Wisconsin as a candidate for the Ph.D. in economics with minors in statistics and history.

1. Much of the information concerning the Young family and Allyn Young's early life and career is condensed from documents and letters in the A. A. Young Manuscripts (AAY MSS) in the archives of the Widener Library at Harvard University, and the Allyn A. Young Collection (AAY COL) in the archives of the Teachout Memorial Library, Hiram College, Hiram, Ohio.

While it is uncertain why he chose to study economics, the times were conducive to it. Economic issues and problems dominated the news and politics of the day. A wave of industrial unrest epitomized by the Pullman strike and the march of Coxey's Army on Washington reflected the burgeoning power of the labor unions. Young's father, a gifted public speaker, had taken a leading role in the 'free silver' debate in Ohio and in the Dakota territory. The rise of the Populist Party with its strength in the Midwest and its programs of control of the railroads and the trusts and monetary reform reached its peak in the presidential election of 1896. A surviving program of Allyn's college literary society lists him as speaking on "The Great Commoner," the popular name of William Jennings Bryan and the leading proponent of free silver.

While at Wisconsin Allyn studied economics with Richard T. Ely and William A. Scott, and history with Frederick Jackson Turner and Charles H. Haskins; and he received instruction in statistics from Edward D. Jones. Ely, impressed by Young's ability, secured a temporary one-year appointment for him in the Bureau of the Census in Washington, D.C. Arriving there in the summer of 1899, Young joined other graduate students from Harvard, Chicago, Johns Hopkins, and the Massachusetts Institute of Technology, working in the Section of Analysis and Research for the Twelfth Census directed by Professor Walter F. Willcox of Cornell University. While there, Young formed friendships which were to be lifelong with Thomas S. Adams of Johns Hopkins, Wesley C. Mitchell of Chicago, and Willcox.

Young returned to Wisconsin in the fall of 1900 and in June 1902 was awarded the Ph.D. in economics. During his Washington stay he had gathered the data, not only for his first professional publication, "The comparative accuracy of different forms of quinquennial age groups" (Young 1900), but also for his dissertation, "A discussion of age statistics." The latter was published as a monograph by the Bureau of the Census in 1904. Young's interest in statistics was to continue throughout his life.

Allyn Young's academic career began with an appointment to the faculty of Western Reserve University in September 1902. After two years in Cleveland he accepted a position in the Amos Tuck School of Banking at Dartmouth College as assistant professor of finance. In the month of August 1904 he married Jessie Bernice Westlake of Madison. Young was not happy at Dartmouth, owing to a misunderstanding about the courses he was to teach and the lack of a good library in economics. In September 1905 he returned to Wisconsin as assistant professor of economics, where his good friend Thomas Adams was lecturing. It was during this year that Young, Adams, and Max O. Lorenz agreed to revise Ely's *Outlines of economics* as co-authors with Ely. The book was to become the leading college principles textbook between 1908 and 1930.

In the summer of 1905 David Starr Jordan, first president of Leland

Stanford Jr. University, was engaged in a search for a chairman of the newly endowed economics department. Meeting his friend, Walter Willcox, by chance in London, Jordan asked him for a recommendation and Willcox suggested Young. Young was offered the position as associate professor and acting head of the department with the understanding that after a trial period, he would be made permanent chairman and promoted to the rank of professor. Although the university suffered extensive damage in the California earthquake of April 1906, it opened as scheduled that fall. Young's tenure at Stanford was not a happy one although he was made permanent chairman and promoted to professor. Jordan was authoritarian in his administration of the university. He was unwilling for Young and the other chairmen to have the major responsibility for recruiting staff or recommending promotions and salary increases. Young recommended Thorstein Veblen twice for promotion to professor, only to have Jordan reject it twice. Jordan was more interested in promoting undergraduate work than graduate studies. The economics department had an inadequate budget for the library acquisitions, visiting scholars, and experienced faculty which were needed for a graduate program. Finally, Young's salary had not been increased, although he felt he had proved himself. Discouraged over the prospects at Stanford he accepted an invitation to be a visiting professor of economics at Harvard for the academic year 1910–1911. This gave him an opportunity to survey faculty positions in the East. He taught a graduate course in mathematical economics and a course in advanced statistics at Harvard. He so impressed the faculty that had a position been open he would have been offered the job. The final break with Jordan came with a misunderstanding about an offer to Young for a professorship at Wisconsin and Jordan's refusal to increase Young's salary. He then decided to go to Washington University at St. Louis as chairman and professor of economics, where he would replace his good friend Thomas S. Adams, who was going to the Wisconsin Tax Commission.

Although St. Louis was satisfactory to Young in terms of salary—he had received a substantial increase over his Stanford contract—he was still bothered by the lack of advanced work in economics and the absence of a superior library. It was during his tenure at Washington University that he published his first major paper in economics, "Some limitations of the value concept" (Young 1911). His main argument in the paper was directed at the almost universal contention of the profession that value, especially exchange value, was antecedent to price, when in fact, he argued, the reverse was true. Young also argued that wealth is measured in terms of imputed price and rests upon the assumption of a stable equilibrium with no substantial increases or decreases in the demand and supply of the commodity. Much of the paper was based upon ideas advanced by Cournot but substantially expanded by Young, one of the few economists of the time who had read Cournot. It was also in St. Louis that Young became associated with the chief engineer of the St. Louis Public Service Commission as a consultant on a rate case. This led to the composition and publication of another article, "Depreciation and rate control" (Young 1914), which challenged the accepted doctrine of public utility regulation as far as depreciation and valuation of investment was concerned.

In 1913 a professorship in economics and finance became vacant at Cornell, and through the influence of Walter Willcox it was offered to Allyn Young. Cornell had a well-established graduate program in economics, a distinguished faculty, and an excellent library, as well as a number of good graduate students. Ithaca was a pleasant community situated in beautiful surroundings, and the years there were happy and fruitful ones for Young. It was at Cornell that he encountered his most famous graduate student and friend, Frank H. Knight. Knight had been working with Alvin Johnson, who left to become editor of a new and liberal magazine, *The New Republic*. At Johnson's suggestion Young took over the supervision of Knight's thesis, "The theory of business profits," later to be revised with Young's help and published as *Risk, uncertainty and profit* (Knight 1921). The association between Knight and Young was to continue until the day of Young's death. While they were not always in agreement, especially on the matter of increasing returns, their professional and personal relationship was marked by a temperate and generous exchange of ideas and criticisms. In 1914 Young was elected secretary of the American Economic Association, a position he was to hold until 1920.

Allyn Young's review of A. C. Pigou's *Wealth and welfare* (Young 1913) attracted widespread professional attention, for in it he corrected a slip in Pigou's reasoning. As Pigou was Alfred Marshall's successor in the Cambridge chair and a leading figure in Anglo-American economics, Young's review, as Taussig remarked, caused "somewhat of a sensation" in academic circles in the two countries. Pigou had argued that in competitive industries subject to increasing costs (diminishing returns) marginal social cost exceeded marginal private cost in equilibrium, while in industries subject to decreasing costs (increasing returns) the reverse was true. This resulted in a misallocation of society's resources; so Pigou advocated a tax on the output of increasing-cost industries and a subsidy to those of decreasing cost in order to bring the marginal social and private costs into equality. Young pointed out that in increasing-cost industries the rise in costs does not represent a using up of society's resources but only an increase in the prices of specialized factors as output expands and those prices are bid up. As such, it is just a transfer of purchasing power from those industries using the specialized inputs to the owners of those factors. Young also hinted in his review that increasing returns are not of the same character as diminishing returns and are not subject to analysis of the partial-equilibrium type. It would be fifteen years before he expanded on these suggestions. Pigou at first attempted to refute Young in the revision of his book, retitled *Economics of welfare* (Pigou 1920, p. 798 n.). However as a result of additional criticisms by Frank H. Knight and D. H. Robertson, Pigou corrected his error in the 1924 edition.

Allyn Young was elected president of the American Statistical Association for 1917, and when the United States entered World War I he was called to Washington to direct the Bureau of Statistical Research for the War Trade Board. Young found a dearth of adequate statistical information for national war purposes and much overlapping and duplication by the various war boards and commissions. In his presidential address to the statistical association in December 1917 he called for a central statistical agency not only for war needs but for peace purposes as well (Young 1917, 873–85). In war time such an organization was essential for the effective mobilization and use of the nation's resources. Not only would this eliminate the duplication and waste but, "there is yet the larger gain that would come from a comprehensive view of our national assets, and more especially of our national product" (ibid. 880). Young closed his talk with the following observation:

> If the statistical problems brought sharply into the foreground by the war hold any lesson that has a significance for times of peace, it is that we have not yet begun to realize the possibilities of federal statistics as a general scheme of national accountancy, or the responsibilities which the future holds for the statistician [Young 1917, 885].

A central bureau was established in June 1918, but did not survive the end of the war. It was not until the 1930s that the government established a national system of accounts.

II *Paris Peace Talks: 1918–1919*

Early in November 1917 James Shotwell, professor of history at Columbia, wrote Young a short letter. He and Shotwell were associated as the history and economics advisers to the textbook division of Houghton Mifflin Company of Boston. Shotwell's letter stated: "I am trying to get light upon the handling of questions of economics in connection with the peace conference at the close of the war and will be needing both contributions and men to help in the work. This is highly confidential and I should very much appreciate a chance to talk things over with you."[2] Young replied that he was very much interested and would be glad to talk with Shotwell at the latter's convenience. The upshot of this contact was

2. J. M. Shotwell to A. A. Young, 1 Nov. 1917, General Correspondence, A. A. Young folder, Inquiry Archives. Young's reply is dated 5 Nov. 1917.

Young's appointment as economics specialist in a group of experts drawn primarily from the nation's universities and colleges to study the problems and lay the groundwork for the peace negotiations. The organization was under the direction of President Woodrow Wilson's confidant Colonel Edward M. House and subsequently became known as 'The Inquiry.'[3] Among the members of the group along with Young and Shotwell were Young's former teacher at Wisconsin Charles H. Haskins, now dean of the Harvard graduate school and specialist on northwest Europe; Isaiah Bowman, president of the American Geographic Society and specialist on Latin America; Charles Seymour, professor of history at Yale and specialist on the Austrian Empire; William E. Lunt, professor of English history at Cornell and specialist on Italy; Clive Day, professor of economic history at Yale and specialist on the Balkans; and Douglas W. Johnson, assistant professor of physiography at Columbia and specialist on boundary geography. The group was headed by Sidney E. Mezes, president of the City College of New York, who was House's brother-in-law; the secretary was Walter Lippmann and the treasurer was David Hunter Miller, a prominent New York City attorney who also served as a specialist on international law.

The problems facing the members of The Inquiry were not only enormous in scope but were new, for the United States had never taken part in a general peace conference and, even though a world power, lacked a world view. The major problems of the organization such as delineating procedures and fields of work, recruiting competent personnel, and securing adequate financing were never fully overcome. The economics division exhibited in microcosm these limitations. In October 1918 the division was manned by just six persons—Young and five assistants. Out of a total budget of $15,000 for September 1918, the economics division received about 10 percent or $1,556.72. Young was forced to rely on outside institutions for much of the economic and statistical information. While some seven hundred reports and documents were prepared in advance of the peace conference, only forty-five or about 6 percent originated from within the division. The external preparers were often uninformed of the purpose of their studies and only in a few cases received any remuneration for them. As a result, there was a wide variation in their usefulness, quality, and viewpoint. Young and his small staff attempted the impossible job of directing, coordinating, and interpreting these reports. A further and more important difficulty for the economists was the fact that The Inquiry was organized along geographical lines. The continent of Europe was divided among regional specialists who prepared the historical, political, geo-

3. Much of the following information, except where specifically noted, is based on the contents of chapters 2 through 10 of Gelfand 1963. Material used by permission, Yale University Press, copyright 1963.

graphical, sociological, and demographic analyses which were to provide the background for the group's recommendations concerning postwar national boundaries. Economic problems were regarded as common to all areas, and special reports on regional and national problems were to supplement the other information. This program had the double disadvantage of both overburdening the staff of economists and focusing on national or regional problems to the exclusion of serious economic problems which involved wide areas or which confronted Europe as a whole. Young recognized this deficiency and in a memorandum dated February 25, 1918, outlining a program for economic studies wrote:

> The economic information in these special regional studies relates for the most part, to definitely circumscribed areas. Very little of it is shaped so as to show the *relations* between different areas. Nor is it sufficiently homogeneous to permit throwing it together in such a way as to show readily the economic significance of different possible boundary lines. . . . In short, there is no way in which these regional studies can be pieced together to form a whole. What is needed is a general background of economic information, organized in a systematic and uniform way, covering those parts of the world in which the problem areas fall. . . . This information must be gathered by men or organizations working on *subjects* rather than on areas.[4]

The problems to which the passage above particularly applied, in Young's view, were those of reparations and the commercial relations between nations. Young's pleas for a larger staff and comprehensive studies were to no avail, since the importance of economic matters in the forthcoming peace discussions and matters associated with the distortions of war were not generally recognized outside the economics division. The latter problems in particular were spotlighted by the collapse of the Central Powers in October 1918 and the armistice on November 11.

Among the members of The Inquiry who were designated by executive order to accompany President Wilson and the American delegation to Paris were Young, Shotwell, Bowman, Day, Haskins, Seymour, Lunt, and Johnson, along with Mezes. They were named as technical advisers to the American Commission to Negotiate Peace. Sailing with the President on the former North German Lloyd liner *George Washington*, they witnessed the excitement of the presidential party's departure from New York and the tumultuous welcome for Wilson in Brest and Paris. President Wilson had only one conference with his technical advisers aboard ship, at which time he told them that peace must be based on justice—for example, in settling boundary questions. On the German indemnity he stated his strong

4. R. G. 256, Box 19, Inquiry Archives.

opposition to any payments except for actual war damages done to civilians by the German armed forces. The President concluded the meeting by saying he hoped his advisers would give him a firm position to establish the justice or injustice of various claims. Although he expected them to work according to the organizational plan of the conference normally, they should, in an emergency, not hesitate to bring to his attention directly any problem which was critical to peace with justice. His final words were: "Tell me what's right and I'll fight for it. Give me a guaranteed position."

From the outset of the conference Young was embroiled in the complex problem of German reparations. Not only did this matter occupy much of the time and efforts of the peacemakers, but it was to continue as a major international concern for the next decade. It was not clearly understood that the questions of what damages Germany was to repair, what amount Germany was to pay, and the manner of payment were all interrelated. There was a naive idea circulating that there was available in Germany a surplus of wealth subject to direct appropriation. It was Allyn Young and J. M. Keynes who provided careful and sober estimates of Germany's cash assets and her ability to pay. Keynes' figures were widely publicized in his book, *The economic consequences of the peace* (Keynes 2: 84–85), while Young's are buried in the records of the American Commission (Miller 1928, Docs. 328 and 446). Both reached independently an identical estimate of Germany's capacity to pay—10 billion dollars. This was a far cry from the initial French demand of 200 billion or the British figure of 120 billion dollars. Another aspect of the indemnity which was not understood nor generally considered was the economic consequences of payment upon the receiving countries. In order to make payments beyond the value of her cash assets outside Germany or transportable outside, Germany had to have a surplus in her international balance of payments. This surplus had to be converted into foreign currencies. The surplus required either an export surplus or foreign capital investment in Germany. The whole situation gave rise to the famous 'transfer problem' which was debated and discussed by economists of repute in the interwar period. Young was involved in the reparations problem throughout the decade.

Young and J. M. Keynes met in Paris, and the subject discussed was the problem of German indemnities (Burnett 1940, Doc. 65, 469). They did not, however, develop a close relationship, and while both left Paris before the signing of the Versailles Treaty, the reasons for leaving were quite different. Keynes' reason for resigning from the British delegation is well-known, but Young did not resign; he was in effect sent home as a result of his role in the 'Italian crisis' which occurred in the spring of 1919.

Italy had entered the war on the Allied side as a result of a secret treaty, the Treaty of London, signed in 1915 by Britain, France, Russia, and Italy. This treaty gave Italy wide territorial concessions plus a share of the indemnity at the war's end. Italy's support of the Allies was the outcome of a deliberate bargain. Italy, therefore, came to Paris with claims in fundamental conflict with Wilson's general principle of "open covenants openly arrived at." Upon his arrival in Paris, Prime Minister Orlando of Italy submitted a memorandum which added the port of Fiume to the Italian demands. Under the London treaty this port had been awarded to the Austrian province of Croatia, now part of the new nation of Jugoslavia (Yugoslavia). President Wilson repudiated the Italian claims based on the secret treaty and asked his technical advisers to prepare a recommendation regarding them. The experts' advice, contained in a memorandum signed by Seymour, Lunt, Day, and Johnson, was to award Italy Trentino, Trieste, most of the Tyrol territory, and part of the Dalmatian coast, but excluding the port of Fiume. This city was to go to Jugoslavia.

Faced with Orlando's intransigence on the matter of Fiume as it had become a *cause célèbre* in Italy, Colonel House proposed a compromise whereby the port city would be divided with the city proper going to Italy but the port becoming a 'free port' under the auspices of the League of Nations. This suggestion caused a split among the American technical advisers, with one group supporting the House compromise, and the signers of the original recommendation joined by Bowman and Young dissenting. The latter group regarded any compromise on the matter as a concession to Italy which they opposed on historical, economic, political, demographic, and moral grounds. When it appeared that the House proposal would go to the President as representing the experts' advice, the six dissenters sent a direct appeal to Wilson reminding him of his promise on the *George Washington* that if he were told what was right and given a strong position he would fight for it (Baker 1924, Doc. 36, 278–80). Unfortunately, in their haste to get to Wilson, they failed to notify House, and when he brought the compromise position to Wilson as being representative of his technical advisers point of view, he was confronted with the letter from the six dissenters. House was very upset, and as a result the six advisers who had signed the letter to Wilson shortly received notice that their services were no longer needed at the conference, as the work was almost complete. Young and Bowman returned to the United States in May 1919 before the signing of the peace treaty took place at Versailles in June.

Allyn Young's sojourn in Paris had a profound influence on his ensuing career. Paris in the winter and spring of 1919 was the center of the world's attention. All the great and near-great in American and European politics were there. Most importantly for Young, the British contingent contained, as did the American, well-known economists and other academicians. A friendly and consultative relationship developed between the American technical advisers and the British delegation. Young was intimately involved both formally and informally in the economic settlements. He served as the American delegate and chairman on the subcommission on commercial treaties, served as alternate for Thomas W. Lamont and Bernard Baruch on the Economic Commission, and was economic adviser to Baruch, Lamont, and Vance McCormack, who were the American representatives on the Reparations Commission. Diaries kept by James Shotwell (1937), David Hunter Miller (1928), and Charles Seymour (1965) all refer to Young's informal consultations regarding reparations, commercial treaties, labor relations, and other matters of an economic nature. It was in these behind-the-scenes activities that he had the most influence and made the strongest mark. There is no doubt that his brilliance as an economist, his persuasiveness in argument, and his personal charm and modesty made a lasting impression on the men with whom he served. His status as an economist of international esteem was established at Paris.

Keynes' indictment of the Treaty of Versailles in his *Economic consequences of the peace* as a Carthaginian peace, his contention that the terms were set secretly by the Council of Four, and in particular, his unflattering portrait of President Wilson as a Presbyterian elder 'bamboozled' by the clever Lloyd George and the sharp-witted Clemenceau dismayed and disturbed Young and the other former members of the American delegation. Reviewing the book for the *New Republic*, Young expressed this opinion:

> It was not the adroitness of Lloyd George or the laconic single-mindedness of Clemenceau that balked the President. It was what he could see over their shoulders. Nothing less than unified and courageous leadership could have lifted public opinion in the Allied countries (including the United States) up to the level of a peace that would have been an honest fulfillment of pre-armistice pledges. Public opinion . . . was always there, in the meeting room of the Council of Four, in the guise of "the domestic political situation." It was Clemenceau's strength and Wilson's weakness.[5]

In his public utterances and writing, as well as in private, Young defended the treaty as the best possible under the circumstances existing in Paris. He summed up his position in a speech prepared for a public forum in Philadelphia:

> My purpose has been to show you that the treaty is not, in reality, the disguised instrument of economic oppression that it sometimes has been held to be. If any are deceived by its economic clauses, it is those who have been counting on its use as just such an instru-

5. Young 1919. Quoted by permission, *The New Republic*, copyright 1920.

ment. . . . It is a hard and exacting document—it could and should have been nothing else—and makes some regrettable but necessary concessions to the prevailing state of mind in Europe, and especially to the political exigencies of the situation. . . . Many of the economic clauses of the treaty are parts of a temporary scaffolding set up to hold things in place until a more enduring structure can be erected. The treaty does not propose to settle the economic relations of the European states for all time. It is a forward looking document. It leaves the way open for new and, it is to be hoped, better adjustments just as soon as the political situation in Europe makes these settlements possible. In the long run the economic settlement will be just what the world makes of it.[6]

Young was extremely disappointed by the Senate's failure to approve the treaty and its refusal to approve United States membership in the League of Nations. He felt that the nation had a moral obligation to work towards a European settlement whether or not the document was approved. He made his view known in an article in *Foreign Affairs*:

The treaty was framed on the assumption that the United States would accept it and would help to administer it. It was on that premise that the other states represented at Paris agreed to its provisions. Our defection virtually revised the treaty for the worse.[7]

Throughout the last decade of his life, Young sought, through his written and oral counsel, to influence and mediate the turbulent economic and political problems created by the war.

III. *The Harvard Years: 1920–1927*

Allyn Young had been offered a professorship at Harvard for 1919–1920, but he felt an obligation to Cornell, as he had been on leave of absence for two years with partial pay; so he turned the Harvard offer down. It was renewed for 1920–1921 with a larger salary, and Young accepted it. Harvard University in 1920 had 180 members in the faculty in Harvard College, 2,534 undergraduate students, and 538 graduate students. On the economics faculty were F. W. Taussig, C. J. Bullock, and Thomas N. Carver; the new Widener Library was among the nation's finest; and there were a large number of brilliant advanced economics students. Young excelled as a graduate teacher, and no summary of his life would be complete without some reference to his teaching. As Schumpeter remarked, "He was first and last a creative teacher, and it was through his teaching rather than his writing that he influenced creative thought"

6. Young 1921. Quoted by permission, Charles Scribner's Sons, copyright 1921.
7. Young 1922. Quoted by permission, *Foreign Affairs*, copyright 1923.

(Schumpeter 1937, 514). Edward S. Mason, a graduate student and instructor at Harvard during Young's tenure, describes him:

> Young was a handsome man, tall and stately, with a shock of gray hair surmounting a face that was more of a poet than an economist. He had, in fact, strong artistic interests, particularly in music, and had in his youth played the organ professionally. He was, for an economist, a singularly unworldly man, careless of his own interest and generous to a fault. It was, perhaps, for this reason that in a department of rather uncongenial personalities his friendship was sought by everyone. Carver enticed him to the golf course; Bullock sought to involve him in the affairs of the Harvard Economic Service; Taussig and Williams were his close friends; and the younger members of the department adored him.[8]

Two of Young's courses became famous among graduate students: "Money and Banking" and "History of Modern Economic Doctrines." Letters and statements from Young's former students attest to his creativeness, personality, and manner of teaching. James W. Angell, explains the basis of Young's influence:

> The foundations of the great influence which Young had on his students, the necessary but not sufficient conditions, were both his own great intellectual capacity, and the wide range of knowledge not only of economics but also of other fields which he brought to bear on specific economic problems. . . . He made our horizons seem wider, and the air fresher. . . . But these things alone might have been insufficient. The key factor, I am sure, was some sort of warm personal magnetism . . . that seemed to flow from him to his students, and that made them both trust him personally and believe in him intellectually.[9]

As a lecturer he appeared to be unsystematic and in some sense unprepared. It seemed as if he left his Widener study hastily gathering together whatever materials he could conveniently find at hand. Indeed, he frequently had to be reminded of class meetings by either students or colleagues, as he would be absorbed in some current interest. While his lectures were unorganized, they were not confusing or rambling to the perceptive student. The lecture went winding around the problem at hand in quest of some new idea, suggestion, or tentative hypothesis. He talked to his students about problems which interested him and which he had been thinking about. Eleanor Lansing Dulles comments on this trait: "Allyn Young

8. Edward S. Mason, "History of the Harvard economics department," *Quarterly Journal of Economics*, Aug. 1982. Used by permission.

9. Letter to the author, 6 April 1973.

was a professor who kept developing his ideas with his class. His students participated in this development—he was nearly a perfect teacher."[10] Lauchlin Currie makes the following observation: "Perhaps the most enduring lesson I learned from Young was that the subject was wide open to modifications and improvements. . . . Young gave the impression of *thinking* as he went along. He continually opened up exciting vistas."[11] His discussion was punctuated by long pauses as he thought through an idea or question. Again Eleanor Dulles comments: "A large, square-shouldered man with slightly rumpled tweeds, he would look into space with a long range perspective while his hands groped for a handkerchief—usually not there, and we wondered whether we should give him one. But his words never failed him." A friend and younger colleague, the late Arthur H. Cole, mentions this characteristic: "Professor Young was quite absent-minded. Also, he had the condition of lapsing into a brown study as he lectured or, according to stories, even as he carved a turkey or roast beef at his table—carved for the family."[12] The student had the sense of being involved with an original and penetrating intellect at work, using facts and theory freely in search for truth. The late Bertil Ohlin wrote: "I took a very stimulating course from Professor Young at Harvard in 1922–23. . . . He impressed me immensely. I am inclined to believe that he was a man, who knew and thoroughly understood his subject—economics—better than anyone else I have met."[13] Young never made a student or any other questioner look ridiculous or stupid. Several former pupils mention this, for example, Overton H. Taylor says: "He had a wonderful trick of taking a student's often 'dumb' question to him in class, restating it with a twist which turned it into a brilliant question, and then answering *that*, to the great benefit of all of us."[14] Under Young economics became no convention to be learned by rote, but an aspect of life itself. Earl J. Hamilton refers to Young's ability to generate in his students an enthusiasm for economic inquiry: "What I treasure most of all is the inculcation of his firm belief that the world is full of interesting problems, about which we know next to nothing and that if one tackles them and really studies them, there is no limit to what one can achieve except limitations inherent in himself. He made me feel this strongly when I left almost every class I ever had under him."[15] As a result of his knowledge, personal charm, and generosity, graduate students flocked to Young for advice, consultation, and direction concerning their theses. His best-known graduate student at Har-

10. Letter to the author, 31 Dec. 1974.
11. Letter to the author, 26 Feb. 1979.
12. Letter to the author, 1 April 1972.
13. Letter to the author, 21 Dec. 1978.
14. Letter to the author, 15 Oct. 1973.
15. Letter to the author, 14 Feb. 1973.

vard was Edward H. Chamberlin, whose dissertation was published as *The theory of monopolistic competition* (Chamberlin 1933).

During his Harvard years Allyn Young was engaged in a wide range of activities other than teaching and research. In 1920 he was appointed to the advisory committee to the Bureau of the Census which not only assisted in interpreting the results of the census of that year but participated in devising index numbers such as the wholesale and consumer price indices. The National Bureau of Economic Research was organized in 1920 with Wesley Mitchell as director. Allyn Young was elected as one of the ten members of the board of directors. As a result of the depression of 1920–21, President Warren Harding, at the urging of the then Secretary of Commerce Herbert Hoover, called a conference of leading economists, statisticians, and business and labor personalities to discuss the proportions, effects, and policies of unemployment. Young, who had known Hoover in Paris, was appointed to the Economic Advisory Committee of the conference. One recommendation of the conference was that Congress should pass legislation to prepare for future fluctuations by accelerating or retarding federal spending for public works. Senator William S. Kenyon introduced such a bill, and Young wrote to him commending the legislation:

> It is sound economics and it seems to me that it would be sound public policy to attempt to counteract the disastrous effects of periods of business depression, so far as possible, by increasing public expenditures on permanent improvements at such times. The flow of individual expenditures, which is what in the last analysis gives employment to labor, is beyond the control of the law, even though wise banking policies may reduce the extent of the cyclical fluctuations in such expenditures. But public expenditures are controllable. It is certainly unwise that public expenditures should be at their maximum when private expenditures are also at their maximum.
>
> The proposals made in the carefully drafted bill do not look forward, as I understand them, to the imposition of heavier taxes or securing of larger public revenues in other ways in depression. The proposals merely are that such public funds as can be conveniently and properly expended at one period rather than another, should so far as possible, be expended at times when such expenditures will be attended by maximum public benefits.[16]

The bill was defeated even though supported by Hoover, the national Chamber of Commerce, and the American Federation of Labor. It was at Young's insistence that a special chapter on business cycles was added to

16. Allyn A. Young to William S. Kenyon, 25 Nov. 1921, AAY MSS.

the 1923 edition of *Outlines of economics*, with the above-mentioned remedy suggested for policy.[17]

Among other activities during his stay at Harvard, Young acted as informal and formal consultant to Benjamin Strong, president of the New York Federal Reserve Bank and member of the Board of Governors of the Federal Reserve System (Dorfman 1969, 4:280 n.). He became an adviser to the Council of the League of Nations, and in 1924–25 assisted Jeremiah Smith, Commissioner General of the League for Hungary, in carrying out the reconstruction plan for the Hungarian economy (Young 1927b). Young was appointed by the Council in 1926 to a committee to plan for a world economic conference to be held in Geneva in 1927. He was elected president of the American Economic Association in 1925 and in his presidential address made a rational and strong plea for international economic cooperation (Young 1927a).

In 1924 a group of younger economists put forward "sort of a manifesto" generally critical of classical and current economics. It was published (Tugwell 1924) under the title of *The trend of economics*. Young, whose tolerance for differing points of view was unusually wide, faulted the writers in an erudite review for their general misunderstanding of the methods and thought of both modern and classical economists "I do not see," he wrote "how one who looks backward with smoked glasses can look forward with open and clear eyes" (Young 1924, 170–71).

As Mason noted, Young was generous to a fault not only with his money but with his time and ideas. A cursory examination of the acknowledgments by authors of various articles in the *Quarterly Journal of Economics* for the issues between 1920 and 1930, for example, reveals that Young's name appears more often than any other. He was an acute, knowledgeable, and gentle critic, often presenting theoretical alternatives or corrections in his reviews. He remarked in his review of Edgeworth's *Papers relating to political economy* that: "Even the book reviews . . . are never mere abstracts. At one point or another the reviewer pushes some thesis advanced by the author a little further, puts it under a new light, or brings it under new relations" (Young 1925, 724). The same sentiments could easily apply to his own book reviews.

It was during his Harvard tenure that Young began a gradual but persistent reorientation of his frame of reference for economic research. One can find in his various letters to his former student and friend, Frank H. Knight, during the 1920s, a rising concern about what is now called the paradigm for economics. For example in a 1922 letter to Knight, he wrote: "What bothers me especially is that, after all, economics, like any other science, must be shaped to fit our needs for an instrument of control. . . .

17. Memorandum, A. A. Young to R. T. Ely and T. S. Adams, undated, *Outlines of economics* folder, AAY MSS.

I have yet to see that the method of general equilibrium gives us anything at all that *gets us anywhere*."[18] Young had a strong empirical bent as a result of his doctoral studies at Wisconsin. Ely, who taught him economics, described his method of research as the 'look and see' method. Students or economists by observing the world as it was could develop new premises and generalizations. Facts should be gathered in accordance with an hypothesis and arranged and analyzed to gain new knowledge and hypotheses. Hypotheses are fundamental to economics, as are empirical observations. Since economic life is consistently changing and given hypotheses are relative to a given state of economic life, economists should involve themselves in public and business affairs so as to give society the benefit of their knowledge and, in turn, gain new knowledge for new hypotheses (Ely 1938). It was natural, therefore, for Young to question a theory which was not grounded securely on an empirical base. His work with Edward Chamberlin on the theory of monopolistic competition also added to his conviction that the perfectly competitive model was deficient in many respects for either description or prediction. Young had access to a large quantity of data and information about the American economy as a consequence of his membership in private and public organizations during the decade. Testing the idea of a static general equilibrium model against the pertinent data confirmed Young's skepticism of the social value of that construct. His mental reconstruction was conceived at Harvard, but it was to be born at the London School of Economics.

IV. *The London School: 1927–1929*

In 1925 the London School of Economics and Political Science received a large grant from the Laura Spellman Rockefeller Fund which provided for, among other things, a chair of political economy in the School. Edwin Cannan, who was currently serving as professor of economics, was retiring in 1926, and Sir William Beveridge, the School's director, was searching for someone to fill the chair. It was offered to Allyn Young, and he accepted it for a period of three years. It was the first time that a chair in a British university had been offered to an American.

Young arrived in London in September 1927, at the height of the so-called cost controversy among economists. Piero Sraffa's famous paper, "The laws of return under competitive conditions" (Sraffa 1926), had recently been published. Sraffa's incisive criticisms of Marshallian economics and his conclusions regarding the competitive model created an intellectual turmoil. One aspect concerned the compatibility of competitive equilibrium with increasing returns. Sraffa argued that wherever decreasing costs prevailed because of 'internal economies' it was necessary

18. A. A. Young to F. H. Knight, 9 Dec. 1922, AAY MSS, F. H. Knight folder.

to use monopoly theory. Young felt that Sraffa's conclusion would be interpreted to mean that increasing returns would always eventuate in monopoly; he therefore felt it was time to present his views on increasing returns and competition.

Shortly after arriving in Britain, Young was elected president of Section F (Economics and Statistics) of the British Association for the Advancement of Science—the first American to be so honored. This gave him an opportunity to address himself to the problem of increasing returns before a large part of the British economic establishment. He gave his speech, "Increasing returns and economic progress" (Young 1928) on September 10, 1928, at Glasgow University—an appropriate place, for the paper was a variation on Adam Smith's theory of economic development. It was widely recognized at the time as a major contribution to economics. Schumpeter, writing a number of years later, states the following opinion of Young's address: "A volume of essays . . . constitute the bulk of his published work and do not convey any idea of the width and depth of his thought. . . . But *ex ungue leonem*—that is to say, the reader may form some idea of that lion from a single claw, namely, his paper 'Increasing Returns and Economic Progress'" (Schumpeter 1959, 875 n. 23).

Young, like Adam Smith, was interested, first of all, in the general problems of the economy as a whole, with only essential references to individual industries and firms as operational elements. He opened his remarks by shunning the use of the partial equilibrium method:

> I do not propose to discuss any of those alluring but highly technical questions relating to the precise way in which some sort of equilibrium of supply and demand is achieved in the market for products of industries which can increase their output without increasing their costs proportionately. . . . I suspect, indeed, that the apparatus that economists have built up for dealing effectively with the range of questions . . . may stand in the way of a clear view of the more general . . . aspects of the phenomena of increasing returns [Young 1928, 527].

Young proposed that a sectoral view of the economy should be taken as an approach:

> Instead, we have to go back to a simpler and more inclusive view, such as some of the older economists took when they contrasted the increasing returns which they thought were characteristic of manufacturing industry taken as a whole with the diminishing returns which they thought were dominant in agriculture [ibid. 528].

Economic progress was engendered by an expanding industrial sector leading to an extension of the division of labor which in turn required capital investment of both the deepening and widening types. Young, along with Smith, thought that manufacturing offered more opportunities for the division of labor than did agriculture. The data that Young had at hand sustained his belief, for it showed a startling advance in manufacturing productivity, with only moderate gains for that of the farm sector.

The central theme of Young's paper was Adam Smith's theorem that the division of labor is limited by the extent of the market. "That theorem," he said, "I have always thought, is one of the most illuminating and fruitful generalisations which can be found anywhere in the literature of economics" (ibid. 529). The division of labor, according to Young, meant something much broader in scope than the pin-making example that Smith had used. It manifested itself in the growth of indirect or roundabout methods of production and specialization among industries. He stressed the point that with the expansion of the market it became economical to use more capitalistic and specialized methods of production. A complex production process for a product is broken up into a number of simpler steps which may lead to the substitution of machinery for labor. As the demand for a given product, for example, increases it may pay the firm to concentrate a single step in production in a specialized plant. With continuing growth of the market the specialized plants may themselves become a new industry. As Young stated it, "certain roundabout methods are fairly sure to become feasible and economical when their advantages can be spread over the output of the whole industry. These potential economies, then, are segregated and achieved by the operations of specialized undertakings which, taken together, constitute a new industry" (ibid. 539). Young used the transformation of the old printing trades into a succession of industries—paper, wood pulp, ink, presses, etc.—as an example. This approach requires the abandonment of the Marshallian concept of industry, for with growth, industry boundaries become blurred and overlapping. It also meant that the traditional market definition had to be altered.

For his purposes Young defined the market in terms of Say's Law:

> In an inclusive view, considering the market not as an outlet for the products of a particular industry, and therefore external to that industry, but as the outlet for goods in general, the size of the market is determined and defined by the volume of production. If this statement needs any qualification, it is that the conception of the market in this inclusive sense—an aggregate of productive activities, tied together by trade—carries with it the notion that there must be some sort of balance, that different productive activities must be proportioned one to another [Young 1928, 533].

In his sketch of a growth model for an advanced industrial economy, Young was to add important qualifications to Say's venerable theorem.

In this sketch of a model of economic progress Allyn Young used the reciprocal demand curve which had been developed by Marshall and extended by Edgeworth. This device shows the quantity of one commodity, say cloth, which one nation is willing and able to trade with another country for various quantities of another commodity, say steel, at each of a series of prices of steel in terms of cloth. Demand and supply are interdependent, as the demand for steel calls forth a supply of cloth just as the supply of steel is a demand for cloth. Applying the concept to the domestic economy, Young assumed that both commodities were produced competitively under conditions of increasing returns and the demand for each was elastic in the sense "that a small increase in its supply will be attended by an increase in the amounts of other commodities which can be had in exchange for it" (ibid. 534). Thus, if the price of steel in terms of cloth fell as a result of an increased supply of steel, and cloth producers' demand for steel is elastic, then they would supply proportionately more cloth in exchange. Young said that under these circumstances an increase in the supply of one commodity *is*, in effect, an increase in the demand for others. In addition, it must be supposed that every increase in demand will evoke an increase in supply (ibid.). It is a long-run notion, and Young is arguing that production under conditions of increasing returns and an elastic demand are the necessary and sufficient conditions for the functioning of Say's Law. Given this situation, Young remarked: "Even with a stationary population and in the absence of new discoveries in pure or applied science" (as contrasted with such new ways of organizing production and such new 'inventions' as are merely adaptations of known ways of doing things, made practicable and economical by an enlarged scale of production, ibid. 534 n. 2) "there are no limits to the process of expansion except the limits beyond which demand is not elastic and returns do not increase" (ibid., 534).

The cornerstone of economic development in Young's view is the creation of markets. He regarded this as the key component:

> It is dangerous to assign any single factor the leading role in that continuing economic revolution which has taken the modern world so far away from the world of a few hundred years ago. But is there any other factor which has a better claim to that role than the persisting search for markets? No other hypothesis so well unites economic history and economic theory [Young 1928, 536].

Like Schumpeter, Young attributes much to the 'entrepreneurial spirit' in economic progress. "The business man's mercantilistic emphasis upon markets," he wrote, "may have a sounder basis than the economist who thinks mostly in terms of economic statics is prone to admit" (ibid. 537). One of the chief tasks of modern industry, said Young, is finding markets, and the search for markets is not only a matter of multiplying profits by multiplying sales but also of adding to sales and profits by reducing costs. He suggests that 'selling expenses' may not be a case of sheer economic waste, but the case depends upon their effect on the aggregate output of industry as opposed to their effect on the profits of individual firms (ibid.). It is obvious that Young's concept of competition is not that of 'perfect competition.' He is harking back to Smith's notion of the 'competition that counts,' competition by free entry and the exploitation of new opportunities for the division of labor.

Young's address was a challenge to the neoclassical paradigm. The phenomenon of increasing returns plays a far more important role in an advanced industrial economy than current competitive theory allowed. The notion that the perfectly competitive general equilibrium model was a suitable frame of reference for research and policy was erroneous.[19] The application of equilibrium methodology in the presence of increasing returns was at best misleading. "No analysis of forces making for economic equilibrium . . . will serve to illumine this field, for movements away from equilibrium, departures from previous trends are characteristic of it" (Young 1928, 528). Young felt that the changes in production methods and techniques as well as in industrial organization induced by the extension of the division of labor were not systematic enough to be subjected to any type of equilibrium analysis, partial or general. In his words:

> the counter forces which are continually defeating the forces which make for economic equilibrium are more pervasive and more deeply rooted in the constitution of a modern economic system than we commonly realize. . . . Every important advance in the organization of production . . . alters the conditions of industrial activity and initiates responses elsewhere in the industrial structure which in turn have an unsettling effect. Thus change becomes progressive and propagates itself in a cumulative way [Young 1928, 533].

Young's point is that static analysis of the traditional mode fails to illuminate the problems associated with economic growth. He intimates that in his own model, time must be explicitly included: "If under these hypothetical conditions, progress were unimpeded and frictionless . . . the realizing of increasing returns might be progressive and continuous. . . . But it would remain a process requiring time" (ibid. 534).

Young's model incorporating increasing returns arising from advances in the division of labor eschewed the assumption that changes in cost and demand conditions were exogenous to the system. The forces making for such changes came from within. Taking a cue from economic history, he

19. Lord Kaldor has expanded on this point. See Kaldor 1972.

argued that the search for markets by entrepreneurs was the mainspring of progress. Market expansion allowed for the expansion of known aspects of the division of labor which would otherwise be too costly. The enlargement of any one market generating increasing returns would create 'external economies' in other markets. Thus, a cumulative advance takes place with action and reaction via the division of labor and market expansion.

Despite the attention it received at the time of delivery, Young's paper has not been utilized for the purpose of constructing a new version of the economic paradigm. His insights and conclusions have not been followed, with the notable exception of Nicholas Kaldor (now Lord Kaldor), a former student of Young's at the London School of Economics. Partly this lapse is due to a succession of events which directed economists' attention to other problems: the onset of the worldwide depression, the monopolistic competition and Keynesian 'revolutions,' the outbreak of the Second World War and the subsequent postwar problems. Young's untimely death shortly after the Glasgow conference, before he had time to expand and elucidate his ideas, was a factor in the neglect. Kaldor, commenting upon Young's paper in a recent formal lecture states that it was premature: "it was so many years ahead of its time that the progress of economic thought passed it by. . . . Economists ceased to take notice of it long before they could grasp its full revolutionary implications. . . . It was partly also because its importance as a basic criticism of general equilibrium theory could not be appreciated at a time when that theory itself was not properly understood" (Kaldor 1972, 1243).

Shortly before making his presidential appearance in Glasgow, Young had received a generous offer from the University of Chicago to become head of the department there at the end of his contract in London. His friend and former student, Frank Knight, was on the Chicago economics faculty. Young returned to the United States in December 1928 to attend the American Economic Association meeting in Chicago and to explain to Knight and others his decision to return to Harvard at the close of his London agreement. There was an influenza epidemic in England in the winter of 1929, and shortly after his return from America Young fell ill. He got up from his sick bed to deliver a talk on reparations at the Political Economy Club of London, of which he was an honorary member. He suffered a relapse and pneumonia set in. He died in the early morning of March 7, 1929. J. M. Keynes, in a letter of condolence to Mrs. Young on behalf of the Royal Economic Society, appended the following apt sentiments:

> I must add too a word on my account. I do not think we have ever met, but I knew your husband well. . . . His was the outstanding personality in the economic world and the most lovable. His influence as a teacher and a critic and as one who would always share

with others all his best ideas was far greater than anyone would suppose who knew only of his printed words; for it was his own work—unfortunately perhaps—which always came last.[20]

The author wishes to thank the following for helpful suggestions and pertinent criticisms: Professor A. W. Coats, Dr. Lauchlin Currie, Professor George J. Stigler, Professor E. T. Nevin. Above all, the author wants to acknowledge the encouragement, interest, and willing help of Lord Kaldor, King's College, Cambridge University, in this project. All errors of course are the sole responsibility of the writer. Partial financial support was received from the Old Dominion University Research Foundation.

Bibliography

MANUSCRIPT COLLECTIONS AND UNPUBLISHED MATERIALS

The Archives of the Inquiry, The National Archives, Washington, D.C.

Edward S. Mason, "History of the Harvard economics department."

Allyn A. Young Manuscripts, Archives of the Widener Library, Harvard University.

Allyn A. Young Collection, Archives of the Teachout Memorial Library, Hiram College, Hiram, Ohio.

PUBLISHED BOOKS AND PAPERS

Baker, Ray Stannard 1924. *Woodrow Wilson and the world settlement*, vol. 2. New York.

Burnett, Philip M. 1940. *Reparations at the Paris Peace Conference*, vol. 1. New York.

Chamberlin, Edward H. 1933. *The theory of monopolistic competition*. Cambridge, Mass.

Dorfman, Joseph 1969. *The economic mind in American civilization*, vol. 4. New York.

Ely, Richard T. 1938. *Ground under our feet*. New York.

Gelfand, Lawrence E. 1963. *The Inquiry*. New Haven.

Kaldor, N. (Lord Kaldor) 1972. "The irrelevance of equilibrium economics." *Economic Journal* 82: 1237–55.

Keynes, J. M. 1971. *The economic consequences of the peace*. In *The collected writings of J. M. Keynes*, vol. 2. London.

Knight, Frank H. 1921. *Risk, uncertainty and profit*. Chicago.

Mason, Edward S., "History of the Harvard economics department," *Quarterly Journal of Economics*, Aug. 1982.

Miller, David Hunter 1928. *My diary at the Paris Peace Conference*. Washington, privately printed.

Pigou, A. C. 1912. *Wealth and welfare*. London.

———1920. *Economics of welfare*. London.

Robbins, Lionel (Lord Robbins) 1971. *Autobiography of an economist*. London.

Schumpeter, Joseph A. 1937. "Allyn A. Young." in *Encyclopedia of the Social Sciences* (New York), 15: 514–15.

———1959. *History of economic analysis*. New York.

20. J. M. Keynes to Mrs. Allyn A. Young, 17 March 1929, AAY COL., Letters of Condolence folder.

Seymour, Charles 1965. *Letters from the Paris Peace Conference*. New Haven.

Shotwell, James T. 1937. *At the Paris Peace Conference*. New York.

Sraffa, Piero 1926. "The laws of return under competitive conditions." *Economic Journal* 36: 535–50.

Tugwell, Rexford G., ed. 1924. *The trend of economics*. New York.

Young, Allyn A. 1900. "The comparative accuracy of different forms of quinquennial age groups." *Publications of the American Statistical Association* 7 (1900–1901): 27–39.

———1911. "Some limitations of the value concept." *Quarterly Journal of Economics* 25: 409–28.

———1913. "Pigou's Wealth and Welfare." *Quarterly Journal of Economics* 27: 672–86.

———1914. "Depreciation and rate control." *Quarterly Journal of Economics* 38: 630–63.

———1917. "National statistics in war and peace." *Publications of the American Statistical Association* 16 (1917–18): 873–85.

———1919. "The economics of the treaty." *New Republic* 21 (1919–20): 388–89.

———1921. "The economic settlement." In Edward M. House and Charles Seymour, eds., *What really happened at Paris*. New York.

———1922. "The United States and reparations." *Foreign Affairs* 1 (1922–23): 35–47.

———1924. "The trend of economics, as seen by some American economists." *Quarterly Journal of Economics* 39 (1924–25): 155–83.

———1925. "Papers relating to political economy." *American Economic Review* 15: 721–24.

———1927a. "Hungary in 1925." In Allyn A. Young, *Economic problems new and old* (Boston), pp. 37–62.

———1927b. "Economics and war." In Allyn A. Young, *Economic problems new and old* (Boston), pp. 1–20.

———1928. "Increasing returns and economic progress." *Economic Journal* 38: 527–42.

[7]

History of Political Economy 17:1

CCC 0018–2702/85/$1.50

German economists and the Depression of 1929–1933

Michael Hudson

I

The controversy as to Keynes's significance in the history of economic thought has proceeded along two lines of inquiry which, though clearly interrelated, have often been undertaken separately: his contribution to economic analysis, and that to public policy. I shall be concerned primarily with the latter, though in explaining the policy responses made by German economists to the Depression it will be necessary to devote some space to explaining the nature of the model of economic fluctuations with which they worked and the policy conclusions to which those models gave rise. Secondly, in this article I shall be concerned only with *economists*, i.e., professional economists working in the universities and similar type of institutions and publishing the results of their research mainly (but not wholly) in the learned journals and in books clearly intended primarily for other 'academic' economists. The distinction I am drawing is rather similar to that drawn by Schumpeter between economic analysis and economic opinion, where 'economic opinion' as defined by Schumpeter is "the sum total of all the opinions and desires concerning economic subjects, especially concerning public policy bearing upon these subjects that, at any given time and place, float in the public mind," and is unconnected "with any attempt to improve our conceptual apparatus."[1] Obviously, a full analysis of policy responses to the Depression would have to take into account the proposals emanating from that 'economic opinion,' but that is not our concern here.

Moreover, there are inevitably some economists 'active' during the period whose categorisation as either academic or non-academic is equally problematical. Of these, the most famous is probably Wilhelm Lautenbach, sometimes referred to as the German Keynes. In Röpke's words, "in a completely independent way he had already at the beginning of the thirties . . . developed a theory of economic dynamics which paralleled Keynes's way of thinking and was superior to it in many respects in precision, clarity

Correspondence may be addressed to the author, School of Economic Studies, The University of Leeds, Leeds LS2 9JT, England.

1. J. A. Schumpeter, *History of economic analysis* (New York, 1959), 38–39.

and conciseness."[2] But Lautenbach did not publish a great deal, and what influence he did exert on German economic thinking at the time flowed from his personal contacts with other German economists and from his rather shadowy role as *Referent* in the Economic Ministry.[3] In addition, there are several academic economists whose claims to have been anticipators of Keynes have recently been advanced: Ferdinand Grünig,[4] Carl Föhl,[5] and Fritz Mann,[6] the latter of whom believed himself to have anticipated Keynes's fiscal policy.[7] The main problem involved in assessing the claims of such economists is that there is little evidence that they played a noticeable role in the public discussion between economists about policy which is the subject of the present article.[8] Finally, it is also significant that in the compilation of documents by Bombach,[9] aimed at showing the state of the discussion on employment policy in Germany before Keynes, only at most four out of the nine authors excerpted are economists in the sense defined above, and the views of two of the former (Donner and Neisser) are specifically instanced in what follows. In a complete study of economic thought in Germany in the early thirties, which the present author is at present involved in attempting to write, these and many other writers will deserve a full examination of their views.

Finally, we are not concerned directly with the *validity* of the analytical apparatus employed by German economists, or of the policy conclusions at which they arrived during that time, but with (a) what precisely that apparatus and those conclusions *were*, and (b) to what extent, if at all, these conclusions flowed from a body of analysis which may be regarded as Keynesian. In short, the mere advocacy of the necessity of public works

2. Wilhelm Röpke, 'Vorwort' to Wilhelm Lautenbach, *Zins, Kredit und Produktion*, ed. Wolfgang Stützel (Tübingen, 1952), p. ix.

3. Ibid.; and Walter Eucken, *Unser Zeitalter der Misserfolge* (Tübingen, 1951), 34. For a revealing anecdote about Lautenbach's views, see Gottfried Haberler, 'Critical notes on rational expectations,' *Journal of Money, Credit and Banking* 12, 4 (Nov. 1980, part 2):834.

4. Ferdinand Grünig, *Der Wirtschaftskreislauf* (Munich, 1933).

5. Carl Föhl, *Geldschöpfung und Wirtschaftskreislauf* (Munich, 1937).

6. Fritz Karl Mann, *Die Staatswirtschaft unserer Zeit* (Jena, 1930)

7. Ibid. ch. 3, according to a communication from an anonymous referee.

8. The lack of success on the part of the present author in finding evidence for such participation is also characteristic of two recent and broader studies in German relating to the same period. Thus, merely to take Mann as an example, Krohn emphasises Mann's prominence in the field of public finance, but refers only to his 1929 work, *Deutsche Finanzwirtschaft*, not to that of 1930 referred to note 6 above. Similarly, in the section of Krause and Rudolph's book dealing with the Weimar period, Mann does not figure among the extremely large number of economists cited. See Claus-Dieter Krohn, *Wirtschaftstheorien als politische Interessen* (Frankfurt/New York, 1981); and Werner Krause and Günther Rudolph, *Grundlinien des ökonomischen Denkens in Deutschland* (Berlin [East], 1980), ch. 4. This is not to say that the claims of Mann et al. to theoretical priority are without foundation, but merely to reiterate the point about the scope of the present article made in the text.

9. G. Bombach, ed., *Der Keynesianismus II. Die beschäftigungs-politische Diskussion vor Keynes in Deutschland. Dokumente und Kommentare* (Berlin/Heidelberg/New York, 1976).

expenditure on a larger or smaller scale during the period 1929–33 will not be regarded in this context as having any direct bearing on the problem posed in this article.

Thus, Garvey in his 1975 article specifically focuses on "the economic policy guides which have entered history as 'Keynesian' rather than the theoretical underpinning for these prescriptions," and states that "they [were] not presented within the framework of an elaborate and original theoretical analysis."[10] In terms of the Schumpeterian distinction with which we are working, it is largely 'economic opinion' which is being discussed by Garvey, rather than 'economic analysis.' To analyse the policy proposals of German economists in the depression of 1929/33 is therefore to link directly with the work on Keynes and his predecessors which has been so fruitfully conducted in recent years by T. W. Hutchison[11] and J Ronnie Davis[12] for Britain and the United States respectively.

II

There is little dispute that the policies which governments actually followed during the onset and deepening of the depression were actively deflationary in their effects, consisting as they usually did of sharp rises in taxation and cuts in expenditures in an attempt to restore budgetary balance, and wage and other cuts to overcome downward rigidities that had allegedly developed in the economy. The German Government's actions were wholly within this framework, at least until late 1932. Thus, in a succession of emergency decrees under Article 48 of the Constitution and other legislative acts, the Brüning Government introduced compulsory reductions in the prices of trade-marked goods and those of cartellised branches of industry, and in interest rates, wages and salaries, and rents. Similarly, to restore budgetary balance, various taxes, tariffs, and charges for government services were raised, some several times—e.g., turnover, income, and wealth taxes; taxes on beer, tobacco, sugar, and vehicles; duties on coffee, tea, and oil; and contributions to unemployment insurance. As well, new taxes were introduced. Finally, in an attempt to further reduce expenditure, wages and salaries for government employees were cut, the benefit rates on unemployment benefits reduced, and payments under pensions, etc., lowered.[13] The evidence of similar behaviour by other governments during this period is plentiful.

10. George Garvey, 'Keynes and the economic activists of pre-Hitler Germany,' *Journal of Political Economy* 83.2 (April 1975):395.

11. T. W. Hutchison, *On revolutions and progress in economic thought* (Cambridge, 1978), chs. 5–6.

12. J. Ronnie Davis, *The new economics and the old economists* (Ames, Iowa, 1971), 7, 153.

13. Horst Sanmann, 'Daten und Alternativen der deutschen Wirtschafts- und Finanzpolitik in der Ära Brüning,' *Hamburger Jahrbuch für Wirtschafts- und Gesellschaftspolitik*, 10. Jhrg. (1964–65):114–15.

It must be emphasised that the operative phrase in this context is "within this framework," for it cannot reasonably be argued that the economic policy being conducted by governments *at any time* simply constitutes a translation of the then-dominant economic theory into practice. In the case of Germany, in particular, there is powerful evidence that Brüning's drastically deflationary policy and defence of the exchange rate were adopted at least in part for reasons of foreign policy. Thus, when Brüning believed that reparations might finally be eliminated by showing that Germany simply was unable to pay them, despite the efforts it was undertaking to do so, it was obviously inconsistent with this aim to embark upon a deficit-financed program of job creation at a time when no other country (and especially among Germany's creditors) was doing so.[14]

This reservation becomes of particular significance if the question is then posed: Were such actions by governments actually in line with the policy proposals being advanced by *economists* at the time? For Britain and the United States at least, the works of Hutchison and Davis cited above suggest strongly that this question must be answered in the negative. For British economists, for example, Hutchison has shown that there was a wide degree of consensus as to the need for government to undertake actively reflationary policies, and only little support for wage cuts.[15] For the United States, one of the most striking examples, precisely because probably one of the least predictable, was provided by Irving Fisher: not merely did he argue that monetary policy would largely be ineffective given the depth the depression had reached, but he also rejected balancing the budget as the "misapplication of the principles of sound economics."[16] More generally for the United States, Davis concluded that "the policy of the 'new' economics and the policy of the 'old' economics during the 1930's seem to have been remarkably alike."[17]

III

That there was a wide body of resistance in Germany to the deflationary actions of German governments between 1929 and 1933 is clear. It is equally clear that it was voiced by circles of economic opinion who were very far indeed from being outsiders in the sense of (say) Silvio Gesell. Grotkopp's[18] work and the compilation of documents by Bombach,[19] as well as Garvey in his article,[20] show the respectability of many of the

14. Knut Borchardt, 'Zwangslagen und Handlungsspielräume in der grossen Wirtschaftskrise der frühen dreissiger Jahre: Zur Revision des überlieferten Geschichtsbildes,' *Jahrbuch der Bayerischen Akademie der Wissenschaften 1979* (Munich, 1979), 96.

15. Hutchison, op. cit.

16. Michael Hudson, 'Irving Fisher's plan for the stabilisation of the dollar: a study in monetary theory and history.' Unpublished Ph.D. thesis, University of Leeds, 1977.

17. Davis, 153.

18. Wilhelm Grotkopp, *Die Grosse Krise* (Düsseldorf, 1954).

19. G. Bombach, op. cit.

20. See n. 7 above.

proponents of programs for large-scale public works advanced during the period. But what they also show is that very few of them were economists in the sense defined at the beginning of this article, although some "junior members of the academic community" did figure among them.

Our main concern must therefore be to relate the policy proposals being advanced by *economists* in Germany to the theoretical explanations they put forward as to the causation of 'business cycles' or fluctuations and the course they took. There have been many general surveys, both by contemporaries and by later writers,[21] of the general body of cycle theory prevalent at the time we are discussing, and here I set out a number of conclusions that may be drawn as to their general features.

(a) In all such theories, the proximate cause of the upswing and downswing is located in the behaviour of the producer-goods industries, especially in the 'disproportionalities' that emerge between those industries and the industries producing consumer goods in the course of the upswing. Thus, in what was probably the most famous of the 'monetary' theories of the cycle, Mises argued that, given the forcing down of the interest rate below a natural rate by the banking system, an upswing took place beginning from the producer-goods industries, since the more abundant and cheaper credit would go primarily to facilitating a rise in the demand for the product of such industries, hence lead to a rise in their output, and then extend itself to all other sectors of the economy. Yet during this process, Mises argues, a point will come at which 'overcapitalisation' now emerges: the essential conditions of saving and investment have remained unchanged, so 'too much' is being invested, especially in durable capital equipment, 'too much' in the sense that the actual level of demand for finished goods cannot possibly justify such an increase in the volume of equipment installed.[22] Even those who took an eclectic position, in which monetary factors played only a role (though a significant one) in inducing the upswing, agreed that such disproportionalities could be significant in still further intensifying the disturbances which would arise during an upswing from more fundamental features of an advanced capitalist economy: "the normal crisis ultimately stems from a false estimate of future possibilities of production or better of individual lines of production [i.e.] where such production is speculative in nature."[23]

(b) The various phases of the cycle, the sequence depression-upswing-

21. For contemporary surveys, see: Simon Kuznets, 'Monetary business cycle theory in Germany,' *Journal of Political Economy* 38.2 (April 1930); Rudolf Stucken, 'Neue deutsche Konjunkturliteratur,' *Zeitschrift für die gesamte Staatswissenschaft* 86.Bd. (1929). For a modern treatment, see T. W. Hutchison, *A review of economic doctrines, 1870–1929* (Oxford, 1953), ch. 23, "Crises and Cycles (II): From c. 1900."

22. Mises's views are thoroughly summarized in the article by Kuznets cited in n. 21 above.

23. Peter Quante, 'Arbeitsbeschaffung und Rentabilität,' *Schmollers Jahrbuch* 57.Jhrg. (1933), 1:42.

boom-crisis-downswing-depression, were regarded as inevitable. As Stucken put it, trade cycle theory assumed that "to every peak of activity a depression ensued, and to every depression an upswing."[24] Similarly, Baracs regards it as self-evident that the expansion of the economy always takes place cyclically.[25]

(c) All the theories employed 'equilibrium' models, and in two senses: (i) the initiation of the upswing required some *exogenous* shock;[26] and (ii) the system itself possessed adjustment mechanisms which would ultimately tend to restore the equilibrium that had been disturbed.

Perhaps the classical example of this reasoning appears in the Report of the Brauns-Kommission of 1931:

> The crisis is a necessary if also painful reaction by the economic organism to the violence done to it in the preceding boom. . . . Every crisis constitutes a self-cleansing process [and a] recovery can be reckoned upon with certainty.[27]

The cleansing function of the crisis is likewise a commonplace among cycle theorists. In Schumpeter's terms,

> the essence of what occurs in depression periods . . . is the fitting of the new into the organism of the economy, the elimination of what has ceased to be viable, and the re-organization of the system of values and prices of the economy, a *fumbling for a new equilibrium*.[28]

And the *causal* linkage between the various phases of the cycle is likewise regarded as inevitable: in particular, that between depression and upswing. In a formulation which combines both the inevitability of the crisis and the necessary consequence of a new upswing with this cleansing function, Quante writes:

> this period of downswing must be followed directly by a new upswing, since after the necessary "cleansing" of the system has occurred, after elimination of enterprises which have become unprofitable, and so on, a better balance can be found between supply and current demand.[29]

(d) This did not mean, however, that the fluctuations had to be accepted passively; the severity of the upswing and the violence of the downswing

24. Stucken, 147.

25. Johann Baracs, 'Zins, Kredit und Konjunktur,' *Archiv für Sozialwissenschaft und Sozialpolitik* 59 (1928):587.

26. Adolph Löwe, 'Wie ist Konjunkturtheorie überhaupt möglich?' *Weltwirtschaftliches Archiv* 24.2 (Oct. 1926).

27. Quoted in Wilhelm Röpke, 'Praktische Konjunkturpolitik: Die Arbeit der Brauns-Kommission,' *Weltwirtschaftliches Archiv* 34 (1931, no. 2): 427, 429.

28. Joseph Schumpeter, 'Dauerkrise?' *Der deutsche Volkswirt*, 25 Dec. 1931, 419.

29. Quante, 46.

could be and should be moderated, most particularly through measures of monetary policy.[30] It was in this context, in fact, that Keynes was very influential upon German economic thought, though it was, of course, the Keynes of the *Treatise*.[31]

Yet, despite the possibility of such amelioration, it is impossible to escape the conclusion that not merely was it believed that it was not possible to iron out fluctuations, but that also it would not actually be beneficial to do so. Schumpeter was not the only economist to argue that it was precisely during the upswing that there took place the new investment which raised the overall output capacity of the economy, and that not all such advances were lost in the subsequent crisis and depression.[32] Moreover, the crisis and depression were in their own way productive of health for the economic organism: they forced the elimination of obsolete methods of production and inefficient firms, spread the innovations through industry, and prepared the ground for the subsequent, inevitable, recovery.[33]

IV

That the system might not work with such automaticity, however, or that it might once have done so but did so no longer, was increasingly widely accepted by economists even before the Depression. At that time, concern was being expressed with 'structural,' i.e., long-run, unemployment rather than 'cyclical' or short-run, but some of the arguments which were to figure in later discussion were already being emphasised. The immediate stimulus to such concern was the relatively sluggish performance of the German economy in the 1920s, even abstracting from the upheavals of the immediate postwar period and the Great Inflation. Why was it, German economists asked, that even in such periods of upswing as the German economy had enjoyed during that time, the level of unemployment remained at relatively high levels?[34]

Saitzew, for example, argued that all the causes of long-term unemployment in the German economy during this period could be compounded into a single factor: the World War. But he then listed, as part of a more detailed discussion, the following factors: directly politically determined

30. Baracs, 589, even concludes that the proposition that the expansion of the economy need not be marked by recurrent crises if policy is appropriately applied during the upswing "belongs among the platitudes of modern business cycle theory."

31. For an extremely sympathetic review of Keynes's *Treatise*, see Wilhelm Röpke, 'Geldtheorie und Weltkrise,' *Der deutsche Volkswirt*, 25 Sept. 1931, 1742–47.

32. Schumpeter, 'Dauerkrise,' 420. For a similar view of the 'normal' crisis, see Gerhard Colm, 'Wege aus der Weltwirtschaftskrise,' *Die Arbeit*, Heft 11, 8.Jhrg. (1931): 820.

33. Hans-Joachim Rüstow, in Franz Böse, ed., *Deutschland und die Weltkrise* (Munich/Leipzig, 1932), 87.

34. Deitmar Petzina and Werner Abelshauser, 'Zum Problem der relativen Stagnation der deutschen Wirtschaft in den zwanzigen Jahren,' in Hans Mommsen et al., *Industrielles System und politische Entwicklung in der Weimar Republik* (Düsseldorf, 1974).

causes, such as the imposition of reparations on the defeated nations; the emergence of new, competitive industries in markets previously supplied by Europe; the growth of neo-mercantilism; causes stemming directly from domestic industrial change—rationalisation, monopolisation, and technical progress; state intervention and social policy; the problems of agriculture; population changes; and the psychological factor.[35] The existence of an alleged scarcity of capital was also widely accepted. In the classic work on this subject by Welter, the scarcity was attributed to a wide range of factors, most notably the overall tax burden, its disincentive effects on ability and willingness to invest, the effect of cartellisation and state intervention in misallocating capital.[36] The meeting of the Verein für Sozialpolitik in 1932, on 'Germany and the World Crisis,' is a summarisation of all these themes.

The factors in this list that contemporary economists emphasised in their initial response to the Depression were monopolisation, and hence insufficient flexibility of commodity prices; and state intervention and social policy, which both made possible the creation of price rigidities and removed the necessary degree of flexibility from wages. In this period, therefore, it was to these phenomena that the economists turned to explain the depth of the Depression and its duration.

Those who emphasised state intervention and social policy as the root of the problem had a very simple diagnosis to offer and an equally simple policy conclusion to advance. As Alexander Rüstow, one of the architects of the later Social Market Economy argued:

> The basic point of all these [state] interventions and subsidies is usually that, if through structural change . . . the competitive conditions of any part of the national economy deteriorate, interventions are undertaken to compensate for this deterioration, to protect the economic sector concerned. The only possible behaviour in this situation is to do nothing at all, to let things work themselves out according to the maxim: laissez faire, laissez passer. . . . [Eventually, equilibrium will be restored] but . . . how long will it be till [then], and how great will be the sacrifices and injuries that will be inflicted upon those concerned in the meantime? . . . the capacity of the economy to resist, to suffer, has obviously been greatly underestimated. Certainly, if one had done nothing at all, with the sole exception of unemployment benefits, and let things run their course, the mischief would not have been remotely as great as it has become through the accumulation of perverse interventions.[37]

35. Manuel Saitzew, ed., *Die Arbeitslosigkeit der Gegenwart*, Schriften des Vereins für Sozialpolitik, 185/1 (Leipzig, 1932).

36. Erich Welter, *Die Ursachen des Kapitalmangels in Deutschland* (Tübingen, 1931), 197f.

37. Rüstow, *in* Böse, 62–64.

Similarly, Eucken argued that what was at basis an orderly, rule-governed economy had been plunged into anarchy by the capture of the state by powerful, organised interest-groups, chief among whom were, of course, workers and employers. The result is that the regulatory power of the free price had been greatly weakened, and the inherent tendency of the system to full employment had been eliminated:

> In an economy disorganised by the State in this way, an equilibrium on the market can occur at most fortuitously and disproportions must necessarily emerge.[38]

Schumpeter too may be counted among this group.[39] For Mises, finally, who saw the problem as stemming wholly from the privilege the banks possessed of creating credit, the issue was equally simple: to remove this privilege from them by imposing upon them the duty to maintain 100 percent cover for their note issue.[40]

Responses such as these may safely be regarded as considerably more extreme than most economists would have supported; but there *was* general agreement among them that, wherever possible, rigidities must be removed. And this implied that the Government should not merely cease to do certain things; it was also called upon to undertake purposive action. Especially: if wages had become rigid, and the price system thereby prevented from exercising its regulative function, they must be *forced* to fall. It may seem a caricature of this position to introduce the following quotation:

> Unemployment of *some duration* must *always* be traced back to an incorrect level of wages. For the wage has the property of being able to operate, with flexibility, as a regulator, and unemployment as a long-run phenomenon supplied irrefutable evidence that the wage has lost the capacity to do so.[41]

And even if unemployment has originated, not because the wage level was too high, but for some other reason,

> it is incorrect to say that, in such cases, the level of wages is not an issue. . . . For the wage is a price which as such reacts sensitively to all changes in economic circumstances—or better, should react.[42]

38. Walter Eucken, 'Staatliche Strukturwandlungen und die Krisis des Kapitalismus,' *Weltwirtschaftliches Archiv* 36 (1932, no. 2): 315.
39. Schumpeter, 'Dauerkrise,' 419.
40. Kuznets, 156.
41. Georg Halm, 'Zum Problem der Lohnsenkung,' *Schmollers Jahrbuch* 55 (1931, no. 2): 47.
42. Ibid.

But in terms of what most economists believed wages should be made to do, in the early stages of the Depression, it is by no means the most extreme statement that can be found. Thus,

> Since the total income can be distributed among as many people as conceivable, and prices can fall as low as can be imagined, . . . there is only one limit to the fall in prices that can be brought about: when the *last* unemployed worker has found work and the last piece of equipment seeking employment has found it. . . . So long as there is an *excess* supply of workers, equipment and commodities, price cuts are possible and necessary.[43]

There is little evidence, therefore, that the first deflationary steps of the Brüning Government met with any significant resistance among economists. Nor, more significantly, when the current of opinion in the profession later changed, was there any departure from the basic principle that 'loosening,' i.e., removal of rigidities especially on the side of wages, must take place alongside and supplementing measures of re-expansion. The one argument I have discovered in relation to price and wage cuts during this period involves, not whether such cuts were necessary or desirable, but rather precisely *what prices* should be lowered.[44]

In what may be regarded as a middle-of-the-road analysis, Heinrich Mannsteadt (Professor at Rostock) began by affirming that, as soon as unemployment takes on or threatens to take on the character of a long-run phenomenon, this shows that the price mechanism is being prevented from fulfilling its role as the central adjustment mechanism of economic life. The obstacles to its doing so, he continued, were mainly to be found in (a) the larger burden of fixed costs arising from the preceding rationalisation movement in German industry, but also from increased taxes and social security impositions; and (b) the growth of monopolistic organisations on the part of both the employer (e.g. cartels) and employees (e.g. trade unions). The conclusion he drew as following from this analysis was that a policy of wage and price cuts was now essential.[45]

V

The shift to active advocacy of public works programmes among German economists came from 1931 onwards, when unemployment continued to rise and both directly and indirectly was seen to constitute a threat to

43. Otto Conrad, 'Die Möglichkeiten einer Erweiterung des Arbeitsbedarfes,' *Jahrbücher für Nationalökonomie und Statistik* 138 (1933): 46.

44. Fritz Machlup, 'Zur Frage der Ankurbelung durch Kreditpolitik,' *Zeitschrift für Nationalökonomie* 4 (1933); Alfred Amonn, 'Zur gegenwärtigen Krisenlage und inflationistischen Krisenbekämpfungspolitik,' *Zeitschrift für Nationalökonomie* 5 (1934).

45. Heinrich Mannsteadt, '*Lohn- und Preissenkungspolitik im Lichte der Wirtschaftswissenschaften* (Jena, 1931).

the maintenance of the present system. As Dobretsberger summed up the shift:

> the creation of jobs requires an immediate solution without respect to the other problems which economic policy faces; for the fate of millions of unemployed, the burden which has been imposed on the trade unions since the beginning of the deflationary policy, the strain placed on the State budget by subsidies for social insurance etc., cannot be maintained for as long as necessary to allow the success of overall stabilisation policy to emerge or the automatic easing of the position to occur. The urgency of an "emergency aid" [is evident], even if it is purely a temporary one not founded in economic principle.[46]

What may also have played a role in this respect, it has been suggested by Borchardt, is that the economic crisis *until mid-1931* appeared to the German authorities and the economists to be no different *in essence* from others in Germany's preceding economic history. It had not begun in any sense dramatically, and in the first few months of 1931 some signs of upswing had actually appeared to have shown themselves. It was only with the monetary collapse of summer 1931 that the realisation grew that this might not be a crisis of the 'usual' type and that direct government intervention to reflate the economy, or at least to check the downward movement, was now called for.[47] The advocacy of public works expenditure for the purpose now grew in volume and respectability.

The theory developed to justify such public works expenditures began with an attempt to answer the question, Why had unemployment continued to rise and no signs of recovery appeared? The argument from rigidities now looked inadequate, though not irrelevant: wages and prices *had* fallen—under the pressure both of systematic forces and of the markedly deflationary policy of the Brüning Government—and yet the economy continued to decline. There must be, it was concluded, some other reason for this.

That reason was found in the theory of 'secondary deflation.' The primary deflation, it was argued, had been prolonged by the rigidities that had become characteristic of the system; but they had by now largely been weakened, or the depth of the depression could no longer be explained by their existence: what had happened is that the primary deflation had given way to a purely destructive downward spiral, the 'secondary deflation.' Röpke[48] gives probably the most concise analysis of what the second de-

46. Josef Dobretsberger, 'Bemerkungen zu den Arbeitsbeschaffungs-plänen,' *Jahrbücher für Nationalökonomie und Statistik* 137, 3.Folge, 82 (1932, no. 2): 261.

47. Borchardt, 91–93.

48. Wilhelm Röpke, 'Trends in German business cycle policy,' *Economic Journal*, Sept. 1933. See also the comment by Otto Donner in 'Voraussetzungen und Konsequenzen öffentlichen Arbeitsbeschaffung': "The opponents of work creation now find themselves on the

flation involved and I shall follow him here, though other economists arguing in a similar fashion will be cited at various places in what follows.

Röpke agrees with those he calls the "restrictionists" that the primary crisis may truly be regarded as the unavoidable form in which the process of liquidation and adaptation takes place, so that a policy designed to counteract it merely results in a prolongation and intensification of the crisis. But the secondary deflation is due to totally different causes: in particular, the circular flow of income is interrupted by hoarding, as a general collapse of confidence takes place. Firms maintain themselves in as liquid a position as possible, instead of using their income to replace old equipment or for new investment; householders are unwilling to spend such incomes as they do obtain for consumption, but save it instead. In this situation, any attempt by producers to get rid of their surplus output by cutting prices, lowering costs, and cutting output is self-defeating: the general economic contraction is thereby merely widened. The result of this is to still further reduce confidence, which in turn serves as a kind of death blow to the willingness of entrepreneurs to undertake new investment. Moreover, Röpke sees the process, if left to itself, as eventually giving rise to an underemployment equilibrium: the rate of saving will have been pushed down to the level of the rate of investment by the impoverishment of consumers, and it will moreover become impossible, except at the cost of revolution, to continue with the budget-balancing exercise that has been conducted by governments up to this point. Hence, he concludes, "those are after all right who maintain that even the severest crisis will cease in the end"—provided, he adds, "the political and social framework will stand the formidable pressure" exerted by the secondary deflation.[49]

What emerges from this is in fact a theory of pump-priming: state initiative must replace private initiative if the system is to be set in motion again. But equally clearly, the implication of the theory seems to be this: once the secondary deflation has been overcome in this way, the creative destruction and unfreezing done by the primary deflation will ensure that the system will then expand of its own accord.

But why did Röpke and other economists end up with a theory of pump-priming? Why do they not suggest that the aim of policy should be to restore, at least, the cuts in government expenditure that have already taken place, especially on social expenditures, and proceed to run a budget deficit in this way? Two reasons were advanced. On the one hand, as part of the primary deflation process, these cuts had had an economic role to play, though their social effects were readily agreed to have been deplorable. Or, in Colm's terms: it has doubtless been necessary to cut expenditures

defensive . . . the paradox of yesterday becomes the commonplace of today." *Die deutsche Volkswirt* 7, no. 43 (1933):1221–23.

49. Röpke, 'Trends,' 438.

in order to adjust them to the diminished revenue of the Government and the increased claims on it for social purposes, and "a very desirable simplification and economy in administration has been achieved." On the other hand, to restore cuts in government expenditure, and even more to expand it, would imply that the government budget deficit would again increase, with subsequent effects on confidence.[50] A long-run factor also had a role to play here: one of the reasons advanced for the alleged "shortage of capital" during the 1920s had been government competition on the market for long-term funds. At the present time, when the effects of the bank crisis of 1931 and the general collapse of confidence had "frozen" the long-term capital market, budget deficits and the consequent need to finance them by borrowing would prevent the "unfreezing" of that market and keep interest rates at too high a level.[51] Moreover, if, under present circumstances, "even an interest rate approaching zero may be insufficient to induce entrepreneurs to enter upon new investment,"[52] it is restoration of the demand for commodities, rather than merely the supply of liquidity, that is the essential step to be taken. And it is the role of public works to do this. Even in this context, however, the need for caution was voiced: only when we can be sure that the economy has indeed reached its (depression equilibrium) lowest point should public works be embarked upon. While arguing that a rise in private investment requires a strengthening of confidence and that "work creation" was appropriate to achieve this, Donner concluded that it could only do this when all the "real presuppositions" for it to do so were fulfilled, i.e., if prices have ceased to decline, the credit markets are characterised by plentiful liquidity, and profitable investment opportunities have become available.[53]

What remains sacrosanct in all this is the exchange rate. In fact, since July 1931 Germany had to all intents and purposes been off the gold standard; but an equally important political fact was that the German exchange rate was in effect part of a system of international treaty obligations and could not be freely (unilaterally) altered.[54] But the basic economic argument against devaluation was that given the high degree of commodity stocks and excess capacity currently existing, there was no reason why there should be any upward pressure on the price level for some time; hence a devaluation was unnecessary. Even more, a devaluation would be *fatal* to the success of the expansionary policy; given their experience of

50. Colm, 824.

51. Thus the Brauns-Kommission's proposals for the floating of a large long-term *foreign* loan to finance its public works recommendations.

52. Röpke, 'Trends,' 436.

53. Donner, 1221.

54. Gert Hardach, 'Währungskrise 1931: Das Ende des Goldstandards in Deutschland,' in Derek Aldcroft et al., *Finanz- und wirtschaftspolitische Fragen der Zwischenkriegszeit* (Berlin, 1973).

inflation in 1923/24, the German population would respond rapidly and adversely to any currency change, and the resultant shock to confidence would outweigh the expansionary effects of the job-creation activities.[55] The significance of maintaining confidence in the stability of the mark had implications for the *scope* of the reflationary activities as well; e.g., Neisser, while arguing for a change in the legislation governing the activities of the Reichsbank so as to permit it to undertake open-market operations, nevertheless concludes that it must be granted to the Bank only under stringent provisions, so that it cannot undertake "inflationary" credit expansions; and precisely the same was argued by Colm for the extent of credit-financed public works.[56] Similarly, Marschak argued that a limit must be set right from the beginning to the granting of credit to public authorities and that such credit must be suspended as soon as a rise in private confidence has occurred.[57]

Of course, given the recent experience of the 1923–24 Great Inflation, the desire to see that any credit expansion for public works should not create dangers for the stability of the mark is quite explicable, as is the explicit ruling-out of devaluation. But it meant inevitably that rather narrow limits were set to any reflation that Germany might undertake independently of the course of economic activity in other nations. Once again, Donner posed the issue squarely:

> in the long run, the only way out for the country conducting work creation is either to check its upswing to protect its currency, or else to clear the path for its upswing by devaluing its currency to the extent that its prices have risen relatively to those abroad.[58]

Yet although exchange control had been operative since mid-1931, too open an advocacy of devaluation was also sheered away from by economists, since it would give aid and comfort to a group, the autarkists, with whom most economists (and, for that matter, most writers on economic affairs) had little sympathy.[59]

VI

Röpke claimed that his views reflected majority opinion among German economists of the time, with Donner adding that "the paradox of yesterday has become the commonplace of today," and the opponents of work crea-

55. Colm, loc. cit.; Hans Neisser, 'Ankurbelung oder Inflation?' *Der deutsche Volkswirt* 6.3 (1932).

56. Ibid.

57. Jacob Marschak, 'Einige Thesen zur Krisenpolitik,' *Wirtschaftsdienst*, Heft 51, 18 Dec. 1931, 2042.

58. Donner, 1223.

59. See Grotkopp, 210 f.

tion finding themselves now on the defensive.[60] It would be interesting to test these claims, though it is significant (a) that Röpke later became a bitter opponent of Keynes and especially of Keynesians, for the stimulus the Keynesian theory had given to inflationary activities on the part of the State:[61] and (b) that the contemporary reception among German economists for *The general theory* was a very negative one.[62] But it is in fact unnecessary for the purposes of this article to undertake such a test. For even if Röpke's claim was true, and the majority of German economists were in agreement with his views and those of the other economists cited, the basic problem would still remain: To what extent was the type of analysis Keynesian in the more formal sense referred to in page 36 above? To ask this question is immediately to raise another and far more intensively debated question: What does Keynes *really* mean?

The framework provided by Leijonhufvud in his article 'Effective demand failures'[63] seems to represent almost a summary of the views of the economists involved. He argues that if the system is displaced far enough from its full coordination path, i.e., moves outside what he calls the "corridor," the system's homeostatic mechanisms become weaker until at some point they may be so weak that "for all practical purposes the Keynesian 'unemployment equilibrium' is as sensible a representation of its state as economic statics will allow." Within the corridor, on the other hand, the self-adjusting mechanisms work well. Clearly, this was precisely the structure of argument employed by German economists: the primary deflation process sees the system's own adjustment mechanisms working to push the system back toward equilibrium; once the deflation has gone over into a secondary process, however, the system is outside the corridor. However, Leijonhufvud argues, the self-adjusting forces may be prevented from operating by "institutional obstacles [which] intervene to make them ineffective at some point": in the contemporary discussion, state intervention and social policy had acted to prevent the forces of wage and price flexibility from working. Finally, within the corridor, Leijonhufvud sees the presumption as being in favour of "monetarist" propositions, outside it in favour of "fiscalist"; the contemporary discussion is very interested in monetary policy as a means of smoothing out the more violent fluctuations of the business cycle as it follows its normal course, but eventually plumps for fiscal policy during the secondary deflation, for it then sees monetary policy as having become quite ineffective. There thus exists a high degree of correspondence between the model constructed by Leijonhufvud and

60. See n. 31 above.

61. Grotkopp, 237.

62. Krause & Rudolph (n. 8 above), ch. 4.

63. Axel Leijonhufvud, 'Effective demand failures,' *Swedish Journal of Economics* 75 (March 1973).

the progression in policy proposals advanced by German economists in 1929–33.

It follows, then, that if Leijonhufvud's model can be regarded as catching the essentials of Keynes's analysis, we appear to have a group of economists who, in the formal analytical sense, are Keynesians before Keynes. However, one problem immediately arises: the type of analysis they present is fundamentally one of pump-priming. The system behaves well enough normally; indeed, in the 'primary phase' of the downswing, there takes place a loosening-up of rigidities that have developed. It is only when the economy moves into a secondary deflation that state intervention is necessary. The state's function is then simply to get the mechanism working again in the way in which it normally does, after which state intervention appears to once again become unnecessary. To apply the phrase 'pump-priming' to this type of analysis therefore seems reasonable, and it is interesting to note that Röpke himself is usually credited with introducing into economic discourse in Germany an equivalent phrase (*Initialzündung*).[64]

But was this what Keynes really 'meant'? Davis would appear to imply a negative response to this question, when he says that "as late as mid-1934, Keynes was still a pump-primer," since the implication is that it is not pump-priming we find in Keynes's mature work,[65] and this is surely a view that would find ample support in (e.g.) Keynes's 1937 article.[66]

The question whether there were Keynesians before Keynes in Germany by 1933 can then admit of two responses, one positive and one which must remain open until the economics profession itself has arrived at consensus in the interpretation of Keynes's analysis. Positively, there *were* economists in Germany who by 1933 were advancing policies to combat the Depression which a later generation can agree upon in labelling 'Keynesian.' What a later generation will have yet to agree upon is whether those policies flow from, are based upon, an analysis similar to that presented by Keynes.

64. Helmut Marcon, *Arbeitsbeschaffungspolitik der Regierungen Papen und Schleicher* (Bern and Frankfurt a.M., 1974), 45.

65. Davis, 144.

66. J. M. Keynes, 'The general theory of employment,' *Quarterly Journal of Economics*, Feb. 1937.

[8]

History of Political Economy 18:4

CCC 0018-2702/86/$1.50

Hayek's Ricardo effect: a second look

Laurence S. Moss and Karen I. Vaughn

I. *Introduction*

In this article we review a long-standing controversy in twentieth-century economic thought: the debate over Hayek's Ricardo effect. Hayek developed his interpretation of the Ricardo effect in the context of his theory of business cycles primarily in the late 1930s and early 1940s. At that time Hayek's use of the familiar proposition was held up to close scrutiny by many talented critics, including Nicholas Kaldor, H. D. Dickinson, and R. G. Hawtry, all of whom, according to Hayek, failed to understand what he was saying.[1] In each case Hayek countered their criticism with a restatement of his proposition which in turn failed to satisfy the critics.[2] Indeed, this apparent miscommunication was still taking place as late as 1969 when Hayek wrote his last piece on the Ricardo effect in answer to a criticism leveled by Sir John Hicks.

Correspondence may be addressed to Professor Moss, Dept. of Economics, Babson College, Babson Park (Wellesley) MA 02157-0901; or to Professor Vaughn, Dept. of Economics, George Mason University, 4400 University Drive, Fairfax VA 22030.

1. A partial list of English language writers includes, in chronological order, Nicholas Kaldor, 'Capital intensity and the trade cycle,' *Economica*, Feb. 1939, 40–66, reprinted in idem, *Essays on economic stability and growth* (Glencoe, Ill., 120–47; Tom Wilson, 'Capital theory and the trade cycle,' *Review of Economic Studies* 7 (1938–40): 169–79; H. D. Dickinson, Review of Hayek's *Freedom and the economic system*, in *Economica*, Nov. 1940, 435–37; R. G. Hawtrey, 'The trade cycle and capital intensity,' *Economica*, Feb. 1940, 1–22; Hugh Townshend, Review of Hayek's *Profits, interest and investment*, in *Economic Journal*, March 1940, 99–103; Nicholas Kaldor, 'Professor Hayek and the concertina effect,' *Economica*, Nov. 1942, 359–82, reprinted in idem, *Essays on economic stability*, 148–76; Sho-Chieh Tsiang, *Variations of real wages and profit margins in relation to the trade cycle* (London, 1947), reprinted, W. Germany, 1970; Sho-Chieh Tsiang, 'Rehabilitation of time dimension of investment in macrodynamic analysis,' *Economica*, Aug. 1949, 204–17; William J. Baumol, 'Income effect, substitution effect, Ricardo effect' *Economics*, Feb. 1950, 69–80; Friedrick Lutz and Vera Lutz, *The theory of investment of the firm* (Princeton, 1951), 137–42; R. G. Hawtrey, *Capital and employment* (1937; London, 1952), 248–255; John Hicks, 'The Hayek story,' in idem *Critical essays in monetary theory* (Oxford, 1967), 203–15; Mark Blaug, *Economic theory in retrospect* (Homewood, Ill., 1968), 543–48; Walter Adolf Johr, 'Note on Professor Hayek's "True theory of unemployment,"' *Kyklos* 30 (1977): 713–723; and David H. Howard, Review of Hayek, *Denationalisation of money, Journal of Monetary Economics* 3 (1977): 483–85.

2. Hayek adopted the name 'Ricardo effect' toward the end of the 1930s, but the effect itself is discussed in some detail in the following references: F. A. Hayek, *Prices and production* (London, 1935), 69–100 and 148–57; idem, *Profits, interest and investment* (London, 1939), 3–71; idem, 'A comment,' *Economica*, Nov. 1942, 383–85; idem, 'Three elucidations of the Ricardo effect,' *Journal of Political Economy*, 1969, 274–85.

The purpose of our article is to discover whether in this debate it was Hayek who was out of step with the profession or the profession that was out of step with Hayek. We shall argue that the reason that Hayek's argument seemed so elusive to his contemporary colleagues (and some later critics) was that his method of analysis was foreign to their way of thinking. While English economists in the 1930s (especially after Keynes published the *General theory*) were concerned primarily with the static problem of balancing income and expenditure flows at acceptable levels of employment, Hayek was attempting to develop a dynamic theory of business cycles that involved tracing out the path of adjustment of the capital stock of an economy from one equilibrium state to another. This problem of describing the transitional process only became the subject of serious professional attention long after the debate over the Ricardo effect was concluded.[3]

In the course of our exposition, we will demonstrate that Hayek's Ricardo effect was not, in Blaug's words, "only another instance of the vice of neoclassical economics: the hasty application of static theorems to the real world."[4] Indeed, we shall argue that this is the *last* accusation one could logically hurl at Hayek's analysis. The very reason why Hayek encountered so much difficulty in communicating his message was precisely that he was not presenting an exercise in comparative statics but was rather hypothesizing a particular adjustment process where the final equilibrium state depended upon the particular path of adjustment followed in the economy.

In recent years the founders of the 'new classical economics' have praised the broad outlines of Hayek's approach to the business cycle. Robert Lucas pointed out that as early as 1929 Hayek articulated what remains today the single most important theoretical question in business cycle research. Hayek asked, How can cyclical phenomena be incorporated "into the system of economic equilibrium theory?"[5] Lucas goes on to regret the unfortunate Keynesian diversion of research effort from a thoroughgoing theory of the business cycle to what, in Lucas's words, is the "simpler question of the determination of output at a point in time."[6] It is well known that Hayek also regretted the unfortunate "Keynesian diversion" and resisted the redirection of research away from what he considered to be one of the most important macroeconomic questions: how production

3. E. Burmeister, *Capital theory and dynamics* (Cambridge, 1980).

4. Blaug, 548.

5. F. A. Hayek, *Monetary theory and the trade cycle* (London, 1933), 33 n. The German edition of Hayek's essay appeared in 1929. Cf. Robert E. Lucas, Jr., 'Understanding business cycles,' in K. Brunner and A. Meltzer, *Stabilization of the domestic and international economy* (Amsterdam, 1977), reprinted in R. Lucas, Jr., *Studies in business cycle theory* (Cambridge, Mass., 1981), 215.

6. Lucas, 215.

structures adjust to the underlying demand conditions and savings patterns of the community. It was this concern that made him wary of an economic theory that made it appear possible to push an economy into a perpetual state of boom.[7] He feared that instead of perpetual boom, inflationist policies would only result in short-term, illusory gains followed by a collapse with all of its undesirable macroeconomic effects.

Hayek's approach (much like the modern approach of Lucas and others) was to derive macroeconomic consequences from an analysis of the self-interested behavior of market participants. This was a continuation of the Misesian research program of reducing aggregative relationships to statements about individual action in markets.[8] Hayek's particular analytic structure combined elements of a Wicksellian cumulative expansion that included Cantillon effects with an 'Austrian' description of production as consisting of a succession of stages that had to be synchronized and coordinated with each other through appropriate price signals.[9] This framework allowed Hayek to argue that changes in the quantity of money would have non-neutral effects on individual prices and on the allocation of resources. All this led Hayek to admit the stimulative impact of Keynesian monetary policies but severely criticize the Keynesian claim that unemployment could be permanently cured by government-engineered expansions of aggregate demand. If governments try such engineering, they will be thwarted by the Ricardo effect.

We have organized our discussion as follows. In Section II we identify two uses of the Ricardo effect in Ricardo's *Principles,* each of which bears a certain similarity to the mechanism Hayek finally developed. In Section III, we trace the intellectual roots of Hayek's theory to the 'reverse movement' problem in the trade cycle theory of Ludwig von Mises. Mises' theory was itself a variant of the 'cumulative process' analysis first presented by K. Wicksell at the turn of the century. In Section IV, we summarize Hayek's main concern during the 1930s, that economic development required voluntary savings on the part of the economy and that government-created booms would prove to be self-defeating. The Ricardo effect served as the trigger that would bring on the crisis. In Section V we review the substance of the Hayek-Kaldor debate over the micro-

7. See for example the selected passages from Hayek's writings in F. A. Hayek and S. Shenoy, *A tiger by the tail* (London, 1972); idem, *Full employment at any price?* (London, 1975).

8. On the Misesian 'research program' see L. S. Moss and K. I. Vaughn, 'Ludwig von Mises and the Austrian tradition,' paper read at the 1980 meeting of the American Economic Association in Denver, MS; and L. S. Moss, 'The monetary economics of Ludwig von Mises,' in idem, *The economics of Ludwig von Mises: toward a critical reappraisal* (Kansas City, Mo., 1974), 13–49.

9. G. O'Driscoll, *Economics as a coordination problem* (Kansas City, Mo., 1977), pp. xv–xxi, 1–11. and 153–55.

foundations of the Ricardo effect. This debate was especially important to the development of Hayek's theory. It was by responding to Kaldor's formidable criticisms of that mechanism that Hayek finally realized why the comparative static approach based on perfect information was totally out of step with the type of phenomena Hayek was trying to model.

II. *Ricardo's Ricardo Effect*

As a proposition in comparative statics, the Ricardo effect compares two equilibrium states of the economy—before and after a change in relative factor prices has induced a switch in production techniques. As part of a dynamic theory, the Ricardo effect examines the path by which an economy reestablishes equilibrium after a disequilibrating shock to the system occurs. Both uses of the Ricardo effect appear in Ricardo's *Principles*, and both uses influenced Hayek in naming his own composite mechanism of relative price changes after the work of his English predecessor.[10] It may be helpful to explain the Ricardo effect as it appeared in Ricardo's *Principles* so as to better appreciate the way in which the mechanism functions in Hayek's trade cycle theory.

Comparative static statement

In his famous first chapter "On Value" in the *Principles*, Ricardo explained why the labor theory of relative commodity prices breaks down in a capital-using economy. It breaks down because of different durabilities of capital or, as Ricardo noted elsewhere, the varying role of time in the production of commodities.[11] More specifically, Ricardo demonstrated why a sudden across-the-board rise in wages must raise the prices of commodities manufactured with labor-saving machinery by a lesser amount than that same wage increase will raise the prices of commodities produced without any machinery at all. His analysis proceeded in two steps.

First, at the 'firm level,' the manager finds himself indifferent between two techniques of production, Technique A and Technique B, each capable of producing a given volume of output at the same identical cost. Technique A, consists of a $5,000 machine lasting one year and capable of performing 100 man-years of work. Technique B, consists of directly hir-

10. See David Ricardo, *On the principles of political economy and taxation*, in *The works and correspondence of David Ricardo* (Cambridge, 1951) 1:39–43, and 386–397. Hayek cited both places in Ricardo's *Principles* as the location of what he (Hayek) termed the 'Ricardo effect' (see Hayek, 'The Ricardo effect' in idem, *Individualism and economic order* (London, 1949) 220. O'Driscoll, a recent commentator, emphasized the dynamic Wicksellian nature of Hayek's analysis 'The specialization gap and the Ricardo effect: comment on Ferguson,' *History of Political Economy* 7.2 (1975): 268—but did not emphasize the close connection between the argument of Ricardo's machinery chapter and Hayek's Ricardo effect mechanism; cf. O'Driscoll, *Economics as a coordination problem*, 92–128.

11. David Ricardo, Letter to McCulloch, 13 June 1820; cf. P. Sraffa, Introduction to Ricardo, *Principles*, p. xlv.

ing 100 man-years of labor to do the work unaided by any machinery at all. At a supposed wage of $50 per man-year, both techniques cost $5,000. Ricardo explained that it is obviously a "matter of indifference" to the manager which of the two techniques is used.[12]

The second step of Ricardo's argument requires that we upset this state of indifference by supposing wages unexpectedly rise from $50 per man-year to $55 per man-year—a 10 percent rise in wages. Technique B, the labor-intensive technique, will now cost $5,500. The machine-intensive technique, Technique A, will also increase in price, but not by as much. The price of the machine cannot increase to $5,500 because if it was formerly profitable to sell those machines at $5,000 (the price of the machine prior to the rise in the price of labor), then each machine had to have contained *less than* 100 man-years of labor to allow for profits to the machine makers. As a general rule, a machine must contain less labor than it displaces, and so a rise in wages will raise its price by *less than* 10 percent.[13] Faced with a cheaper way of getting the work done, the manager will substitute the machine method for the direct-labor method of production.

Now moving from the firm level of analysis to the economic system as a whole, Ricardo was quite explicit about the role competition plays in keeping machine producers from increasing the prices of their machines by the full 10 percent. Such an effort would elevate profits among machine manufacturers above the going rate established by the productivity of marginal investments in agriculture.[14] This would create a situation in which an "unusual quantity of capital" would flow into machinery manufacture expanding the supply of machines and forcing their prices down.[15] Competitive forces would therefore drive the price of machines down again.

A corollary of Ricardo's argument is that the substitution of machinery for labor causes the prices of commodities produced with machines to decline relative to the prices of commodities produced entirely with direct labor. In other words the adoption of labor-saving machinery by capitalist-managers, in an effort to maximize profits, eventually results in a decline in specific consumer-goods prices.[16] Thus, we can summarize the conclu-

12. Ricardo, *Principles*, 40.

13. Ibid.

14. On Ricardo's so-called 'agricultural theory of profit' see P. Sraffa, Introduction to Ricardo, *Principles*, pp. xxx–xxxvii. For an application of that theory to how it 'regulates' the overall market rates on competing investments and a summary of the recent doctrinal debate surrounding that application, see L. S. Moss, 'Professor Hollander and Ricardian economics,' *Eastern Economical Journal* 5 (Dec. 1979): 503.

15. Ricardo, *Principles*, 41. Our discussion is entirely consistent with S. Hollander's claim that Ricardo's "intention" was to show that a once-and-for-all rise in wages would not raise the level of prices, but only alter relative commodity prices; cf. L. Moss, 'Professor Hollander and Ricardian economics,' 503–6.

16. Ibid. 37–38.

sions of the comparative static version of Ricardo's Ricardo effect as follows:

(i) A rise in wages will encourage managers to substitute machine-intensive for labor-intensive methods of production; and
(ii) In the new equilibrium position, the prices of consumer goods made with (labor-saving) machinery will decline relative to the prices of other commodities.[17]

The Ricardo effect in a dynamic context

Hayek refers to a second place in Ricardo's *Principles* to support his use of the Ricardo effect: Chapter 31 "On Machinery." In that now famous chapter, Ricardo addressed the problem of whether the introduction of a new technology could ever make workers worse off. Added only in the third edition, his surprising conclusion was that under certain circumstances, the introduction of a technological innovation could reduce the real wages of labor and lead to unemployment in the short run.[18] He argued that if the introduction of the new technology is sudden and there is no growth in the economy, the fact that labor will have to be diverted from the production of consumer goods to the production of capital will lead to a reduction in the real wage of labor and to reduced employment.[19] That is, during the transition period while new capital goods are being produced, less food can be produced with the same total resources as one had before. Hence in the next time period, workers find that there is less for them to buy with their money, reducing their real wages, and they find that some of the labor that was previously employed has now become 'redundant' because of the increased productivity of the new machinery. Here we have the germ of the idea that later appears in the Austrian theory of the boom—that capital-intensive methods of production cannot be instantly installed; rather, a costly transition period must be financed and this financing requires real savings on the part of the community. It was an idea, however, that Ricardo himself did not explore further.

After raising this extremely interesting problem about the process by

17. Although Ricardo did not specifically discuss the economic impact of a sudden decline in the wages of labor, we can infer from his comparative-static framework that a once-and-for-all decline in wages will encourage managers to substitute labor-intensive or direct methods of production (Technique B) for labor-saving (i.e., capital-intensive) methods of production (Technique A). Also, the decline in wages will bring about a decline in the prices of consumer goods made without machinery relative to the prices of consumer goods manufactured with the aid of machinery. This is the form of Ricardo's comparative-static theorem that most closely resembles the one Hayek tried to develop—see the text.

18. On the details of Ricardo's controversial chapter, see P. Sraffa, Introduction, pp. lvii–lx; and S. Hollander, 'The development of Ricardo's position on machinery,' *History of Political Economy* 3.1 (1971): 105–35.

19. Ricardo, *Principles*, 390.

which new capital goods are financed, Ricardo assured his readers that the practical significance of his example of an innovation crisis was slight. These conditions could occur only in an economy without net investment, and even then it would only be during the temporary transition period that the workers would experience distress.[20] As a practical matter, sudden switches from "circulating to fixed capital" occur concurrently with capital accumulation. This meant that there is typically enough real community savings available to sustain the flow of consumer goods while some labor is being diverted to constructing capital goods. In the context of capital accumulation all that happens is wages rise less quickly than they otherwise would. The financing of the new capital goods does not require that wages fall absolutely. Thus, with net investment, the introduction of new technology during the process of accumulation improves the economic welfare of the workers. The worker's wage is lower than it would otherwise be, but higher than it was in the past.

Hayek's version

As recently as 1969 Hayek articulated his Ricardo effect theorem that "an increase in the demand for consumer goods will lead (in conditions of full employment) to a decrease in the demand for the kind of investment goods appropriate only to more highly capital-intensive modes of production."[21] Hayek demonstrated that the Ricardo effect can be presented as a theorem in comparative statics by comparing two equilibrium positions identical in all respects except one—the ratio of product-to-factor prices is higher in one than in the other.[22] But as the rest of his 1969 restatement made clear, Hayek's Ricardo effect was employed to do a great deal more than simply compare the logic of choice under varying patterns of relative prices. The raison d'être of the mechanism was to explain why the end of the boom phase of the trade cycle nearly always consists of a depression.

Much as Ricardo had used his proposition to draw out the possible disequilibrium consequences of the attempt to introduce a new technology before adequate savings are available, Hayek used the Ricardo effect as an important component of a dynamic theory of the trade cycle to elucidate the implications of a disequilibrium phenomenon. Drawing on the comparative static proposition in Ricardo's chapter I, Hayek employed the notion that changing real factor prices induce entrepreneurs to switch from labor-saving methods of production back to labor-intensive methods, thereby ending the boom. But what is it that caused the factor prices to change in the first place? As early as 1931 Hayek elaborated that success-

20. Ibid. 395.

21. F. A. Hayek, 'Three elucidations of the Ricardo effect,' 275–77. See also Hayek, *Profits, interest and investment*, 3–72.

22. Hayek, 'Three elucidations,' 275–76.

fully switching from a labor-intensive to a labor-saving technology requires that there be a diversion of national product from consumption to investment so as to "finance the transition." According to Hayek it was "voluntary savings" that provided this "diversion" and nothing else could do as well. An inflationary process seldom succeeds, because it relies on "forced savings" rather than voluntary savings, and forced saving is rarely if ever adequate. As we shall explain below the inadequacy of forced savings manifests itself in a change in factor prices ultimately inducing the switch back to labor-intensive methods of production and the crises.

Hayek referred his readers to *both* chapters in Ricardo's writings to support his analysis. Several commentators compare Hayek's mechanism to Ricardo's first version and fail to emphasize the close connection between the argument of Ricardo's chapter "On Machinery" and the central problem of Hayek's theory.[23] In addition to the influence of Ricardo's *Principles* on Hayek, we must also consider the impact of a particular unresolved problem in the so-called Austrian theory of the business cycle on Hayek's thinking about economic problems.

III. *The Reverse Movement Problem*

During the 1920s Ludwig von Mises' 'circulation-credit' theory of the business cycle (now commonly called the 'Austrian' theory) was widely regarded as the most important of the contributions of the younger generation of Austrian writers to modern, neoclassical economics.[24] Mises took issue with the phenomenon Wicksell described in his *Interest and prices* of a steady and evenly accelerating increase in prices so long as the market rate of interest is held below the natural rate and the quantity of money steadily increased.[25] According to Mises the injection of new money into the economy has to raise certain prices ahead of others as entrepreneurs try to construct more capital-intensive investment projects. When new money enters the economy through the loan market, after a period of economic expansion consumer-goods prices will rise ahead of wages, and this will encourage entrepreneurs to substitute labor-intensive for capital-intensive techniques of production. This will discourage the sales of capital

23. Except for this omission, see G. P. O'Driscoll's useful critique of Ferguson's remarks about Hayek's version of the Ricardo effect in 'The specialization gap and the Ricardo effect.' Hayek refers to both of Ricardo's versions in 'The Ricardo effect,' *Economica* 34 (May 1942): 127–152 n. 3. One major difference between the two versions has to do with Ricardo's suggestion that technological changes induce the substitution of machines for labor, while Hayek's analysis is restricted to a choice of techniques that is induced by a change in factor prices.

24. G. Haberler, *Prosperity and depression* (Geneva: League of Nations, 1941), 33–35; H. S. Ellis *German monetary theory 1905–1933* (Cambridge, Mass., 1934), 335–74.

25. Knut Wicksell, *Interest and prices* (1898; London, 1936), 102–21.

goods and bring about an economic crisis. The process of capital-goods construction cannot go on indefinitely. Mises insisted that a 'reverse movement' must inevitably set in, ending the boom and ushering in the crisis even if entrepreneurial expectations were to remain optimistic and even if the operation of the international gold exchange standard did not produce contractionary pressures on the banking system.[26] Mises' discussion of the reverse movement problem was incredibly terse:

> This is one of the ways in which the equilibrium of the loan market is reestablished after it has been disturbed by the intervention of the banks. The increased productive activity that sets in when the banks start the policy of granting loans at less than the natural rate of interest at first causes the prices of production goods to rise while the prices of consumption goods, although they rise also, do so only in a moderate degree, viz., only insofar as they are raised by the rise in wages. Thus the tendency towards a fall in the rate of interest on loans that originates in the policy of the banks is at first strengthened. But soon a counter-movement sets in: the prices of consumption goods rise, those of production goods fall. That is, the rate of interest on loans rises again, it again approaches the natural rate.[27]

While this analysis set forth a broad outline of a theory of the trade cycle, it left several theoretical questions unanswered. The most important from the Austrian point of view were these: What was the market mechanism that could bring about the counter-movement? How can one explain how each entrepreneur pursuing his own interest can be led to make decisions which, when reconciled with the decisions of other managers, produce the end of the boom and the subsequent crisis? In other words, what are the microeconomic foundations for the "spontaneous *dis*order" that seems to characterize the business cycle?

Shortly after Hayek arrived in London, he was invited to deliver the special university lectures at the London School of Economics (1930–1931). Hayek used this occasion to elaborate on the Mises account of the boom and crisis in a way that made more explicit use of the Austrian description of production as a succession of stages through which resources must pass toward their ultimate destination of becoming consumer goods. This course would enable him to explain, he believed, why a credit-financed boom would necessarily have to end in crisis. The published version of his lectures, *Prices and production* (1931) immediately attracted the interest and commmentary of most of the leading economists of his

26. L. v. Mises, *Theory of money and credit* (1912; London, 1934), 362–63. Cf. John S. Mill, *Principles of Political economy with some of their applications to social polity*, 2 vols. (Toronto, 1965), 2:528 n.

27. Mises, ibid.

day and led to his appointment to the prestigious Tooke chair at the London School.[28]

Hayek analyzed the reverse-movement problem in Lecture 3. According to Hayek, a credit-induced boom leads entrepreneurs to bid resources away from consumer-goods industries without any compensating voluntary savings on the part of consumers. This resulting relative decrease in the supply of final goods and services at a time when wage incomes are rising due to the newly created money causes final goods prices to rise faster than the price of labor. There is a consequent decline in the real wage of labor (where real wage means the ratio of product price to per-unit labor cost). This is most pronounced in the stage of production nearest to the consumer and leads to a surge in profits on short-term investment projects. This surge encourages entrepreneurs to turn away from machine-intensive methods of production in favor of more labor-intensive methods, thereby discouraging sales of capital goods.[29] Entrepreneurs, determined to complete their endangered long-term capital projects, turn to the banks for more bank credit, and a tug of war begins. Producers seek new bank loans, the banking system accommodates the new loan demand by creating new money, product prices rise ahead of wage costs. In each market period the process repeats itself, with product prices always rising ahead of wages.[30] Hayek argued that any attempt to reduce the flow of bank credit will bring this

28. According to Abba Lerner, "I had just learned about the average period of production from Professor Friedrich von Hayek's first course at the London School of Economics on capital theory [1931–32]. At the time, a group of my fellow students (who were avid discussants of economic theory in the third year undergraduate study room) were very excited about my essay and its three-dimensional diagram. We persuaded the editor of the *Clare Market Review*, the LSE student magazine to print it in the magazine." Lerner, shortly before his death, revised the exposition under the title 'Paleo-Austrian capital theory,' and it has been published posthumously in A. Lerner, *Selected economic writings of Abba P. Lerner*, ed. D. Colander (New York, 1983), 563–83. Other responses to the main argument of *Prices and production* include John R. Hicks, 'Equilibrium and the trade cycle,' *Zeitschrift für Nationalökonomie* 4 (June 1933), reprinted in *Economic Journal* 18 (Oct. 1980): 523–34; Hans Neisser, 'Monetary expansion and the structure of production,' *Social Research* 1 (Nov. 1934): 434–57; and E. F. M. Durbin, *Purchasing power and trade depression: a critique of underconsumption theories* (London, 1933; revised 1934); R. G. Hawtrey, *Capital and employment* (London, 1952), 220–55. Last, but by no means least, was Piero Sraffa's stinging review, 'Dr. Hayek on money and capital,' *Economic Journal*, March 1932, 42–53. Also cf. Hayek's response, 'Money and capital: a reply,' *Economic Journal*, June 1932, 236–49, followed by Sraffa's 'Rejoinder,' ibid. 249–51. The Sraffa-Hayek debate has only in recent years inspired discussion; see M. Desai, 'The task of monetary theory: the Hayek-Sraffa debate in modern perspective' (working paper at Institut des Sciences Economiques in Belgium); M. Milgate, 'On the origin of the notion of "Intertemporal Equilibrium,"' *Economica* 46 (Feb. 1979): 1–10; and L. M. Lachmann, 'Austrian economics under fire: the Hayek-Sraffa duel in retrospect' (MS, 18 pp.).

29. See F. A. Hayek. 'The paradox of savings,' in idem, *Profits, interests and investment* (New York, 1939), 199–263. See C. Menger's discussion of the various 'orders' of production in his *Principles of economics* (Glencoe, Ill., 1950), 149–74. Cf. Hayek, *Prices and production*, 32–50; and J. R. Hicks, *Capital and time* (Oxford, 1973), 3–26.

30. Hayek always emphasized that the appropriate measure of real wages was the nominal wage divided by the price of the immediate product that labor helped produce. To

process of competing errors to a halt, turning the boom into a bust and leading to a readjustment of the capital-goods industry to a new equilibrium consistent with real patterns of consumer demand.[31]

In his 1969 restatement of the Ricardo effect, Hayek objected to Hicks's description of the mechanism presented in *Prices and production* as being predicated on wages "lagging" behind consumer-goods prices.[32] Hayek argued that his explanation did not depend upon a lag, if that meant that one incorrect market value is somehow trying to catch up with a correct value with which it must be in harmony. Rather, *both* product prices and wages are incorrect in the sense of being inconsistent with the underlying objective conditions of supply and demand for consumer goods. The fact that consumer expenditures are ultimately used to pay for intermediate goods creates the objective conditions in the market that generate a particular price sequence. As he argued in 1939 and 1942, when capital creation is financed through expanding bank credit, the signals that communicate the objective conditions to entrepreneurs are distorted, and incorrect investment decisions are made. The incorrect decisions are corrected by way of a crisis.

In essence, the Ricardo effect as Hayek described it occurred in the context of a process of genuine macroeconomic disequilibrium in which a crisis could not be averted. The crisis, he argued, was a necessary consequence of a boom brought about by money creation and characterized by a constant incompatibility between relative prices and the growing structure of real capital.

IV. *The Inevitability of the Crisis*

The first major point Hayek was making during his lectures and in several articles he published in the years immediately following *Prices and production* was simply that any real growth in the capital stock takes time and requires voluntary net savings. There is no way for an expansion of the money supply in the form of bank credit to short-circuit the process of economic growth. His second major point was more difficult. He argued that forced savings can only distort the mix of capital and consumer goods, by generating false relative price signals. These false signals throw the economy into a genuine macroeconomic disequilibrium that cannot be sustained over time. Eventually, the underlying consumer preferences will

---

distinguish this concept of the real wage from the usual nominal wage divided by the price index, Hayek spoke of the "own-wage" of labor. We have glossed this distinction in the text, since none of our conclusions is affected by it. See Hayek, 'The Ricardo effect' in idem, *Individualism and economic order*, 251–53.

31. F. A. Hayek, *Prices and production*, 90–94. On the tug-of-war thesis, see Murray N. Rothbard, *America's great depression* (Princeton; 1963), 17–21.

32. F. A. Hayek, 'Three elucidations,' 278–79. Curiously, Hayek had earlier described his theory as involving "lags"; see idem, *Prices and production*, 146.

reassert themselves. All that credit can do is to encourage competition between consumers and producers for the same pool of scarce resources, leading ultimately to a state of affairs in which producers switch from capital-intensive to labor-intensive methods of production. This switch, when carried out by a large number of managers, will choke off investment and bring on a full-scale crisis. But was either the switch or the crisis inevitable? Hayek argued that they are, but most of his early critics disagreed.[33]

Suppose the inflation caused by an expansion of bank credit could only last for, say, twenty-two months, but that a larger (i.e., 'more roundabout' or 'deeper') capital structure could be erected in less time. Wouldn't that mean that even when the eventual halt to credit expansion came, the economy would be richer with a larger per capita capital stock that could potentially produce enough income to generate the savings to maintain itself without collapse? If this scenario were possible—say, under conditions of less than full employment of resources—it would seem that a deliberate policy of credit creation could bootstrap the economy into a permanently larger flow of consumer goods without suffering the consequences of a disruptive crisis.[34]

At one place Hayek did agree that under certain restricted conditions a credit expansion could occur that did not end in collapse with a misplaced collection of capital goods. He warned, however, that the conditions were so stringent that they were unlikely to have much empirical relevance. This happy state of affairs could only occur in a 'progressive economy' where credit expansion did not lead to increased prices, but only managed to keep price levels constant as output grew. In this case, where voluntary saving was already high and the proportion of capital formation financed by forced saving was very low, it was just possible that a crisis could be averted if the credit expansion had been gradual and the contraction equally gradual. However, even in this case, he argued, forced saving did not actually increase the capital stock that can be accumulated in the long run, but only speeded up the process of creating it, since once the credit expansion stopped, "for a time the current voluntary savings will be used to take over, as it were, the capital created by means of forced saving; and current savings would then have to serve, not to make further new investment possible, but merely to maintain capital which has been formed in

33. Apparently, consumers must change their *flow* of savings in order to build up a *stock* of capital. Once the stock is built up (i.e., completed), savings can be reduced. H. Neiser, 'Monetary expansion,' 439–42, and also P. Sraffa, 'Dr. Hayek on money and capital,' 46–48. Cf. Haberler, *Prosperity and depression*, 54–56. Cf. L. Lachmann, *Capital and its structure* (London, 1956), 100–127.

34. Hayek, 'The present state and immediate prospects of the study of industrial fluctuating,' trans. from the German, 'Der Stand und die nächste . . . ,' in Hayek, *Profits, interest and investment*, 180.

anticipation of these savings."[35] Under these circumstances, there would still be a relative price change for real wages and real cost of capital that would trigger a switch of techniques. But in this case, the switch would not lead to a crisis. Thus, as a theoretical matter, the crisis need not inevitably follow the boom. The likelihood of such a set of events, however, was extremely limited. As Hayek explained, this was not a scenario upon which to build one's plans for smooth economic growth, since the conditions under which it might obtain were extremely restrictive. As a practical matter, credit expansions followed by economic crises were the norm, not the exception.

In Hayek's early book, *Monetary theory and the trade cycle,* he presented a theory of trade cycles that made them endogenous to a monetary economy.[36] Cyclical fluctuations were simply the consequences of information problems inherent in an economic system that relied on credit banking. In *Prices and production* he described a process of economic growth that consisted of a time-consuming transition from one full-employment equilibrium to another. Business cycles were a consequence of attempting to finance this transition process by an expansion of the money supply via bank credit creation. In both these books, Hayek was well on his way to working out a macroeconomic theory that incorporated money and time into a theory of growth from one equilibrium state to another.

However, after the publication of Keynes' *General theory,* the rules of the game changed and professional attention shifted from the problem of economic growth as a transition process from one equilibrium to another, to the problem of the determination of flows of income and expenditure at a moment in time. The limelight shifted from Hayek to Keynes.

In 1939 Hayek produced a restatement of his view of the trade cycle more in line with these contemporary trends. Instead of starting from a position of full-employment equilibrium as he had before, he tried to meet Keynes and his followers on their own ground by making standard Keynesian assumptions of unemployment, rigid wages and interest rates, immobile labor, in order to show how the economic system would nevertheless still find itself unable to sustain a boom.[37] It was here that he first used the term the 'Ricardo effect' to underline the venerable pedigree of the mech-

35. Ibid.

36. Hayek, *Monetary theory*, 147.

37. This claim was asserted by Mises in 1912 and restated toward the end of the 1930s by Hayek. See esp. *Profits, interest and investment* where Hayek states: "What I am concerned with is to show how [the rate of profit] would act if the rate of interest failed to act at all" (6–7). At another place in his essay Hayek concludes, "We might get the trade cycle even without changes in the rate of interest" (64). Cf. O'Driscoll, *Economics as a coordination problem*, 94–96.

anism that figured so prominently in his attempt to give a microeconomic account of how individual maximizing decisions on the part of entrepreneurs will lead to the switch of techniques that brings about an economic crisis. In 1939, then, the debate over the Austrian theory of the business cycle focussed explicitly on the choice-theoretic foundations of the turning point in business cycles.

V. *Microfoundations of the Ricardo Effect*

Let us suppose along with Hayek that during the boom, consumer-product prices do rise ahead of wages, and hence real wages fall. Is this alteration in relative prices by itself sufficient to produce a crisis? As we have shown, Hayek believed that the price effect would induce entrepreneurs to substitute labor-intensive for labor-saving methods of production. Although each entrepreneur makes the decision to alter investment priorities independently of other entrepreneurs, the aggregative effect of their decisions is to produce a decline in net investment (that is, a decline in the sales of capital goods) and the onset of the crisis. By 1939 Hayek was arguing that the crisis will begin even if the monetary authorities stand ready to continue to supply bank credit at less than the natural rate.[38] Indeed, one important corollary of Hayek's Ricardo effect was to show that while a commodity standard (that is, a gold standard) might by itself be sufficient to arrest a boom, it was by no means necessary. A boom would end because of the incentives created by changes in the relationship among wages, prices, and profits.

In order to appreciate the choice-theoretic foundations of Hayek's Ricardo effect, it will be helpful to think of entrepreneurs as managing a number of on-line investment projects. In fact, the firm itself may be construed as a "portfolio of investment projects" rather than, as in standard Marshallian terms, an organization that produces a single product.[39] Now each investment project can be identified with a particular product and calculable rate of return. The entrepreneurs are assumed to reshuffle the amount of liquid capital available to them so as to maximize the present value of the firm: they calculate the rate of return on each separate project and then allocate money capital among the projects so as to equalize returns at the margin.[40]

38. Hayek, *Profits, interest and investment*, 64.

39. Members of the Austrian school were never endorsers of the Marshallian firm/industry distinction. See M. Rothbard, *Man, economy and the state*, 2 vols. (Princeton, 1962), 1:304–8). The modern 'management view' of the firm (similar to the Austrian view) sees the firm as a bundle of investment projects, see B. Henderson. *Henderson on corporate strategy* (Cambridge, Mass., 1972), 145–66. In the example taken from Hayek (to be discussed below) Hayek speaks of three "firms" rather than three investment projects within a single firm. This modification allows us to clarify our exposition considerably.

40. See Tsiang, *Variations of real wages*, 133–34. F. A. Hayek, 'The Ricardo effect,'

In his 1939, 1942, and 1969 expositions of the Ricardo effect mechanism, Hayek started his analysis (much as Ricardo did) with the firm in "long-period investment equilibrium" earning the same rate of return on the investments in each different project. In some projects capital turns over rapidly (bakery products), while in other projects (selling rare books) funds are typically tied up for years on end. Offsetting these 'waiting periods' of varying lengths are the actual returns on the different projects which differ in absolute amounts so as to yield an identical internal rate of return among all projects. The internal rate of return (I) is equal to the product of the rate of turnover (T) and the profit margin (M). In equilibrium then, $M = I/T$ for all projects.[41]

Now, let us disturb this equilibrium situation by permitting a sudden unexpected rise in product prices (relative to wages) and we discover that the rate of return on quick-turnover projects will have risen relative to the returns on slow-turnover projects. Entrepreneurs would obviously attempt to shift their money capital to quick-turnover projects in which the returns are now relatively greatest. These quick-turnover projects are necessarily more labor-intensive, and hence the demand for capital investment relative to labor will fall. Now it is absolutely vital to keep in mind the following arithmetic facts in order to appreciate the controversy surrounding Hayek's mechanism: (i) the internal return on quick-turnover projects has indeed risen relative to slower-turnover projects but (ii) all rates of return are necessarily higher than they were prior to the rise in product prices.[42]

The second of the two facts led T. Wilson, Nicholas Kaldor, and the majority of Hayek's critics after 1940 to accuse Hayek's theory of being

---

227. Hayek's firm-manager tries to maximize the "internal rate of return on investments"; see Lutz and Lutz, 16–26. For a general critique of using the internal rate of return as an index of investment success see Hirshleifer, *Investment, interest and capital* (Princeton, 1970), 51–56, and K. E. Boulding, 'The theory of a single investment,' *Quarterly Journal of Economics* 49 (May 1935).

41. According to Hayek, "the per annum net percentage return on the whole capital of a firm (or on any part of it for which we find it necessary to compute separately), net of 'wages of management' and of risk premium, we shall designate as the 'internal rate of return.'" Initially, the internal rate of return is equal on all projects. Hayek explained: "If we call the internal rate of return I, the rate of turnover T, and the profit margin M, the relationship will be presented by $I = TM$ or $M = I/T$. If . . . the internal rate is 6 percent, [then] the profit margin of a firm turning over its capital six times a year will have to be 1 percent, while a firm turning over its capital only once in two years will have to earn 12 percent on all sales, and a firm turning over its capital only once in every ten years will have to earn a profit of 60 percent" (Hayek, 'Ricardo effect,' 227).

42. "For the three [investments] which we have just considered by way of illustration, the first (with an annual rate of turnover $T = 6$) will find its profit margin increased from 1 to 6 percent; the second [with $T = ½$] from [12] to [17] percent; and the third (with $T = \frac{1}{10}$) from 60 to 65 percent. Multiplying these profit margins by the corresponding rates of turnover, we obtain the new internal rates of return of $6 \times 6 = 36$ percent for the first, [$½ \times 17 = 8.5$] percent for the second, and $\frac{1}{10} \times 65 = 6.5$ percent for the third [investment activity]" (Hayek, 'Ricardo effect,' 227).

logically inconsistent.[43] According to Hayek's critics the rational firm-manager would not simply switch from one kind of project to another, but would try to invest more in each and every project. If before the rise in product prices all returns were equal to the firm's cost of capital, then in the next equilibrium position the scale of the firm must increase because the firm will invest in all its investment projects until each internal rate of return falls back down to equal the cost of capital.[44] The cost of capital remains fixed throughout the analysis because Hayek has assumed that during the boom the banking authorities are making loanable funds freely available at a rate of interest below the natural rate.

According to Kaldor:

> [Hayek committed the same fallacy as those who argue that] a rise in demand for a commodity will cause a rise in its price, and the rise in price causes a restriction in demand (because less is bought at a higher price than a lower price), the increase in demand will lead to a reduction in the amount bought. No doubt the rise in price will make the increase in purchases (following upon the increase in demand) less than it would have been if the price had not risen. But it cannot make it less than before, since the price has only risen because the amount bought has gone up. In the same way, the reduction in capital intensity will make the rise in investment expenditure less than it would have been if capital intensity had remained constant. But it cannot eliminate it altogether because capital intensity would not have fallen if investment expenditure had not risen.[45]

In short, Kaldor claimed that Hayek had assumed a situation in which the substitution effect outweighed the scale effect, a situation which a comparative static analysis of the Ricardo effect mechanism demonstrated to be impossible.

Hayek responded to Kaldor's criticism by claiming that it missed the point. Kaldor along with other critics seemed unable to understand his mechanism for two basic reasons: (i) their stubborn attachment to the 'perfect competition' model of market structure even when the descriptive realism of that model was at odds with the particular market under study and (ii) their insistence on evaluating his Ricardo effect mechanism solely within a comparative statics framework.

Consider the first charge. If the loanable-funds market were perfect in that the cost of capital facing the firm were to remain constant regardless of the absolute volume of funds the firm wished to borrow, then the rational manager would indeed expand the size of the firm in all directions

43. Kaldor, 'Professor Hayek and the concertina effect,' *Economica*, Nov. 1942. Reprinted in Kaldor, *Essays on economic stability and growth* (London, 1960), 2:148–76.

44. Ibid. See also Wilson, 'Capital theory and the trade cycle,' 177; Hawtrey, *Capital and employment*, 240–45; and Tsiang, *Variations of real wages*, 141–44.

45. Kaldor, ibid.

as Kaldor insisted he would. But, Hayek argued, the market for loanable funds is not and cannot be modeled as 'perfect' under these conditions. Under any real conditions, the cost of capital facing the firm could not remain equal to the external market rate of interest while the firm expanded in size; there is a "limit beyond which [the firm-owner] can raise capital only at higher costs."[46] Loans to the same borrower will never represent the "same commodity" in the sense in which the term is used in theory of competition. Bankers will not lend infinite amounts of bank credit to any single borrower at a uniform rate because they will perceive an increased risk associated with a higher debt-to-equity ratio.[47] But are the bankers' perceptions based on an understanding of the real underlying conditions that prevail in the market or are their perceptions based instead on the imperfect and incomplete information available to the creditors at the time the applications for the loans are received?

Hayek later clarified this point. He admitted that creditors "misjudge" the credit-worthiness of borrowers because they fail to take into consideration the favorable impact inflation will have on the firm's revenues. In the long run, increasing product prices might imply that the credit-worthiness of a firm has increased and therefore should justify increased loans at no additional risk premium. But long before creditors perceive that this sort of long-run equilibrium adjustment has occurred, the Ricardo effect will have already asserted itself. Hayek's argument then rested on the assumption that increasing product prices increased the firm's demand for loanable funds more quickly than the banks could subjectively reevaluate the credit-worthiness of the firm itself. Under these circumstances, the firm is constrained by the upward sloping portion of the supply curve of credit which acts as a brake on the firm's expansion.[48] Hence, with incomplete knowledge the scale effect cannot outweigh the substitution effect as Kaldor maintained. In this way Hayek readily admitted what several of his critics had pointed out: the upward sloping supply of credit to the firm acted as a kind of rationing device to constrain the growth of the firm. The manager adjusts by investing his limited capital in short-term (that is, labor-intensive) investment projects.

Hayek's resort to this kind of credit rationing was by no means *ad hoc*. The credit rationing was a rational response to the informational lags that occur during a period of accelerating inflation. The assessment of the credit-worthiness of the firm in one period imposes a "finance constraint" on the amount it can borrow (at the old interest rate) in the next period.[49]

46. Hayek, 'Ricardo effect,' 237.

47. Ibid. 236. Cf. M. Kalecki, 'The principle of increasing risk,' *Economica*, Nov. 1937.

48. Hayek, 'Ricardo effect,' 235–37.

49. Cf. M. Kohn, 'In defense of the finance constraint,' *Economic Inquiry* 19 (181): 177–95.

Consider, now, the merits of Hayek's charge that his critics misunderstood his theory because of their preoccupation with perfectly competitive equilibrium conditions and comparative statics. According to Hayek, even if the supply of credit were infinitely elastic to the economy as a whole, the Ricardo effect would still occur because of the finance constraints encountered along the path of business expansion. However, one cannot see that point simply by comparing two equilibrium states. Such a comparison, Hayek argued, would disguise precisely the mechanism he was interested in discussing. As he put it:

> The situation which we consider . . . is indeed the classical instance of a cumulative process. . . . the perfectly elastic supply of credit at a rate of interest lower than the internal rate of all or most of the firms will be the cause of continuous changes of prices and money incomes where each change makes further changes necessary. There is no point in saying with respect to such a situation that "in equilibrium there must" exist such and such a relationship, because it necessarily follows from the assumptions that the relationship between at least some prices must be out of equilibrium.[50]

This disequilibrium is a situation in which the different price-determining tendencies in the economy are inconsistent with one another and lead to perpetual change. Hayek tried to explicate his problem by resorting to an imaginative analogy: "The question is rather similar to that whether, by pouring a liquid fast enough into one side of a vessel, we can raise the level at that side above that of the rest to any extent we desire." Of course, we cannot, since this depends upon the viscosity of the liquid itself. Hence, "the speed at which an increase of incomes leads to an increase in the demand for consumers' goods limits the extent to which, by spending more money on factors of production, we can raise their prices relative to those of the products."[51] In the end, real wages will have to fall, if for no other reason than the unavailability of consumer goods to meet the demand; and hence it is inevitable that the Ricardo effect will be triggered.

To throw Hayek's problem into relief, consider the subsequent Hicksian construct of the 'progressive economy.'[52] In a progressive economy the managers expect the demand for their products to be rising. Based on this expectation they proceed to invest and expand the scales of their firms. They do this over a market period long enough for the net investment that takes place to generate exactly enough extra income and new savings for

50. Hayek, 'Ricardo effect,' 239.
51. Ibid. 241. Cf. idem, 'Three elucidations,' 281.
52. J. R. Hicks, *Capital and growth* (Oxford, 1956), 90–93. This is not to be confused with Hayek's use of the term 'progressive economy,' referred to earlier in this article.

savings and investment to remain equal to each other. In Hicks's progressive economy, investment generates income without delay—the period of construction of capital goods is assumed to be zero.[53] In the new equilibrium position, managers find out that they have constructed exactly the quantity and variety of capital goods they wished to have at the beginning of the market period. Thus, the economy started out in stock equilibrium and ended up in stock equilibrium. In addition, the flow of net investment during the market period was exactly matched by a flow of net savings. Flow and stock equilibrium occur together in the progressive economy. The boom, to return to Hayek's terminology, has proceeded smoothly and without the slightest possibility of ending in crisis.

Now clearly this construction of a progressive economy rules out the Mises-Hayek crisis phenomenon as a matter of definition. If all plans are coordinated at the beginning of the market period and also at the end, then where is the "cluster of business errors" that constitutes the crisis? In this sense, Hayek was quite correct when he objected to Kaldor's use of comparative static methodology. The methodology of comparing isolated equilibrium states rules out precisely the phenomenon of the crisis.

Suppose on the other hand, that Hayek's entrepreneurs only *believe* they are in a progressive state. The lowering of the interest rate suggests that consumers have provided a larger amount of real savings and the managers eagerly begin the task of constructing the new equipment.[54] But the entrepreneurs have only been deceived into thinking the flow of new voluntary savings is larger than it really is because (as we know) it is only the money supply that is increasing. Now the flow of actual net savings is brought exactly into balance with the flow of actual net investment through the familiar forced-saving mechanism. Still, at the end of the period the actors come to realize that their stocks of capital goods are inappropriate to satisfy consumer demand. In old-fashioned terminology, there is too much fixed capital and not enough circulating capital—a realization brought on by Hayek's Ricardo effect mechanism. In summary, we have stock equilibrium at the beginning of the market period, flow equilibrium within the period, and stock *dis*equilibrium at the end.

Hayek's point is that precisely because the entrepreneurs are mistaken about the true real savings of the consumers, a time must come when they have evidence of their mistakes and take steps to correct them. A comparative static analysis of the economy at two points in times, where the capital structure at T_2 is larger than at T_1 compares two equilibrium situations. Hayek preferred a market period approach over a comparative static analysis because it enabled him to identify the sequence of events by which

53. Ibid. 91.

54. Hayek, *Monetary theory and the trade cycle;* and cf. Rothbard, *America's great depression*, 16–17.

the entrepreneurs come to realize that the equilibrium toward which they are all heading is no longer economic. They come to that conclusion because the underlying structure of production makes the simultaneous realization of their business plans impossible. This information is transmitted to the entrepreneurs through the price system by way of the internal rates of return on investment projects. Hayek's objection to applying comparative statics to this problem of dynamical change and adjustment seems to us remarkably cogent. The problem is not to learn about maladjustments by comparing states of equilibrium but rather to ask if the conditions prevailing at T_1 make the transition to T_2 at all possible. Kaldor's approach indeed assumed away the very problem that Hayek's theory was designed to analyze, the problem of the transition an economy undergoes in moving from one coordinated capital structure to another. The revival in the 1970s of interest in modeling this transition process gives Hayek's favorite mechanism a decidedly modern ring.[55]

VI. *Conclusion*

By emphasizing the inapplicability of the perfectly competitive model especially in the supply of loanable funds, and by insisting on the disequilibrium nature of the cumulative process, Hayek was speaking a different language from his peers in the 1930s, 1940s and, surprisingly, in the late 1960s as well. Hayek challenged the relevance and appropriateness of comparative static analysis to an expanding economy. His struggle to free himself from the precepts of comparative static analysis constitutes, in our view, the elusive element in his thinking and explains why so much miscommunication occurred. Hayek's most formidable opponent, Kaldor, seemed unable to structure the problem except in comparative static terms, and this we believe is what prompted Hayek to focus on their methodological differences.

It is gratifying that by the 1970s Hayek's favorite problem of the process of adjustjment from one coordinated state of equilibrium to another was finally recognized and tackled by some of the finest minds in the profession, including one of Hayek's own critics—Hicks.[56] While the particular solution and the methods of analysis Hayek proposed may be controversial, there is now no longer any question that the problem Hayek raised about the feasibility of reaching one equilibrium based on the conditions

55. Hicks, *Capital and time*, 47–80. See also E. Burmeister, *Capital theory and dynamics*. See, however, Lachmann's 'A reconsideration of the Austrian theory of industrial fluctuations,' *Economica* 7 (May, 1940); in idem, *Capital expectations and the market process* (Kansas City, 1977), 267–86.

56. Hicks, *Capital and time*, 81–150. Hicks like Hayek harks back to Ricardo's machinery chapter for doctrinal precedent. See Hicks.

prevailing prior to reaching that equilibrium is an important one. The issues Hayek raised during the 1930s have their counterpart in the modern debates about the structural limits placed on short-run macroeconomic policy. This, of course, remains a central concern of the 'new classical economists,' some of whom have recognized Hayek as a pioneer investigator.[57] We have taken a second look at Hayek's Ricardo effect in order to illuminate certain novel elements in Hayek's thinking and their relevance to contemporary economic theorizing.

57. Hayek did not reach the same conclusion as certain radical exponents of the "new Classical economics." For one thing, Hayek would not agree that a fully announced set of policy changes will have no effect on real macroeconomic variables as has been maintained by T. Sargent and N. Wallace in '"Rational expectations," the optimal monetary instrument and the optimal money supply rule,' *Journal of Political Economy* 83 (April 1975): 241–54. Hayek argued that Keynesian stimulative policies would have short-run beneficial effects. Hayek disagreed with Keynes when Hayek insisted these beneficial effects would be at the expense of long-run disruptions.

[9]

History of Political Economy 20:1

CCC 0018-2702/88/$1.50

Ugo Mazzola and the Italian theory of public goods

Orhan Kayaalp

I. *Introduction*

That the Scandinavian theory of public goods has earned an important place in the Anglo-Saxon public finance curriculum does not necessarily mitigate Buchanan's assertion that English-language students of public finance are seriously afflicted by a "long-continued failure to make comparable extensions of their basic framework or to acknowledge an interest in the continental efforts" (1975). In fact, despite the accommodation of the Scandinavian theory, another important continental body of scholarship, the Italian theory of public goods, continues to lie on the fringes of Anglo-Saxon fiscal thought, appreciated, perhaps, by only a handful of aficionados. The failure of this theory to generate interest in Anglo-Saxon public finance circles can, of course, be explained away by another assertion of Buchanan's that it was simply too "rudimentary [an] effort to analyze the public economy [compared to] the most sophisticated contributions made by Knut Wicksell and Erik Lindahl" (1975). But such a conclusion would be unfair; for it can be demonstrated that, just like its Scandinavian counterpart, the Italian theory not only possesses a convincing economic logic regarding the very core of public finance—that is, the demand and supply of public goods—but also a surprising capability for providing insights into the public-choice related aspects of the discipline such as voting and constitutions. And more important, the Italian theory manages to integrate all these within a collective decision-making framework that is much simpler and more realistic than the one prescribed by the Scandinavians (Kayaalp 1985).

The present article reassesses the Italian fiscal tradition, since it seems that once some lingering misconceptions are cleared up, the much-needed unification of continental and Anglo-Saxon fiscal theories will be closer at hand. With this primary mission, the article examines the "standard" Italian model of the public economy which is owed to Ugo Mazzola, a late nineteenth-century fiscal theorist. Additionally, since in spite of his seminal contributions Mazzola remains the least-known figure among the three

Correspondence may be addressed to Professor Kayaalp at Lehman College of The City University of New York, Bronx NY 10468-1589.

fountainheads of the pure theory of public finance,[1] the article attempts to indicate his important place in the development of the discipline, and thus to close a gap in the history of economic doctrines.

II. *The Italian Theory of Public Goods in a Neoclassical World*

Despite Musgrave's, Peacock's, and Buchanan's efforts, the English-language literature on Italian work in public finance remains inadequate. Musgrave's classic book of 1959 displays only a secondary interest in the Italian tradition. His main objective is evidently to trace back his multiple-branch theory of budgetary control to the "benefit" approach to taxation. With this in mind, he introduces Pantaleoni, De Viti, and Mazzola as the first economists who transformed the benefit principle from a dictum of justice into a condition of efficiency.

Similarly, Musgrave's and Peacock's *Classics* of 1958 makes no specific claim to creating a sense of the Italian tradition. But it nonetheless achieves this result to a certain degree, as the reader naturally gains an insight into that tradition after studying the excerpts from the works of Barone, Montemartini, Pantaleoni, and Mazzola contained in the book. It is Buchanan's 1960 essay that proves most effective in that regard. It addresses itself directly to the task of presenting to the English-language economist the essence of the Italian tradition in fiscal theory and achieves its goal admirably. Yet, because Buchanan's aim is to follow the development of this tradition in a sixty-year period (between 1880 and 1940) the essay does not sufficiently stress the earlier part, which constitutes the emphasis of the present article. Also, Buchanan's essay inexplicably omits Mazzola's contributions, which the present study finds to have been fundamental in the development of that tradition.

That political economy and public finance had always been an Italian specialty was long recognized in the Anglo-Saxon world.[2] But Italians go to the extent of asserting that they were the true founders of these disciplines. As to primacy in political economy, Italians can indeed muster much evidence from their rich history of economic thought.[3] They can

1. The other two, Maffeo Pantaleoni and Antonio De Viti de Marco, were hailed as the founders of the positive theory of public finance as early as in 1934 (Benham 1934a). That honor was extended to Ugo Mazzola much later by Musgrave 1959 and Musgrave & Peacock 1958. De Viti's main work (1888) became available in English in 1936, and that of Pantaleoni (1889) in 1957. Mazzola's 1890 *I dati scientifici della finanza pubblica (Scientific elements of public finance)* is unfortunately still not translated into English, except for a chapter that is included in Musgrave & Peacock 1958, 39–47. So far as the author is aware, Mazzola's *Il fondamento scientifico dell'economia dello Stato* (1888) has never been referred to in the English-language literature.

2. See, for example, Weinberger 1940 and Benham 1934a, 1934b.

3. This claim was defended most ardently by Pantaleoni in *Giornale degli Economisti* 69. 1(1924).

proudly point out, for example, that Muratori (1749), Beccaria (1763), Verri (1763), Genovesi (1769), and Paoletti (1772) had pleaded for "the greatest happiness of the greatest number" many years before the publication of Bentham's well-known work and that Ortes had indicated twenty-five years before Malthus the disproportion between the increase of population and that of subsistence—even stating and discussing the geometrical growth of population—in his *Riflessioni sulla popolazione* of 1790 (Weinberger 1940).[4] It seems, however, that these claims may never be settled, since it is unlikely that it will be proved whether the classical British economists had actually read the Italian work.

But the Italians' claim that they were the founders of the theory of public finance is indisputable. The optimum condition analysis of public goods certainly had its origin in Pantaleoni 1883 and De Viti 1888, and found its classical expression in Mazzola's *I dati scientifici della finanza pubblica* (1890). The three founders of the positive fiscal theory gained much insight from British political economists; but Italy also provided a few splendid names. For instance, the concept that the value of a good was derived from its "perceived utility" and not from its "*rareté*" or its "cost of production" was clearly established in Italy by Ferrara 1934 at least fifteen years before the publication of Jevons' *Theory* (1871). Ferrara was aware of the contributions of Briganti 1780, who defined economics as "mechanics of pleasure, or hedonism," and of Ortes 1790b, who earnestly investigated the link between subjective utility and the market value. But Ferrara was a step ahead of Briganti and Ortes in this regard: he argued that utility constituted the basis of the prices of *all* goods, private or public.

As the Walrasian system took root in Italian political-economic circles in the early 1880s, Pantaleoni, De Viti, and Mazzola discerned the possibility of extending the concept of individual valuation to the public economy. But unlike Edgeworth and Marshall who ventured to do this in a straightforward manner, they reasoned that the public economy could not be analyzed adequately without taking the political context into account. Based on this premise, Pantaleoni and De Viti went on to develop certain political assumptions that seemed necessary for producing a fiscal optimum that was not only efficient but also equitable.[5]

Mazzola, meanwhile, focused directly on the nature of "public" ends and "public" wants and the capacity of certain (public) goods for satisfying

4. The claims of the Italian economists were defended also by British authors. Bonar (1922) and M'Culloch (1925), for example, attest respectively that Bentham's and Malthus's theories were based on Italian thought.

5. See my 1985 essay for a discussion of Pantaleoni's and De Viti's seminal contributions to the *Scienza della finanze* in this regard.

such ends and wants. He devoted his entire life—which came to an abrupt end when he was only thirty-five—to prove that public finance was an autonomous discipline because "it had a subject matter—public ends, public wants, public goods—which was quite different from that of" political economy (Einaudi 1936). Mazzola appreciated fully the low regard in which public finance was held in the 1880s, when political economy was making tremendous strides while the "science" of public finance (*"scienza" delle finanze*) was still in search of a positive foundation. He agreed with Loria 1886 that "Public finance was falling seriously behind the general progress that other social sciences were making and that, unlike them, it was not being rejuvenated from the font of historical research and positive methodology" (Mazzola 1890, p. vii).

Mazzola reminds Loria, however:

> Political economy [too] was treated initially only as a political "art." But it made progress continuously, and has only now taken the shape of a "science." This occurred because it has adopted objective methods of analysis. Thanks to the efforts made in theoretical research, it has discovered laws according to which economic events proceed. Thus, it is now possible to account for the influences underlying conflicting interests [in the private economy]. Because political economy did not limit research only to everyday problems that took place in the market, it provided new theoretical insights so that it is now possible to analyze effectively the problems associated with money, banking, insurance, transportation, etc. In the discipline of public finance, in contrast, the search for general principles was either given secondary place or was mingled with extraneous judicial and political elements. For example, discussion of the problems of the "most equitable" taxation was not preceded by investigation of the causal links on which certain facts were based. We do not have a prejudice against applied work. On the contrary, we are in favor of finding practical solutions to urgent fiscal problems; but we would like "pure" scientific research to have a major part in illuminating the true state of fiscal affairs [1890, viii–ix, all excerpts are the author's translation unless otherwise indicated].

With *I dati* (1890), Mazzola clearly attained his goal. He demonstrated for the first time that the "science" of public finance was capable of attaining the dual goals of the fiscal optimum by adopting a purely positive algorithm.

III. *Mazzola and the Science of Public Finance*

When Mazzola set out to analyze the public economy systematically, certain premises applicable to the public economy had already been established in Italy by his close colleagues Pantaleoni and De Viti.[6] To begin with, Pantaleoni had extended the concept of individual valuation to the "expenditure" side of the fiscal account (1883) and De Viti postulated that since there always existed an economic exchange between the State and the citizens, to each service offered by the State then must correspond a tax claim (1888).[7] Thus, when Mazzola set out to formalize the Italian theory of public goods (1888, 1890) the two parts of the fiscal account had already been integrated in Italy within a marginalist framework.

Mazzola bases his "pure" theory of public finance directly upon the behavior of economic man. The *homo œconomicus* that emerges in *I dati* (1890), however, is quite different from that imagined by contemporary Anglo-Saxon (or, for that matter, German) political economists. According to Mazzola:

> There exist, in the first place, the aims of the individual. To attain these, however, it is necessary [that he first] accomplish other aims. . . . [Economic] man does not set as his ultimate or direct aim such things as national defense or general security. He wants to accomplish his material aims in life or his spiritual aims in the field of moral or intellectual improvement. He cannot arrive at these ends, however, unless he is able to live in such a way that he feels secure against his foreign and internal enemies and is prepared to co-operate with other men for the achievement of aims denied to men who live in a state of isolation. Therefore the "public" aims are distinguished as being "conditional" to the attainment of the ultimate aims of man and as being attainable only through political co-operation. The vol

6. Pantaleoni, De Viti, and Mazzola became professors at the University of Camerino when they were in their early twenties. They also shared the editorship of the *Giornale degli Economisti*, the foremost economic journal of Italy. They then moved to Pavia, where Mazzola eventually took over the chair of public finance that was vacated when Luigi Cossa died in 1896. Mazzola remained in that position until his death in 1899. De Viti and Pantaleoni, meanwhile, returned to their alma mater, Rome, as chair professors in 1887 and 1901 respectively.

7. De Viti greatly transcended Pantaleoni, who expected of the finance minister the "standard" economic behavior, that is, rationality and self-interest . . . The minister's task, according to Pantaleoni, consisted of equating the marginal yields of alternative public expenditure projects. De Viti, meanwhile, assumed that the minister was "sentient," that is, receptive to the conflicting social wants of different groups and motivated to produce a public-economic solution that, in the long run, would be in the best interests of all the key coalitions. That a "behavioral" assumption lay at the heart of De Viti's patently "positive" theory of public goods threw off many competent Anglo-Saxon public finance specialists. For example, Henry Simons went to the extent of describing De Viti's theory as "a mass of intellectual confusion and of dangerous half-truths which, along with other vestiges of continental thought, are likely to plague us still for many years" (1937, 717). Simons' criticism appears to have stemmed, in turn, from a severe obsession with the "sacrifice" principle. This leads him to believe that De Viti's assertion that 'individuals 'demand' public goods . . . [and that] taxes are the 'prices' against which people set the utilities of these goods . . . [would leave] the reader in confusion" (p. 713).

untary association of private individuals would not serve the purpose; what is needed is rather a political cooperation [Einaudi 1936, referring to Mazzola 1890, 23].

Mazzola thus indicates an important feature of public goods, that is, they are "complementary" to private goods. Then he discovers another characteristic: public goods, unlike private ones, are "indivisible." It is because of this that the price theory cannot be extended "directly" to the public economy. In Mazzola's usage, the term "indivisibility" covers also "non-excludability" and "non-rivalry." The following passage may help illustrate this point:

> The utility of most public goods is complementary and indivisible. The services of law and order, public health, etc., are contributory causes to private satisfactions. But although their consumption produces individual satisfaction, the quantities consumed by each individual cannot be divided up and measured. What is known is simply that public goods enter into individual satisfaction in certain proportions. The indivisibility of consumption constitutes the technical reason preventing the formation of a single market price in the public economy. In the case of a private good, anyone who cannot pay the price is excluded from consumption. But if a public good had a price exceeding its marginal utility for some classes of consumers, their inability to pay the price would not effectively exclude them from consuming the good. To achieve this, the public good must be withdrawn from the market altogether—even from the use of those who are willing to pay the price—for, otherwise, those who wish not to pay would still enjoy the public good. This occurs because the market price is the maximum the consumer would pay for the amount of marginal utililty that the good offers. The concept of indivisibility of public goods also explains why the public economy sometimes resorts to a device very similar to private prices—namely, duties or fees—whenever the quantity of a public good consumed can in fact be imputed to the individual [1890, 171–72.].

Consequently, Mazzola postulates that in some instances the price theory as political economists have it can be extended directly to the public economy:

> Fees, or fixed charges, as we have had occasion to observe, represent a price phenomenon in the public economy resembling private prices. For example, the delivery of mail may have different marginal utilities for various users, but the price is uniform. The reasons underlying public fees are well-known. The fee is a price, and most often a monopoly price, fixed by the government in conformity with certain purposes [1890, 178].

The prices of "pure" public goods, meanwhile, are determined as follows:

> In the private as well as the public economy, utility-maximizing behavior dictates that the available resources be allocated among various uses in such a way that marginal utilities of all the goods are, after the allocation, equal. The prices of public goods too are formed in this way, that is, by equating the marginal utilities of public goods after considering the accompanying fiscal burden. This price formation is different from that of the private market, however, since it [results in multiple prices; 1890, 180].

That multiple prices existed in the public economy is by no means an original idea. Mazzola agrees with Wieser, who observed that if indeed the laws of political economy governed both the private and the public economy, as Emil Sax 1883 was arguing, *everyone* would be required to pay a price comensurate with the intensity of the need one felt (Wieser 1889). This would mean that wealth would cease to offer any ascendancy, and poverty would cease to constitute a hindrance. Wieser remarks, however, that only in the public economy can this phenomenon be observed, whereas in the private economy there is gross inequality in the distribution of satisfactions. He is appalled by the spectacle of a society which is governed by two sets of rules, those of the private economy as explained by the laws of political economy, and those of the public economy that is governed, perhaps, by the rules of sociology, philosophy, and law rather than economics (Wieser 1889). Mazzola disagrees with the second part of Wieser's conclusion and replies:

> The analysis of this matter does not lie outside of the limits of the theory of value. We do not need historical or philosophical study; we simply need to know why the prices of certain goods are formed in one way and the prices of certain other goods in another way. This is a question of economics pure and simple, and not of philosophy or jurisprudence [1890, 165].

In the final analysis, the overall allocation of resources between private and public goods is governed by the principle of utility maximization (Mazzola 1890, 180). It is the amount of the "complementary" utility accorded by the individual to the available public goods that determines the share of his private resources allocated to those goods. Mazzola states: "It will be readily appreciated that [in the public economy] differential utility can arise only from faulty valuation . . . or when the equilibrium of the scale of utilities is disturbed" (Musgrave & Peacock 1958, 44). The former problem is not endemic to the *public* economy. In the private economy too marginal utilities are not always known or knowable. In this connection, De Viti asked: "when Jones buys a ticket for a theatrical performance, could it be said that [he knows] the share of utility which he would derive from the performance? Yet no one can doubt that there does exist an economic-exchange relationship between the price of the ticket and the enjoyment that the buyer hopes to derive from its use" (1936, 118). It is simply that in the public economy goods and services of this sort happen to be typical (Kayaalp 1985). Consequently, there will be occasional divergences between the benefits expected from and the price attributed to a public good. The serious problem that public finance has to deal with is the latter. For, it is quite possible that the finance minister, who is, after all, an elected politician, will alter the average valuation of public goods to favor any given constituency. According to Mazzola:

> Such a disequilibrium might occur when agencies to which valuation is entrusted decide to serve the interests of a predominating class or person. If they do so, some members of the community would be obliged to allocate a greater part of their private resources to public goods than would correspond to the complementary utility which these goods provide for them, and hence obtain inadequate satisfaction. Some other members, in the meantime, would have at their disposal a larger quantity of private goods, obtained at the expense of other economic units. . . . Apart from these deviations, however, the law is valid for the entire [range of pure public goods; 1890, 175].

IV. *Conclusion*

Thanks especially to the contributions of Samuelson 1954, Musgrave 1959, and Buchanan 1968, to the typical English-speaking student of modern public finance, the central position accorded by Mazzola to the demand and supply of public goods may now seem only too reasonable. It should be borne in mind, however, that traditional Anglo-Saxon public finance was totally devoid of this core for six decades.

Admittedly, Mazzola's share in the development of Marshallian public finance from a relatively minor subdiscipline to "'public economics,' which, at least conceptually is on all fours with 'private economics'" (Buchanan 1975, 383) has been at best an indirect one, as it reached American soil through Sweden via the works of Wicksell and Lindahl. The two Swedish authors make clear in their works (1896 and 1919, respectively) that their main goal is to explore some possible ways to place Mazzola's manifestly positive model of the public economy in a satisfactory normative context. According to Wicksell, who seems to have become familiar with Mazzola's work through Conrad's *Jahrbücher*, July 1890 (Musgrave & Peacock, 75), despite Mazzola's sanguine attitude about it, coercion is still present in his theory and it would be a flagrant injustice to force someone to contribute to the financing of a public activity which did not enhance his own interest (Musgrave & Peacock, 89). Mazzola indeed underplays this problem. His economic "law" perhaps explains the determination of the prices of public goods in a logical manner, but definitely circumvents the issue of coercion. According to Wicksell, Mazzola's reasoning would lead the fiscal economist to the corollary that

> The imposition of taxes is just and applies without arbitrariness and error when each taxpayer succeeds in distributing his resources in such a manner that his utility is maximized. . . . [But] this requirement of tax policy is really meaningless. If the individual is to spend his money for private and public uses so that his satisfaction is maximized, he will obviously pay nothing whatsoever for public purposes. . . . Of course, if everyone were to do the same, the State would soon cease to function. . . . Equality between the marginal utility of public goods and their price cannot, therefore, be established by the single individual, but must be secured by consultation between him and all other individuals or their delegates. How is such consultation to be arranged so that the goal may be realized? On this point Mazzola does not say a word, as I see it, [although] this is precisely the question which ought to be decided [Musgrave & Peacock, 81–82].

From there Wicksell goes on to develop his own theory of public goods, which ingeniously provides an escape from the free-rider dilemma. He thus demonstrates that a "pure" theory of demand and supply of public goods can be formulated in such a way that it also affords justice for *all*. Unfortunately, however, Wicksell's theory is afflicted by *his* convenient assumption of perfect competition and unanimity in voting. It should be remarked at this point that Lindahl's solution did not fare any better than that of his teacher. According to Head 1974, although Lindahl's "cooperative democracy construct" avoids Wicksell's improbable condition of unanimity, there is still "nothing in Lindahl's requirement of 'free agreement,' reasonably interpreted, which can guarantee the achievement of the fiscal optimum through 'government' any more than that of Mazzola" (p. 145, in Kayaalp 1985, 407).

At any rate, Mazzola's contributions to public finance must be compared not with those of Wicksell and Lindahl, who, after all, directed their efforts at *improving* Mazzola's doctrine, but with those of his contemporary Anglo-Saxon counterparts such as Marshall, Edgeworth, and Sidgwick, in whose hands public finance was reduced to "little more than utiliarian ethics applied to certain economic problems" (Whittaker, 311). Furthermore, Mazzola's model must be considered as an example of the *marginalist* revolution. Although a second revolution severely restricted the concept of utility acceptable to any field of economics (Cooter & Rappoport 1984), the author of this article presented the Italian fiscal theory in relation to the first revolution. Within that framework, the Italian corpus certainly displayed much strength that the Marshallian-Pigovian theory sadly lacked.

This essay is dedicated to Professor Herbert Geyer of the City University of New York who some years ago assigned the author, then a graduate student of his, a term paper on Ugo Mazzola. The author is also indebted to Professor Charlotte Muller of CUNY for providing many helpful insights that concerned not only the fiscal theory but also elements of style. But only the author is responsible for any errors. Part of the research was done at University of Pavia, Italy, where the author was a visiting professor in Fall 1986. An early version of this manuscript was presented at the Fourteenth Annual Meeting of History of Economics Society, Harvard University, June 21, 1987.

References

Beccaria, Cesare Bonesana, Marchese 1968. *Dei delitti e delle pene* (1763), in *Opere*, Firenze.

Benham, Frederick 1934a. Book review of De Viti de Marco's *Principii di economia finanziaria*. *Economica*, no. 3:365–67.

——— 1934b. 'Notes on the pure theory of public finance (suggested by the "Ottima Imposta" of Professor Einaudi).' *Economica*, no. 4:436–58.

Bonar, James 1922. *Philosophy and political economy in some of their historical relations*. London.

Briganti, Filippo 1780. *L'esame economico del sistema civile*, reprinted in *Economici classici Italiani*, Milano, 1804.

Buchanan, James M. 1960. 'La scienza delle finanze: the Italian tradition in fiscal theory.' In *Fiscal theory and political economy: selected essays* (Chapel Hilll, N.C.), 22–74.

——— 1975. 'Public finance and public choice.' *National Tax Journal* 28.8: 383–94.

——— 1968. *The demand and supply of public goods*. Chicago.

Cooter, Robert, and Peter Rappoport 1984. 'Were ordinalists wrong about welfare economics?' *Journal of Economic Literature*. (June): 507–530.

De Viti de Marco, Antonio, Marchese 1936. *First principles of public finance*. London. This is the English translation of De Viti's *I primi principii dell'economia finanziaria* (Roma, 1928), which is in turn based on his 1888 book *Carattere teorico dell'economia finanziaria* (Roma).

Einaudi, Luigi 1936. Introduction to De Viti de Marco's *First Principles* . . . (1936), cited.

Ferrara, Francesco 1934. *Lezioni di economia politica*. Bologna. This edition is based on the lectures that Ferrara delivered intermittently between 1856 and 1873. Incidentally, pp. 551–765 of this work includes Ferrara's lectures in public finance.

Genovesi, Antonio 1769. *Lezioni di economia civile*. Reprinted 1803, Milano.

Head, John J. 1974. *Public goods and public welfare*. Durham, N.C.

Jevons, William S. 1957. *The theory of political economy* (1871). Reprinted, New York.

Kayaalp, Orhan 1985. 'Public-choice elements of the Italian theory of public goods.' *Public Finance/Finances Publiques* 3:395–410.

Lindahl, Erik R. 1919. *Die Gerechtigkeit der Besteuerung*. Lund.
Loria, Achille 1886. *La teoria economica della costituzione politica*. Torino.
Mazzola, Ugo 1888. *Il fondamento scientifico dell'economica dello Stato*. Napoli.
——— 1890. *I dati scientifici della finanza pubblica*. Roma. Chapter 9 of this book, translated as 'The formation of the prices of public goods,' is in Musgrave & Peacock's *Classics* (1958), 37–47.
M'Culloch, John R. 1825. *Literature of political economy*. Edinburgh.
Muratori, Lodovico Antonio 1749. *Della pubblica felicità*. Modena.
Musgrave, Richard A. 1959. *The theory of public finance*. New York.
——— and Alan T. Peacock 1958. *Classics in the theory of public finance*. New York.
Ortes, Giammaria 1790. *Riflessioni sulla popolazione*. Venice.
——— 1894. *Calcolo sopra il valore delle opinioni e sopra i piaceri e i dolori* (1790). Reprinted in *Scrittori classici italiani di economia politica*, 24:257–318, Milano.
Pantaleoni, Maffeo 1883. 'Contributo alla teoria del riparto delle spese pubbliche.' *Rassegna Italiana*, Oct. 15.
——— 1957. *Pure economics*. New York. Translated from *Principii di economia pura*, Milano: 1931, which, in turn, was reprinted from an 1889 edition, Florence.
Paoletti, Ferdinando 1894. 'I veri mezzi di rendere felici le società (1772). Firenze. Reprinted in *Scrittori Classici Italiani di Economia Politica*, 20:105–371, Milano.
Samuelson, Paul 1954. 'The pure theory of public expenditure.' *Review of Economics and Statistics* 36 (Nov.): 387–389.
Sax, Emil 1883. *Grundlegung der theoretischen Staatswirtschaft*. Wien.
Schwarzkopf, A. von. 1872. *Beiträge zur Geschichte der nationalökonomischen Studien in Italien im 17. und 18. Jahrhundert*. Strassburg.
Simons, Henry C. 1937. Book Review of *First principles of public finance* by Antonio De Viti de Marco. *Journal of Political Economy* 45 (Oct.): 712–17.
Verri, Pietro, Conte 1804. *Meditazioni sull'economia politica* (1771). Reprinted, Milano.
——— 1954. *Discorso felicità*. In *Del piacere e del dolore ed altri scritti* (1763), ed. De Felici.
Weinberger, Otto 1940. 'The importance of Francesco Ferrara in the history of economic thought.' *Journal of Political Economy* 48:91–104.
Whittaker, E. 1962. *Schools and streams of economic thought*. Chicago.
Wicksell, Knut 1958. 'Ein neues Prinzip der gerechten Besteuerung' (1896). *Finanztheoretische Untersuchungen*. Jena, Pages iv–lvi, 76–87, and 101–159 of this work, translated as 'A new principle of just taxation,' are in Musgrave & Peacock's *Classics*, 73–118.
Wieser, Friedrich von 1889. *Der natürliche Wert*. Wien.

Name Index

Aakerman, Johan 82
Adams, Thomas A. 124–5
Aftalion, Albert 86, 90–91
Allen, William R. 1
Andvig, Jens Christopher 67
Angell, James W. 24, 98–100, 107, 112, 114–18, 120, 134
Arrow, Kenneth J. 38
Attwood, Thomas 99

Baker, Ray S. 131
Baracs, Johann 151
Barone 184
Baruch, Bernard 132
Beccaria, C.B. 185
Bentham, J. 185
'Bernoulli's Theorem' 36
Beveridge, Sir William 138
Black, Fisher 29
Blaug, M. 163
Blitch, Charles P. 122
Bombach, G. 147, 149
Borchardt, Knut 156
Bowman, Isaiah 128–9, 131
Brauns-Kommission (1931) 151
Briganti, F. 185
Brüning, A. 149, 155–6
Bryan, William J. 124
Buchanan, James M. 183–4, 190
Bullock, C.J. 133–4
Burnett, Philip M. 130

Cannan, Edwin 138
Cantillon, A.A. 99, 164
Carver, Thomas N. 133–4
Cassel, Gustav 84, 88, 90, 93
Chamberlin, Edward H. 136, 138
Clark, J.M. 57, 79, 87, 90
Clemenceau, G. 132
Cole, Arthur H. 135
Colm, G. 157, 159
Commons, John 27
Conrad 190
Cooter, R. 191
Copeland, Morris 106, 111, 113
Cournot, A.A. 48–9, 75, 125–6
Coxey 124

Creedy 83
Crockett, John H. Jr. 29
Cross, Melvin 47
Currie, Lauchlin 24, 99, 112–14, 120, 135

da Vinci 83
Davis, J. Ronnie 148–9, 161
Day, Clive 128–9, 131
De Viti de Marco, A. 184–5, 187, 189
Dickinson, H.D. 162
Dobretsberger, Josef 156
Donner, Otto 147, 158–9
Dorfman, Joseph 122, 137
Douglas, Paul 26
Dulles, Eleanor L. 134–5
Dunbar 48
Dupuit, J. 50

Edgeworth, F. 137, 141, 185, 191
Edie, Lionel 105
Einaudi, Luigi 186, 188
Ekelund, Robert B. Jr. 47
Ellet, Charles 50
Ely, Richard T. 123–4, 138
Erickson, E. 49, 62
Eucken, Walter 154

Ferrara, F. 185
Fisher, Irving 1–8, 10–27, 29–45, 48, 58, 75, 99–101, 103, 105, 108, 116, 120, 149
Fisher, Irving Norton 1
Föhl, Carl 147
Foster, William T. 105
Friedman, M. 100, 106, 111, 119–20
Friedman-Savage (paradox) 33
Frisch, Ragnar 7, 67–8, 70, 73–94

Garvey, George 148–9
Genovesi, A. 185
George, Henry 50
Gesell, Silvio 149
Graham, Frank 24, 26
Grotkopp, W. 149
Grünig, Ferdinand 147

Hadley, Arthur T. 47–64
Hamilton, Earl J. 26, 135

Hansen, Alvin 79
Harding, Warren (President) 136
Hart, A.G. 24
Haskins, Charles H. 124, 128–9
Hawtrey, R.G. 99–100, 103–4, 112, 120, 162
Hayek, F.A. 68–71, 77–8, 86, 88, 162–5, 168–82
Head, John J. 191
Heckscher, Eli 7
Hicks, John 162, 172, 179–81
Hirshleifer, Jack 29
Hoover, Herbert 136
Hotelling, Harold 73, 92
House, Edward M. 128, 131
Hudson, Michael 146
Hume, D. 24, 99
Humphrey 108, 112
Hutchison, T.W. 148–9

Jevons, William S. 48–9, 75, 185
Johnson, Alvin 126
Johnson, Douglas W. 128–9, 131
Jones, Edward D. 124
Jordan, David S. 124–5
Juglars (cycle) 77

Kaldor, Nicholas 143, 162, 164–5, 176–8, 180–81
Kalecki, M. 89
Kayaalp, Orhan 183, 190–91
Kemmerer, Edwin W. 1
Kenyon, William S. 136
Keynes, John M. 1, 33, 67–8, 86, 94, 98, 101, 111–12, 130, 132, 143, 146–7, 152, 160–61, 174
Keynesian 117, 120, 148, 163–4
King, Willford 26, 100, 105–6, 108, 111–12, 114
Kitchins (cycle) 77
Kleinwachter 48
Knauth, Oswald 105
Knight, Frank H. 126–7, 137, 143
Koch, Karin 84
Kolko, G. 49
Kondriatiev (cycle) 77, 80, 84, 90
Kuznets, Simon 106

Lamont, Thomas W. 132
Lardner, Dionysius 50
Lautenbach, Wilhelm 146–7
Leijonhufvud, A. 67, 160–61
Leong, Y.S. 107, 111
Leven, Maurice 106
Lincoln, Abraham 3
Lindahl, Erik 68–9, 183, 190–91
Lippmann, Walter 128
Lloyd George 132
Lorenz, Max O. 124
Loria, Achille 186
Lucas, Robert 163–4
Lunt, William E. 128–9, 131
Lutz, Friedrich 38
Lutz, Vera 38

Macaulay, Frederick 105
Malthus 185
Mann, Fritz 147
Mannsteadt, H. 155
Markowitz, Harry 36
Marschak, Jacob 159
Marshall, Alfred 48–9, 68, 126, 138, 140–41, 175, 185, 190–92
Mason, Edward S. 134, 137
Mayer, Thomas 98
Mazzola, Ugo 183–91
McCormack, Vance 132
Meiselman 119
Mezes, Sidney E. 128–9
Miller, David H. 128, 130, 132
Mill, John Stuart 48, 100
Mises, Ludwig von 68, 150, 154, 164, 169–70, 180
Mitchell, W.C. 67, 71–3, 101–2, 105–7, 112, 120, 124, 136
Montemartini 184
Morgenstern, Oskar 34
Moss, Laurence S. 162
Muratori, L.A. 185
Musgrave, Richard A. 184, 189–91
Myers, Stewart C. 40
Myrdal, Gunnar 68, 70

Neisser, Hans 147, 159
Neumann, John von 34
Newcomb, Simon 48, 99–101
Norton, Prof. 38

Ohlin, Bertil 70, 135
Orlando, P.M. 131
Ortes, G. 185

Pantaleoni, M. 184–5, 187
Paoletti, F. 185
Pareto, V. 75
Peacock, Alan T. 184, 189–91
Pearson, Frank A. 11
Persons, Warren M. 72
Pigou, A.C. 50, 54, 57, 70, 101–2, 104–5, 112, 120, 126–7, 192

Pratt, John W. 38
Quante, Peter 151

Ramsey, F.P. 34
Rappoport, Peter 191
Ricardo, David 24, 50, 58–9, 91, 163–9, 172, 174–80, 182
Ripley, W.Z. 57
Robbins, Lionel 122
Robertson, D.H. 67–8, 70, 116, 127
Robichek, Alexander A. 40
Robinson, Joan 54
Roos 92
Roosevelt, Franklin D. (President) 1, 3, 7, 14, 17, 27
Röpke, W. 146, 156–7, 159–61
Rüstow, Alexander 153

Saitzew, M. 152
Samuelson, Paul A. 93, 190
Sax, Emil 189
Say's (Law) 140–41
Schultz, Henry 79
Schumpeter, J.A. 1, 48, 50, 56, 64, 68, 73, 76, 99–102, 104, 112, 120, 122, 133–4, 139, 141, 146, 148, 151–2, 154
Schwartz 106, 111
Scott, William A. 124
Seymour, Charles 128–9, 131–2
Shotwell, James 127, 129, 132
Sidgwick 48, 191
Simons, Henry C. 24
Slutsky 73
Smith, Adam 101, 139–40, 142
Smith, Jeremiah 137, 140
Snyder, Carl 107
Soddy, Frederick 24
Spann, R. 49, 62
Spellman, Laura 138
Sraffa, Piero 138–9
Stickney, Emma M. 123
Strong, Benjamin 13, 137
Stucken, R. 151
Sumner 48
Sweezy, Alan 112

Taussig, F.W. 126, 133–4
Taylor, Overton H. 135
Thornton, Henry 99–100
Tinbergen, Jan 73, 83, 87–8, 92–4
Tooke, Thomas 101
Trescott, Paul B. 98
Tugwell, Rexford G. 137
Turner, Frederick J. 124

Van Horne, James C. 40
Vaughn, Karin I. 162
Veblen, Thorstein 125
Verri, Pietro 185

Walker 48
Walker, F.A. 50
Walras, L. 2, 48–9, 68, 75, 79, 185
Warburton, Clark 100, 118–21
Warren, George F. 11
Weinberger, Otto 185
Wells 48
Welter, Erich 153
Westlake, Jessie B. 124
Whittaker, E. 191
Whittlesey, Charles 26
Wicksell, Knut 68, 99, 101–4, 120, 164, 169, 183, 190–91
Wiener, M. 76
Wieser, Friedrich von 189
Willcox, Walter F. 124–6
Williams 134
Wilson, T. 176
Wilson, Woodrow (President) 128–9, 131–2

Yaari, Menahem 33
Young, Allyn A. 122–43
Young, Sutton E. 123

Pioneers in Economics

Section I: The Forerunners of Classical Economics

1. The Historiography of Economics
2. Aristotle (384–322 B.C.)
3. St Thomas Aquinas (1225–1274)
4. The Early Mercantilists
   Thomas Mun (1571–1641), Edward Misselden (1608–1634), Gerard de Malynes (1586–1623)
5. The Later Mercantilists
   Josiah Child (1603–1699) and John Locke (1632–1704)
6. Pre-Classical Economists Volume I
   Charles Davenant (1656–1714) and William Petty (1623–1687)
7. Pre-Classical Economists Volume II
   Pierre le Pesant Boisguilbert (1645–1714), George Berkeley (1685–1753), Baron de Montesquieu (1689–1755), Ferdinando Galiani (1727–1787), James Anderson (1739–1808), Dugald Stewart (1753–1828)
8. Pre-Classical Economists Volume III
   John Law (1671–1729) and Bernard Mandeville (1660–1733)
9. Richard Cantillon (1680–1734) and Jacques Turgot (1727–1781)
10. François Quesnay (1694–1774) Volumes I and II
11. David Hume (1711–1776) and James Steuart (1712–1780)

Section II: The Golden Age of Classical Economics

12. Adam Smith (1723–1790) Volumes I and II
13. Henry Thornton (1760–1815), Jeremy Bentham (1748–1832), James Lauderdale (1759–1839), Simonde de Sismondi (1773–1842)
14. David Ricardo (1772–1823)
15. Jean-Baptiste Say (1776–1832)
16. Thomas Robert Malthus (1766–1834) and John Stuart Mill (1806–1873)
17. Ramsay McCulloch (1789–1864), Nassau Senior (1790–1864), Robert Torrens (1780–1864)
18. Thomas Tooke (1774–1858), Mountifort Longfield (1802–1884), Richard Jones (1790–1855)

19. William Whewell (1794–1866), Dionysius Lardner (1793–1859), Charles Babbage (1792–1871)

20. George Scrope (1797–1876), Thomas Attwood (1783–1856), Edwin Chadwick (1800–1890), John Cairnes (1823–1875)

21. James Mill (1773–1836), John Rae (1796–1872), Edward West (1782–1828), Thomas Joplin (1790–1847)

22. James Wilson (1805–1860), Issac Butt (1813–1879), T. E. Cliffe Leslie (1827–1882)

23. Karl Marx (1818–1883)

Section III: Neoclassical Economics and its Critics

24. Johann von Thünen (1783–1850), Augustin Cournot (1801–1877), Jules Dupuit (1804–1866)

25. Leon Walras (1834–1910)

26. Carl Menger (1840–1921)

27. Eugen von Böhm-Bawerk (1851–1914) and Friedrich von Wieser (1851–1926)

28. Knut Wicksell (1851–1926)

29. Alfred Marshall (1842–1924) and Francis Edgeworth (1845–1926)

30. Gustav Schmoller (1838–1917) and Werner Sombart (1863–1941)

31. Dissenters
Charles Fourier (1772–1837), Henri de St Simon (1760–1825), Pierre-Joseph Proudhon (1809–1865), John A. Hobson (1858–1940)

32. Thorstein Veblen (1857–1929)

33. Wesley Mitchell (1874–1948), John Commons (1862–1945), Clarence Ayres (1891–1972)

34. Henry George (1839–1897)

35. Vilfredo Pareto (1848–1923)

Section IV: Twentieth Century Economics

36. Arthur Pigou (1877–1959)

37. Frank Knight (1885–1972), Henry Simons (1899–1946), Joseph Schumpeter (1883–1950)

38. Edward Chamberlin (1899–1967)

39. Michal Kalecki (1899–1970)

40. Harold Hotelling (1895–1973), Lionel Robbins (1898–1984), Clark Warburton (1896–1979), John Bates Clark (1847–1938), Ludwig von Mises (1881–1973)

41. Irving Fisher (1867–1947), Arthur Hadley (1856–1930), Ragnar Frisch (1895–1973), Friedrich von Hayek (1899–1992), Allyn Young (1876–1929), Ugo Mazzola (1863–1899)

42. Harry Johnson (1923–1977)

43. Bertil Ohlin (1899–1979)

44. Piero Sraffa (1898–1983)

45. Joan Robinson (1903–1983) and George Shackle (1903–1992)

46. John Maynard Keynes (1883–1946) Volumes I and II